PEARSON          ALWAYS LEARNING

# Economics of Public and Macro Issues

Second Custom Edition

Taken from
*The Economics of Macro Issues,*
Fifth Edition
by Roger Leroy Miller and
Daniel K. Benjamin

*The Economics of Public Issues,*
Seventeenth Edition
by Roger Leroy Miller, Daniel K.
Benjamin, and Douglass C. North

ISBN 10: 1-256-84845-X
ISBN 13: 978-1-256-84845-5

# BRIEF CONTENTS

Chapters 1–5 and 10–20 were taken from *The Economics of Public Issues,* Seventeenth Edition by Roger Leroy Miller, Daniel K. Benjamin, and Douglass C. North.

Chapters 6–9, 21–35, and the Glossary were taken from *The Economics of Macro Issues,* Fifth Edition by Roger Leroy Miller, and Daniel K. Benjamin.

# PART ONE
# Foundations

# CHAPTER 1

# Death by Bureaucrat

How would you rather die? From a lethal reaction to a drug pre-
scribed by your doctor? Or because your doctor failed to prescribe a
drug that would have saved your life? If this choice sounds like one
you would rather not make, consider this: Employees of the Food
and Drug Administration (FDA) make that decision on behalf
of millions of Americans many times each year. More precisely,
FDA bureaucrats decide whether or not new medicines (prescription
drugs) should be allowed to go on sale in the United States. If the
FDA rules against a drug, physicians in America may not legally
prescribe it, even if thousands of lives are being saved by the drug
each year in other countries.

## A Brief History of The FDA

The FDA's authority to make such decisions dates back to the passage of
the Food and Drug Safety Act of 1906. That law required that medicines
be correctly labeled as to their contents and that they not contain any
substances harmful to the health of consumers. Due to this legislation,
Dr. Hostatter's Stomach Bitters and Kickapoo Indian Sagwa, along with
numerous rum-laden concoctions, cocaine-based potions, and supposed
anticancer remedies, disappeared from druggists' shelves. The law was
expanded in 1938 with the passage of the Food, Drug, and Cosmetic
Act, which forced manufacturers to demonstrate the safety of new drugs
before being allowed to offer them for sale. (This law was prompted
by the deaths of 107 people who had taken Elixir Sulfanilamide, an
antibiotic that contained poisonous diethylene glycol, a chemical cousin
of antifreeze.)

The next step in U.S. drug regulation came after a rash of severe birth defects among infants whose mothers during pregnancy had taken a sleep aid known as thalidomide. When these birth defects first became apparent, the drug was already widely used in Europe and Canada, and the FDA was nearing approval for its use in America. In fact, about 2.5 million thalidomide tablets were already in the hands of U.S. physicians as samples. The FDA ordered all of the samples destroyed and prohibited the sale of the drug here. This incident led to the 1962 Kefauver-Harris Amendments to the 1938 Food, Drug, and Cosmetic Act, radically altering the drug-approval process in the United States.

## THE IMPACT OF THE 1962 AMENDMENTS

Prior to the 1962 amendments, the FDA was expected to approve a new drug application within 180 days unless the application failed to show that the drug was safe. The 1962 amendments added a "proof of efficacy" requirement and also removed the time constraint on the FDA. The FDA has free rein to determine how much and what type of evidence it will demand before approving a drug for sale and thus may take as long as it pleases before either granting or refusing approval.

The 1962 amendments drastically increased the costs of introducing a new drug and markedly slowed the approval process. Prior to 1962, for example, the average time between filing and approval of a new drug application was seven months; by 1967, it was thirty months; and by the late 1970s, it had risen to eight to ten *years*. The protracted approval process involves costly testing by the drug companies—$800 million or more for each new drug—and delays the receipt of any potential revenue from new drugs. Because this reduced the expected profitability of new drugs, fewer of them have been brought onto the market.

Debate continues over how much FDA regulation is needed to ensure that drugs are both safe and efficacious, but there is little doubt that the 1962 amendments have resulted in a U.S. "drug lag." On average, drugs take far longer to reach the market in the United States than they do in Europe. Admittedly, it takes time to ensure that patients benefit from, rather than are harmed by, new drugs, but regulation-induced drug lag can itself be life-threatening. Dr. George Hitchings, a winner of the Nobel Prize in Medicine, has estimated that the five-year lag in introducing Septra (an antibiotic) to the United States killed 80,000 people in this country. Similarly, the introduction of a class of drugs called beta blockers (used to treat heart attack victims and people with high blood pressure) was delayed nearly a decade in

America relative to Europe. According to several researchers, the lag in the FDA approval of these drugs cost the lives of at least 250,000 Americans.

## Terrible Trade-Off

In effect, the law requires FDA bureaucrats to make what is truly a terrible trade-off. Lives are saved because unsafe or ineffective drugs are kept off the market, but the regulatory process delays (or even prevents) the introduction of some safe and efficacious drugs, thereby costing lives. Let us now take a more systematic look at this trade-off.

Every time a new drug is introduced, there is a chance that it should not have been—either because it has adverse side effects that outweigh the therapeutic benefits (it is not safe) or because it really does little to help the individuals who take it (it is not effective). When such a drug is introduced, we say that a **Type I error** has been committed. Since 1962, the incidence of Type I error—the thalidomide possibility—has been reduced by the added testing required by the FDA. But other people have been the victims of what is called **Type II error.** Their cost is the pain, suffering, and death that occur because the 1962 amendments have prevented or delayed the introduction of safe, efficacious drugs. Type II error—as with Septra or beta blockers—occurs when a drug *should* be introduced but is held back by FDA regulation.

Over the past twenty or thirty years, outcries over the harm caused by the drug lag have, in some cases, induced the agency to shorten the testing period when the costs of Type I error are small relative to the damages due to Type II error—as in the case of terminally ill patients. One famous example involved azidothymidine (AZT), which emerged as a possible treatment for AIDS. Gay men, among whom AIDS was most prevalent at the time, took the lead in pressuring the FDA to approve the drug quickly, and the FDA responded accordingly, giving it the OK after only eighteen months of testing. Similarly, Taxol, an important new drug used to treat breast cancer, received expedited review by the FDA, in this case because of pressure applied by women in whose families there was a history of breast cancer. The FDA now has a formal program in which it seeks to expedite testing for drugs that seem to offer great promise for alleviating death or suffering. Nevertheless, although the average approval time for new drugs has shortened considerably, it still takes more than ten times as long for a new drug to be approved as it did before the 1962 amendments.

## LESSONS FROM THE FDA STORY

What can we learn from the FDA regulation of new drugs that will guide us in thinking about other public issues of our time? There are several key principles:

1. *There is no free lunch.* Every choice, and thus every policy, entails a **cost**—something must be given up. In a world of **scarcity,** we cannot have more of everything; so to get more of some things, we must give up other things. Although FDA review of drugs saves lives by preventing the introduction of unsafe or ineffective drugs, the cost is billions of dollars of added expenses, plus delayed availability of safe and efficacious drugs, resulting in the deaths of hundreds of thousands of people.

2. *The cost of an action is the alternative that is sacrificed.* Economists often express costs (and benefits) in terms of dollars because this is a simple means of accounting for and measuring them. But that doesn't mean that costs have to be monetary, nor does it mean that economics is incapable of analyzing costs and benefits that are quite human. The costs that led to the 1938 and 1962 amendments were the very visible deaths caused by sulfanilamide and the terrible birth defects due to thalidomide. Subsequent revisions to the FDA process for reviewing drugs, as with AZT and Taxol, have been in response to the adverse effects caused by the regulation-induced drug lag.

3. *The relevant costs and benefits are the marginal (incremental) ones.* The relevant question is not whether safety is good or bad; it is instead how much safety we want—which can only be answered by looking at the added (marginal) benefits of more safety compared to the added (marginal) costs. One possible response to the sulfanilamide poisonings or thalidomide was to have outlawed new drugs altogether. That would guarantee that no more people would be harmed by new drugs. But surely this "solution" would not be sensible, because the marginal cost (due to higher Type II errors) would exceed the marginal benefit (caused by reduced Type I errors).

4. *People respond to incentives.* And this is true whether we are talking about consumers, suppliers, or government bureaucrats. Here the incentive to amend the law in 1938 and 1962 was the very visible death and disfigurement of individuals. The eventual FDA decision to speed up the review process was prompted by intense lobbying by individuals who believed (correctly, as it turned out) that they might be benefited by drugs not yet approved.

5. *Things aren't always as they seem.* Many analyses of the effects of government policies take an approach that doesn't fully recognize the actions that people would otherwise have taken. Thus, official pronouncements about the effects of policies routinely misrepresent their impact—not because there is necessarily any attempt to deceive but because it is often difficult to know what would have happened otherwise. Pharmaceutical manufacturers, for example, have strong incentives to avoid introducing drugs that are unsafe or ineffective because the companies are subject to loss of reputation and to lawsuits. For similar reasons, physicians have strong incentives to avoid prescribing such drugs for their patients. Even without FDA regulation, there would thus be extensive testing of new drugs before their introduction. Hence, it is incorrect to ascribe the generally safe and effective nature of modern drugs entirely to FDA protection. The flip side, however, is that the drug development process is inherently long, complicated, and costly. Even without FDA oversight, some people would die waiting for new drugs because self-interested manufacturers would insist on some testing and cautious physicians would proceed slowly in prescribing new drugs.

The people who work at the FDA (and members of Congress) are publicly castigated when they "allow" a Type I error to occur—especially when it is a drug that kills people. Thus, FDA bureaucrats have a strong incentive to avoid such errors. But when testing delays cause a Type II error, as with Septra, it is almost impossible to point to specific people who died because the drug was delayed. As a result, officials at the FDA are rarely attacked directly for such delays. Because the costs of Type II errors are much more difficult to discern than the costs of Type I errors, many observers believe that there is an inherent bias at the FDA in favor of being "safe rather than sorry"—in other words, excessive testing.

6. *Policies always have unintended consequences, and as a result, their net benefits are almost always less than anticipated.* In the case of government regulations, balancing incremental costs and benefits (see principle 3) fails to make good headlines. Instead, what gets politicians reelected and regulators promoted are *absolute* notions such as safety (and motherhood and apple pie). Thus, if a little safety is good, more must be better, so why not simply mandate that drug testing "guarantee" that everyone is free of risk from dangerous drugs? Eventually, the reality of principle 3 sinks in, but in this case not before the drug lag had killed many people.

As is often true with important public issues, our story has one more interesting twist. Thalidomide is back on the market. In 1998, it was approved by the FDA for use in treating Hansen's disease (leprosy), and in 2006, the FDA gave physicians the OK to use it in treating bone marrow cancer. In each instance, there are strong protections to prevent pregnant women from taking the drug. And so perhaps the very drug that brought us the deadly drug lag will turn out to be a lifesaver for a new generation of patients.

## DISCUSSION QUESTIONS

1. Why don't individuals simply force the FDA to do what is best for consumers of prescription drugs?

2. Why don't the employees at the FDA accurately balance the marginal benefits to drug consumers against the marginal costs to those consumers?

3. Does the structure of the drug industry have any bearing on the types of errors that drug firms are likely to make? That is, would a drug industry made up of numerous highly competitive firms be more or less likely to introduce unsafe drugs than an industry consisting of a few large firms?

4. How could the incentives facing the people at the FDA be changed to reduce the incidence of Type II errors? (*Hint:* Is it possible to compare the FDA approval process with the drug-approval process in other nations?)

5. What would be the advantages and disadvantages of a regulatory system in which, rather than having the FDA permit or prohibit new drugs, the FDA merely published its opinions about the safety and efficacy of drugs and then allowed physicians to make their own decisions about whether or not to prescribe the drugs for their patients?

6. Suppose, for simplicity, that Type I and Type II errors resulted in deaths only. Keeping in mind that too little caution produces Type I errors and too much caution produces Type II errors, what would be the best mix of Type I and Type II errors?

# CHAPTER 2

# The Economics of Oil Spills

At 11:00 A.M. on April 20, 2010, contractors working on British Petroleum's (BP) Deepwater Horizon oil platform met with the platform's BP managers. The well being drilled by the platform was situated in water 5,000 feet deep, some 41 miles off the Louisiana coast line in the Gulf of Mexico. At the time of the meeting, the well had reached a depth of more than 13,000 feet below the sea floor. BP wanted to finish the work on the well because it was much delayed and millions of dollars over budget. The contractors were not happy with some of the cost-saving measures that BP hoped would speed the process, but BP management prevailed at the meeting. By 5:00 P.M. that day, at least some workers on the rig knew that gas was leaking into the well. Gas and oil together are a deadly combination.

Later than evening, in preparation for final work on the project, BP decided to remove from the well the drilling mud used to hold back the high-pressure mixture of gas and oil under the sea floor. This was a critical and deadly decision. At 9:45 P.M., enough mud had been removed that what remained, together with sea water, oil, and natural gas, began shooting out of the oil rig like water from a fire hose. Workers raced to tame the well. When they hit the emergency button to activate a safety device and detach the rig from the well, it was too late. Escaping gas exploded. Eleven workers lost their lives.

The worst oil spill in American history had begun.

## WHO IS TO BLAME?

Of course, no one wanted to accept responsibility for the Deepwater Horizon explosion and oil spill. BP blamed its contractors for the disaster. The contractors blamed each other and BP management. Many of those outside and inside government blamed the "cozy relationship" that the federal government's Minerals Management Service had with the oil industry. Finally, others blamed our continuing reliance on fossil fuels to power our cars and our factories.

According to some experts, BP cut too many corners to make up for lost time and cost overruns. For example, the company shortened a procedure designed to detect gas in the well and remove it before it becomes a problem. BP did not quality test the cement around the pipe, cement that serves as another buffer against gas. And BP used a single pipe drilling method, which is less costly than the double pipe method, but also riskier. Moreover, the BP manager who oversaw the final well tests had almost no experience in deepwater drilling.

Of course, spokespersons for BP claimed that it did not cut corners and that both safety and operational reliability were priorities. Undoubtedly, the "blame game" will continue, particularly as the many lawsuits against BP and its contractors weave their way through the federal courts.

## WHO SHOULD PAY?

Those whose livelihoods depend on tourism and fishing sustained billions of dollars of damages as a result of the BP oil spill. Beaches were closed on the Gulf Coast, as were large inshore and offshore fishing areas. Unlike the response to the 2008 financial crisis, no one argued that federal taxpayers should compensate those who suffered economic (and psychological) damages because of the incident. Instead, BP quickly agreed when President Obama suggested it create a $20 billion pool of funds that would be doled out to those who had been harmed. In principle, this pool will compensate most of those harmed by the spill for most of the damages they sustained.

Overall, there is little doubt that BP shareholders have paid a huge price for whatever real or not-so-accurate blame was placed on BP. Within three weeks of the Deepwater Horizon explosion, the **market value** of the company had dropped by more than $36 billion—about a 20 percent fall. This decline in market value reflects the $20 billion damage fund noted above, as well as other anticipated costs of the spill—damages not covered by the official damage fund, the value of the oil that could have been pumped from the well, and the likely higher costs of drilling in the future.

At issue here is the creation of **negative incentives** that will induce BP and other oil companies to account fully for the risks surrounding offshore oil drilling. The economically **efficient** amount (and location) of drilling occurs only when the companies must pay for the full costs of their drilling—which include the environmental impacts. The creation of a damage pool such as instituted in the Deepwater Horizon case is one way that such incentives can be brought to bear. But the key point is that to achieve economic efficiency, any user of a resource should bear the full cost of using that resource. If not, the resource will be used too intensively and our overall wealth will be lower. "User pays" is a principle that not only seems fair to most people but also minimizes the chances that resources—including, of course, environmental resources—will be wasted.

## What About Long-Lasting Environmental Damages?

One commentator called April 20, 2010, our "environmental 9/11." Although the immediate damage to shorelines and wildlife turned out to be far less than was generally predicted, longer-term issues remain unsettled. For example, we know that escaped oil still sits on the ocean floor in parts of the Gulf of Mexico because of this disaster, and that there is still oil suspended in the deep waters of the Gulf. Because oil has seeped from the floor of the Gulf for millions of years, deepwater bacteria have evolved to feed on the oil. Thus, all of the oil is biodegradable, but we do not know how many years this process will take. Nor do we know what damage might accumulate over this period.

Partly in response to such concerns, President Obama banned all deep water oil drilling in the Gulf of Mexico for six months. Some observers argued that we should also increase subsidies for ethanol production and other alternative forms of energy. The Sierra Club announced that it wanted the permanent phasing out of *all* offshore exploration production.

## Those Nasty Trade-Offs

It is true that if we ban all drilling in the Gulf of Mexico, then in the U.S. portion of the Gulf, there can be no further oil spills. But we cannot ban such oil drilling in *non*-U.S. territorial waters. Brazil, Mexico, and Cuba are already drilling in the Gulf of Mexico and will continue to do so. Therefore, the threat of another oil spill harming the environment near or on our shores cannot be reduced to zero.

About one million barrels per day come from our own offshore oil platforms in the Gulf of Mexico. That constitutes about one-fourth of total domestic oil production. If there were a permanent ban on such oil production, the United States would have to do one of the following:

1. *Increase* onshore *oil production,* perhaps by authorizing exploration in the currently closed Alaska National Wildlife Refuge.

2. *Develop oil shale located in western states.* Currently, such production is uneconomic—the costs exceed the potential revenues. Oil prices would have to rise considerably higher than they are now and stay high for a long time to make oil shale a preferred choice. Also, extraction of oil from oil shale requires huge amounts of water (heated to make steam that is injected into the oil-bearing shale), which would put severe pressure on existing water supplies in the arid western United States.

3. *The United States can import more oil from overseas.* Of course, there is a political argument against this action because we do not want to be "held hostage" to oil-exporting countries. Additionally, more imported oil means more risk of oil spills from oil tankers.

4. *Increase usage of ethanol.* Because most ethanol is made from corn or sugar cane, Midwestern corn farmers and Brazilian sugar cane growers would like this. But the adverse environmental consequences would be considerable. There is already an 8,500-square-mile dead zone in the Gulf caused by farm runoff coming down the Mississippi River. The prime culprit here is nitrogen fertilizer, and the corn used to make ethanol in America is notoriously nitrogen-hungry. So more ethanol means either a bigger Gulf dead zone or damage to Amazonian rain forests that would have to be cut down to make way for more sugarcane.

We could increase the list of alternatives to offshore drilling, but the inference would remain exactly the same. Every alternative to the continued flow of oil from offshore wells in the Gulf of Mexico involves a **trade-off.** Otherwise stated, every alternative action involves an **opportunity cost.** If you are an environmentalist, you might not want to allow oil drilling in now-prohibited parts of Alaska, or a larger Gulf dead zone or smaller Amazonian rain forests. If you are a farmer in the western states, you might not wish to see part of your water supply diverted to help extract oil from shale. And if you are worried about other countries determining our energy fate, you likely are against importing even more oil.

## PUTTING THE DEEPWATER HORIZON
## DISASTER INTO PERSPECTIVE

Eventually, the BP well was capped, and thus far no additional oil has leaked from it. It is estimated that the total spill was about 600,000 metric tons of oil. The closest accidental oil disaster of that size occurred off the Mexican coast in 1979 when the Ixtoc I platform leaked about 500,000 metric tons of oil into the Gulf over a nine-month period. During the Persian Gulf War in 1991, retreating Iraqi troops purposely created the largest oil spill in history—pouring 1.2 million metric tons into the Persian Gulf.

Prior to April, 2010, the biggest oil spill in U.S. territorial waters was caused by the *Exxon Valdez*, which leaked 39,000 metric tons of oil in Prince William Sound in 1989. Over time, for every offshore drilling spill, there have been seven major tanker spills and numerous smaller tanker accidents. Overall, during the 70 years for which there are data, tankers have spilled four times more oil than have offshore drilling accidents.

Perhaps more surprisingly, Mother Nature dumps even more oil into our oceans and waters, by way of natural seeps. Such seepage constitutes over 60 percent of oil in North American marine waters according to the National Research Council. Another one-third of the oil going into the oceans around our country comes from the urban runoffs, spills on land, and discharges from marine vessels. Added to this, every year Americans literally pour one million metric tons of oil down their household drains. This leaves less than 5 percent of oil in North American marine waters that is caused by extraction and transportation. The damage potential of the BP spill was heightened by its concentration in time and space—but its long-lasting effects are likely to be small.

## THE PERILS OF SEEKING ZERO
## ENVIRONMENTAL RISK

Those who worry about our environment—and that includes just about everyone—have sometimes advocated zero environmental risk from oil extraction and transportation activities. Even getting close to zero risk would be extraordinarily costly to society, though.

Consider how much time you spend proofing an important paper you have written for a critical class in college. You might use a spelling and grammar checking program first. Then you might reread your corrected draft. Next, you might put it down for an hour or a day and reread it again. The next time you proof it, you are likely to find very few errors. When do you stop? You stop when the **marginal cost** of doing more would exceed the expected **marginal benefit** (where "marginal" refers to the last or incremental unit).

What is your marginal cost? It is the value you place on the time you would have to spend for an additional proofing. That is your opportunity cost, the value of the best alternative use of your time. This might be studying for another course or it might be the pleasure you get from playing a video game. Your expected marginal benefit is the expected improvement in your grade on the paper and then on your final grade.

The key point, of course, is that you don't spend your entire college career proofreading a single paper. Instead, you take into account the benefits *and* costs of your actions in coming to a sensible decision about the allocation of your time.

## THE EFFICIENT AMOUNT OF POLLUTION

Now use this type of reasoning to ascertain the **efficient** amount of oil pollution in the Gulf of Mexico (or anywhere, for that matter). To make it zero clearly cannot be efficient. The **efficient amount of pollution** occurs when marginal benefit equals marginal cost. To ensure that we have *no* oil spills, we would have to ban not only all offshore drilling but also *any* transportation of imported oil into the United States. If we did that, the price of oil products would skyrocket, thereby creating a severe and long-lasting economic crisis for the entire country.

What about the benefits of reducing the risk of oil spills? They would include less destruction to marine life and fewer damages to those who live on the coasts and those who depend on fishing for a livelihood in the same area.

The last major U.S. offshore oil spill occurred more than 40 years ago, off the coast of Santa Barbara, California. The 2009 *Montara* spill in the Timor Sea was the first major platform spill *anywhere* in the world in more than 20 years. History thus suggests that, despite the events of 2010, oil-drilling safety measures have been effective in keeping significant spills few and far between. To be sure, BP cut many corners and appears to have followed risk reduction procedures that met "industry standards," but did not constitute "industry best practices." Given that BP is now paying for its choices, other oil companies, particularly those that operate in the Gulf of Mexico, have up-to-date information about how much it will cost in the future to cut corners on safety. They will certainly invest in risk-reducing activities more than they did before April 20, 2010. And although we will pay for the risk reduction at the pump, we will also likely benefit from having to put up with even fewer spills in the future.

## DISCUSSION QUESTIONS

1. Why do we use so much oil?

2. How would your life change if there were no offshore drilling and no importation of foreign oil? (*Hint:* The combination of these two changes would reduce the supply of oil in the United States by about 70 percent.)

3. What would be the costs and benefits if the federal government imposed, say, a $3 additional tax on every gallon of gas purchased in the United States?

4. The Deepwater Horizon spill has been called the "Three Mile Island" moment for the oil industry. This is in reference to a core-cooling water leak at a nuclear power plant called Three Mile Island in 1979. Consequent to that disaster, no new nuclear power plants have come online. How has the United States benefited because we have added no new nuclear power plants? What is the trade-off, though, that we have made?

5. Even though you may not consciously calculate the marginal cost and the marginal benefit of studying one more hour for an exam, you still make a choice of whether to study that extra hour or not. Why must you ultimately take into account your opportunity cost for an extra hour of studying (or for any activity, for that matter) if you want to sensibly make choices about how to allocate your scarce time?

6. "The sun is a plentiful source of energy. Therefore, we should be able to harness that energy and slowly wean ourselves from oil imports." What is left out from this statement that has so far prevented solar energy from displacing petroleum products as a source of energy?

# CHAPTER 3

# Supersize It

At least one major fast food company has urged customers to "Supersize It." Americans seem to have been taking the message to heart, putting on pounds at a record pace. In the 1960s, the average American man weighed 166 pounds. Today he tips the scales at a bit over 190. Over the same span, the average American woman put on just as much weight, rising to 164 pounds from her previous 140 pounds. The weight gains have been largest among people who were heavier to begin with, so obesity in America has more than doubled over this period. Over 30 percent of Americans now have a body mass index (BMI, a measure of weight relative to height) in excess of 30, the level at which doctors say a person passes from overweight to obese.[1] What explains these developments? Not surprisingly, economic analysis has a lot to say on this question. In fact, some fairly simple changes in demand and supply explain why waistlines in America and elsewhere in the world have been expanding so quickly.

## WEIGHT IN THE TWENTIETH CENTURY

Actually, Americans put on weight throughout all of the twentieth century, largely as a result of two factors. First, wages in sedentary occupations (those relying on brains rather than brawn) rose relative

---

1 Using the English measurement system, BMI equals 704.5 multiplied by weight in pounds and then divided by the square of height in inches. BMIs in the range 20–25 are considered healthy. Below 20 is thin, 25–30 is overweight, and 30 and above is obese–the range in which significant adverse health effects (ranging from diabetes to heart disease) begin to show up. Someone who is 5′6″) and weighs 185 pounds or more is officially obese, as is true for someone who stands 6′0″ and weighs 220 pounds or above.

to those in active occupations. People responded by leaving jobs in manufacturing and agriculture and by starting work in service and management jobs. This reduced their calorie expenditures on the job and helped push up average weights. Second, the relative price of food declined during the twentieth century. As predicted by the **law of demand,** this induced people to eat more, increasing their caloric intake and their body weights. Between about 1900 and 1960, the weight of the average male rose 16 pounds, with similar but slightly smaller gains for the average female.

These weight gains during the first part of the twentieth century were probably healthful. Many Americans at the beginning of the twentieth century were actually malnourished, and the added poundage led to better health outcomes for them. The excess weight we added during the last 40 years or so is an entirely different matter. By the 1960s, average BMI in the United States was already at the high end of the healthy range of 20–25, so the extra pounds since then have pushed us into the unhealthy categories of overweight and even obese.

## Why the Weight Gains?

How can we explain this surge in poundage? There are three key components. First, as mentioned above, levels of physical activity have declined, although not nearly as much as many popular commentators would have us believe. The big move from active to sedentary employments took place before 1970, so it cannot explain the last 40 years of weight gains. Still, caloric energy expenditures by both men and women in the United States have been falling. Americans are spending less time at work and on household chores, and more time watching TV, looking at computer monitors, and talking on the phone. Overall, per capita caloric energy expenditures have dropped a bit more than 25 percent since the 1960s. This is only a small part of the story, however. Indeed, it can explain only a few of the pounds Americans have added over the past 40 years. The rest comes from higher caloric intake.

By far the most important reason for this added caloric intake appears to be a change in the way food is prepared. Due to major developments in food processing technology, the **time cost** involved in preparing meals has fallen dramatically. This has reduced the **full cost** (money plus time cost) of food, leading to the consumption of significantly more calories. The result has been expanding waistlines.

## CHANGES IN FOOD PREPARATION

In the 1960s, food was prepared in the home by family members and eaten there. Since then there have been numerous technological innovations in food processing, including:

- Vacuum packing
- Flash freezing
- Improved preservatives and flavorings
- The microwave

Much food preparation now is done outside the home by manufacturers who specialize in that activity and then sell the packaged, prepared food to the consumer to be eaten at home. Thus, over the past 40 years, the amount of time spent on food preparation and cleanup in the home has fallen in half. In addition, outside the home convenient, tasty prepackaged foods are now merely a few steps away in a vending machine, rather than being 10–20 minutes away in the nearest store. On both counts, the full cost of consuming food has declined, and people are consuming more calories. Moreover, they are doing it not by eating more calories at each meal, but rather by eating more "meals" (actually snacks) during the day. Caloric intake during the traditional meals of breakfast, lunch, and dinner has remained nearly constant at about 1,800 per day for men and 1,400 per day for women. But both sexes have nearly doubled their intake of calories from snacks, and per capita daily intake has risen to 3,800 calories from 3,100.

## THOSE EXTRA CALORIES

A few questions remain. First, are the additional calories that Americans are consuming each day—the equivalent of a soft drink or a few cookies—really enough to account for the poundage we have been accumulating? The answer is "yes." An extra 150 calories per day for men of average weight and activity levels will eventually lead to 11 pounds of excess waistline baggage. For women, the same 150 calories per day would eventually add an extra 13 pounds. (The weight gain from these extra calories eventually levels off because as people get heavier they burn more calories just doing the things they usually do.)

The second question is: What started the revolution in food processing that made these extra calories cheaper? Although the answer to this is not completely settled, the most likely source may be found in the workforce decisions of women. Beginning about 40 years ago, women began entering the workforce in unprecedented numbers. Indeed, the **labor force participation rate** of women nearly doubled over this period. Moreover, they have been moving into occupations and professions, such as medicine, law, and the upper ranks of business, in which annual earnings are much higher than in the traditional fields of female employment, such as teaching and nursing. Thus, the **opportunity cost** of women's time has been rising, in turn increasing the demand for labor-saving conveniences, such as prepared foods. The food industry has responded just as economic analysis would predict.

## DOES CHEAP FOOD MAKE US WORSE OFF?

A third question being asked by some people is: Are Americans really better off due to the lower cost of food? Ordinarily, economists would argue that a technological improvement that lowered the costs of a good definitely would improve the lot of consumers. But in the present case, the adverse health effects of the extra calories are starting to become significant. Obesity is implicated in diabetes, heart disease, strokes, depression, and some cancers, and the number of people who are disabled due to obesity-related injuries or other health problems is rising sharply. It is estimated that more than $150 billion per year is now spent on obesity-related health problems, about 10 percent of our total health care spending.

As the poundage has piled up across the country, so too have the sales of diet books, as well as the rates of expensive bariatric surgery (in which the stomach is reduced in size to cut caloric intake and absorption). All in all, some analysts have suggested, maybe the lower cost of food has made people *worse* off, by inducing them to do something that they would rather not do—put on weight. This might be particularly the case for people who are said to have little self-control of the amount they eat. There may be something to this argument, but it's also true that people who live in cold weather climates, such as Montana, the Dakotas, and Minnesota, routinely complain about the weather in the winter. People in such climes also spend far more than the average person on clothes to offset the adverse effects of the cold weather. Surely we would not want to argue that such people are worse off for having chosen to live where they do, rather than in warmer locales. Similarly, in the case of people who are said to lack control over the amount they eat, just who is it that shall decide—and enforce—their caloric intake?

## THE ROLE OF SMOKING

There is one final point to our story, one that illustrates that even the best of intentions sometimes yield adverse unintended consequences. Over the same period that Americans have been packing on the pounds, the taxes on cigarettes have risen sharply, even while the number of places where it is lawful to smoke has shrunk significantly. On both counts, the full cost of smoking (price per pack, plus the hassle) has been rising, and one consequence is that smoking has declined in the United States. It is well known that people have a tendency to eat more when they stop smoking, and this very fact seems to be showing up in the national statistics on excess poundage. Where the full costs of smoking have risen the greatest, so too has the incidence of obesity. In effect, people are being induced to substitute eating for smoking. Despite the adverse health effects of the resulting weight gains, the *net* health trade-offs here are likely positive, given the highly lethal effects of smoking. Still, this development reminds us that although people's behavior can easily be understood by examining the incentives they face, sometimes it is difficult to determine ahead of time what the full range of incentives will be.

## DISCUSSION QUESTIONS

1. Calculate your own BMI, based on the formula in footnote 1, but keep it Top Secret. For comparison purposes, consider the following data for approximate average height and weight of major college football players, by position:

| Position | Height (Inches) | Weight (Pounds) |
|----------|-----------------|-----------------|
| Quarterback | 75 | 220 |
| Running back | 71 | 215 |
| Wide receiver | 73 | 195 |

    Is the average player at any of these positions officially obese? What factors other than just weight and height might be important in assessing the "healthy" BMI for an individual?

2. Many insurance companies now impose a surcharge (in effect, a higher premium) for people who use tobacco products. What effect on tobacco usage do you predict such surcharges to have? What

would be the expected effect of an insurance surcharge for people who are obese?

3. Over the past twenty years, many state and local governments across America have (i) sharply raised cigarette taxes and (ii) sharply limited the number of places where people may smoke. Both policy changes have helped reduce the amount of cigarette smoking in the United States. If these same governments decided that they wished to reduce obesity, how might they go about doing so?

4. The technological changes in food preparation seem to have had the greatest effect on the time costs of a "meal," rather than affecting the time cost of consuming extra calories during any given meal. What does economics predict about what we should observe has happened to the number of meals consumed each day, compared to the number of calories consumed per meal?

5. The change in food preparation technologies over the past 30–40 years caused the biggest reduction in time costs for married women. What does economics predict should have happened to the weight of married women relative to other people?

6. During the twentieth century, the cost of the automobile fell drastically, leading to a dramatic rise in the number of miles driven. But all of this driving led to automobile accidents, which now kill more than 30,000 people each year and maim hundreds of thousands more. Is it possible that the fall in the price of the automobile actually made Americans worse off? How much would your answer depend on whether those fatalities were among the people driving the cars as opposed to innocent bystanders, such as pedestrians and children? (*Hint:* Take a look at the chapters in Part Four.)

# CHAPTER 4

# Flying the Friendly Skies?

Most of us hop into our car with little thought for our personal safety, beyond perhaps the act of putting on seat belts. Yet even though travel on scheduled, commercial airlines is safer than driving to work or to the grocery store, many people approach air travel with a sense of foreboding, if not downright fear.

If we were to think carefully about the wisdom of traveling 600 miles/hour in an aluminum tube 7 miles above the earth, several questions might come to mind: How safe is this? How safe should it be? Because the people who operate airlines are not in it for fun, does their interest in making a buck ignore our interest in making it home in one piece? Is some form of government regulation the only way to ensure safety in the skies?

## THE ECONOMICS OF SAFETY

The science of economics begins with one simple principle: We live in a world of **scarcity,** which implies that to get more of any good, we must sacrifice some of other goods. This is just as true of safety as it is of pizzas or haircuts or works of art. Safety confers benefits (we live longer and more enjoyably), but achieving it also entails **costs** (we must give up something to obtain that safety).

As the degree of safety rises, the total benefits of safety rise, but the marginal (or incremental) benefits of additional safety decline. Consider a simple example: Adding exit doors to an airplane increases the number of people who can escape in the event of an emergency evacuation. Nevertheless, each *additional* door adds less in safety benefits than the previous one; if the fourth door enables, say, an extra ten people to escape, the fifth may enable only an extra six to escape. (If this sounds implausible, imagine having a door for each person; the last door added will enable at most one more person to escape.) So we say that the marginal (or incremental) benefit of safety declines as the amount of safety increases.

Let's look now at the other side of the equation: As the amount of safety increases, both the total and the marginal (incremental) costs of providing safety rise. Having a fuel gauge on the plane's instrument panel clearly enhances safety because it reduces the chance that the plane will run out of fuel while in flight.[1] It is always possible that a fuel gauge will malfunction, so having a backup fuel gauge also adds to safety. Because having two gauges is more costly than having just one, the total costs of safety rise as safety increases. It is also clear, however, that while the cost of the second gauge is (at least) as great as the cost of the first, the second gauge has a smaller positive impact on safety. Thus, the cost per unit of additional (incremental) safety is higher for the second fuel gauge than for the first.

## How Safe is Safe Enough?

How much safety should we have? For an economist, the answer to such a question is generally expressed in terms of **marginal benefits** and **marginal costs.** The economically *efficient* level of safety occurs when the marginal cost of increasing safety just equals the marginal benefit of that increased safety. Put somewhat differently, if the marginal benefits of adding (or keeping) a safety feature exceed the marginal costs of doing so, the feature is worthwhile. But if the added benefits of a safety device do *not* exceed the added costs, we should refrain from installing the device. Note there are two related issues here: How safe should we be, and how should we *achieve* that level of safety?

Both of these issues took on added urgency on the morning of September 11, 2001, when terrorists hijacked and crashed four U.S. commercial jetliners. This episode revealed that air travel was far less safe than previously believed. Immediately, it was clear that we should devote additional resources to airline safety; what was not clear was

---

1 Notice that we say "reduces" rather than "eliminates." In 1978, a United Airlines pilot preoccupied with a malfunctioning landing gear evidently failed to pay sufficient attention to his cockpit gauges. When the plane was forced to crash-land after running out of fuel, eight people died.

how *much* additional resources should be thus devoted and precisely *what* changes should be made. For example, almost everyone agreed that more careful screening of passengers and baggage at airports would produce important safety benefits. But how should we achieve this? Should carry-on bags be prohibited or just examined more carefully? How thoroughly should checked luggage be screened for bombs? Even now, our answers to these questions are evolving as we learn more about the extent of the threat and the costs of alternative responses to it. Nevertheless, throughout the process, economic principles can help us make the most sensible decisions.

In general, the efficient level of safety will not be perfect safety because perfection is simply too costly to achieve. For example, to be absolutely certain that no one is ever killed or injured in an airplane crash, we would have to prevent all travel in airplanes—an unrealistic and impracticable prospect. This means that if we wish to enjoy the advantages of flying, we must be willing to accept *some* risk—a conclusion that each of us implicitly accepts every time we step aboard an airplane.

## THE IMPORTANCE OF CIRCUMSTANCES

Changes in circumstances can alter the efficient level of safety. For example, if a technological change reduces the costs of bomb-scanning equipment, the marginal costs of preventing terrorist bomb attacks will be lower. It will be efficient to have more airports install the machines and to have extra machines at large airports to speed the screening process. Air travel will become safer because of the technological change. Similarly, if the marginal benefits of safety rise for some reason—perhaps because the president of the United States is on board—it could be efficient to take more precautions, resulting in safer air travel. Given the factors that determine the benefits and costs of safety, the result of a change in circumstances will be some determinate level of safety that generally will be associated with some risk of death or injury.

Airplanes are complex systems, and an amazing number of components can fail. Over the century that humans have been flying, airplane manufacturers and airlines have studied every one of the malfunctions thus far and have put into place design changes and operating procedures aimed at preventing recurring error. The efforts have paid off. Between 1950 and 2010, for example, the fatal accident rate on U.S. commercial airlines was cut by almost 97 percent.

## DOES THE GOVERNMENT KNOW BEST?

Consumers have the greatest incentive to ensure that air travel is safe, and if information were free, we could assert with some confidence that the actual level of safety supplied by firms was the efficient level of safety. Consumers would simply observe the safety offered by different airlines, the prices they charge, and select the degrees of safety that best suited their preferences and budgets, just as with other goods. But information is not free; it is a **scarce good,** costly to obtain. As a result, passengers may be unaware of the safety record of various airlines or the competence of the pilots and the maintenance procedures of an airline's mechanics. Indeed, even the airlines themselves may be uncertain about the efficient level of safety, perhaps because they have no way of estimating the true threat of terrorist attacks, for example. Such possibilities have been used to argue that the federal government should mandate certain minimum levels of safety, as it does today through the operation of the Federal Aviation Administration (FAA). Let's look at this issue in some detail.

One argument in favor of government safety standards rests on the presumption that, left to their own devices, airlines would provide less safety than passengers want. This might happen, for example, if customers could not tell (at a reasonable cost) whether the equipment, training, and procedures employed by an airline are safe. If passengers cannot cheaply gauge the level of safety, they will not be willing to reward airlines for being safe or punish them for being unsafe. If safety is costly to provide and consumers are unwilling to pay for it because they cannot accurately measure it, airlines will provide too little of it. The conclusion is that government experts, such as the FAA, should set safety standards for the industry.

## DO CONSUMERS KNOW BEST?

This conclusion seems plausible, but it ignores two simple points. First, how is the government to know the efficient level of safety? Even if the FAA knows the costs of all possible safety measures, it still does not have enough information to set efficient safety standards because it does not know the value that people place on safety. Without such information, the FAA has no way to assess the benefits of additional safety and hence no means of knowing whether those benefits are greater or less than the added costs.

The second point is that people want to reach their destinations safely. Even if they cannot observe whether an airline hires good pilots or bad pilots, they can see whether that airline's planes land safely or crash. If it is *safety* that is important to consumers—and not the obscure, costly-to-measure *reasons* for that safety—the fact that consumers cannot easily measure metal fatigue in jet engines may be totally irrelevant to the process of achieving the efficient level of safety.

Interestingly, evidence shows that consumers are indeed cognizant of the safety performance of airlines, and that they "punish" airlines that perform in an unsafe manner. Researchers have found that when an airline is at fault in a fatal plane crash, consumers appear to downgrade their safety rating of the airline (i.e., they revise upward their estimates of the likelihood of future fatal crashes). As a result, the offending airline suffers substantial adverse financial consequences over and above the costs of losing the plane and being sued on behalf of the victims. These findings suggest a striking degree of safety awareness on the part of supposedly ignorant consumers.

## WHAT ABOUT TERRORISM?

Of course, this discussion leaves open the issue of how to handle safety threats posed by terrorists and other miscreants. For example, much of the information that goes into assessing terrorist threats is classified as secret, and its revelation to airlines or consumers might compromise key sources of the data. Hence, there could be an advantage to having the government try to approximate the efficient safety outcome by mandating certain screening provisions without revealing exactly why they are being chosen. Similarly, because airlines are connected in networks (so that people and baggage move from one airline to another in the course of a trip), achieving the efficient level of safety might require a common set of screening rules for all airlines. Even so, this does not inform us whether the government should impose those rules or the airlines should come to a voluntary joint agreement on them.

We began this chapter with the commonplace observation that airlines are safer than cars. Yet many people still worry for their safety every time they get on an airplane. Are they being irrational? Well, the answer, it seems, is in the eye of the beholder. Measured in terms of fatalities per mile traveled, airplanes are about 15 times safer than cars (and 176 times safer than walking, we might add). But this number masks the fact that 68 percent of aircraft accidents happen on takeoff and landing, and these operations occupy only 6 percent of flight time. It is presumably this fact that quite sensibly makes people nervous whenever they find themselves approaching an airport.

# DISCUSSION QUESTIONS

1. Is it possible to be too safe? Explain what you mean by "too safe."

2. Suppose it is possible to observe (or measure) four attributes of airlines: (i) the size of their planes (measured in passenger-carrying capacity), (ii) the experience levels of their pilots, (iii) the age of their planes, and (iv) the length of the typical route they fly. Which airlines would be likely to have the fewest fatal accidents? Which would be expected to have the most?

3. Is safety likely to be a "normal" good (i.e., something people want to consume more of as they get richer)? Use your answer to this question to predict likely safety records of airlines based in North America and Europe, compared to those based in South America and Africa. Then go to www.airsafe.com to see if your prediction is confirmed or refuted by the facts.

4. Many automobile manufacturers routinely advertise the safety of their cars, yet airlines generally do not mention safety in their advertising. Can you suggest an explanation for this difference?

5. Many economists would argue that private companies are likely to be more efficient than the government at operating airlines. Yet many economists would also argue that there is a valid reason for government to regulate the safety of those same airlines. Can you explain why the government might be good at ensuring safety, even though it might not be good at operating the airlines?

6. Professional football teams sometimes charter airplanes to take them to their away games. Would you feel safer on a United Airlines plane that had been chartered by the Washington Redskins than on a regularly scheduled United Airlines flight?

# CHAPTER 5

# The Mystery
# of Wealth

Why are the citizens of some nations rich while the inhabitants of others are poor? Your initial answer might be "because of differences in the **natural resource endowments** of the nations." It is true that ample endowments of energy, timber, and fertile land all help raise wealth. But natural resources can be only a very small part of the answer, as witnessed by many counterexamples. Switzerland and Luxembourg, for example, are nearly devoid of key natural resources, yet the real incomes of citizens of those lands are among the world's highest. Similarly, Hong Kong, which consists of a few square miles of rock and hillside, is one of the economic miracles of modern times, while in Russia, a land amply endowed with vast quantities of virtually every important resource, most people remain mired in economic misery.

A number of studies have begun to unravel the mystery of **economic growth.** Repeatedly, they have found that it is the fundamental political and legal **institutions** of society that are conducive to growth. Of these, political stability, secure private property rights, and legal systems based on the **rule of law** are among the most important. Such institutions encourage people to make long-term investments in improving land and in all forms of **physical capital** and **human capital.** These investments raise the **capital stock,** which in turn provides for more growth long into the future. And the cumulative effects of this growth over time eventually yield much higher standards of living.

## THE IMPORTANCE OF LEGAL SYSTEMS

Consider first the contrasting effects of different legal systems on economic growth. Many legal systems around the world today are based on one of

**TABLE 5–1** Differing Legal Systems

| Common Law Nations | Civil Law Nations |
|---|---|
| Australia | Brazil |
| Canada | Egypt |
| India | France |
| Israel | Greece |
| New Zealand | Italy |
| United Kingdom | Mexico |
| United States | Sweden |

two models: the English **common law system** and the French **civil law system.** Common law systems reflect a conscious decision in favor of a limited role for government and emphasize the importance of the judiciary in constraining the power of the executive and legislative branches of government. In contrast, civil law systems favor the creation of a strong centralized government in which the legislature and the executive branches have the power to grant preferential treatment to special interests. Table 5–1 shows a sampling of common law and civil law countries.

Research reveals that the security of **property rights** is much stronger in common law systems, such as observed in Britain and its former colonies, including the United States. In nations such as France and its former colonies, the civil law systems are much more likely to yield unpredictable changes in the rules of the game—the structure of **property and contract rights.** This unpredictability makes people reluctant to make long-term fixed investments, a fact that ultimately slows the economic growth of these nations and lowers the standard of living for their citizens.

The reasoning here is simple. If you know that the police will not help you protect your rights to a home or a car, you are less likely to acquire those assets. Similarly, if you cannot easily enforce business or employment contracts that you make, you are less likely to make those contracts—and hence less likely to produce as many goods or services. And if you cannot plan for the future because you don't know what the rules of the game will be in 10 years or perhaps even one year from now, you are less likely to make the kinds of productive long-term investments that take years to pay off. Common law systems seem to do a better job at enforcing contracts and securing property rights and so would be expected to promote economic activity now and economic growth over time.

## The Economic Impact of Institutions

Research into the economic performance of nations around the world from 1960 to the 1990s found that economic growth was one-third higher in the common law nations, with their strong property rights, than in civil law nations. Over the more than three decades covered, the standard of living—measured by real **per capita income**—increased more than 20 percent in common law nations compared to civil law nations. If such a pattern persisted over the span of a century, it would produce a staggering 80 percent real per capita income difference in favor of nations with secure property rights.

Other research has taken a much broader view, both across time and across institutions, in assessing economic growth. Institutions such as political stability, protection against violence or theft, security of contracts, and freedom from regulatory burdens all contribute to sustained economic growth. Indeed, it is key institutions such as these, rather than natural resource endowments, that explain long-term differences in economic growth and thus present-day differences in levels of real income. To illustrate the powerful effect of institutions, consider the contrast between Mexico, with per capita real income of about $14,000 today, and the United States, with per capita real income of about $50,000. Had Mexico developed with the same political and legal institutions that the United States has enjoyed, per capita income in Mexico would today be equal to that in the United States.

## The Origins of Institutions

Given the great importance of such institutions in determining long-term growth, one might ask another important question: How have countries gotten the political and legal institutions they have today? The answer has to do with disease, of all things. An examination of more than seventy former European colonies reveals that a variety of strategies were pursued. In Australia, New Zealand, and North America, the colonists found geography and climates that were conducive to good health. Permanent settlement was attractive, so colonists created institutions to protect private property and curb the power of the state. But when Europeans arrived in Africa and South America, they encountered tropical diseases, such as malaria and yellow fever, which produced high mortality rates. This discouraged permanent settlement and encouraged a mentality focused on extracting metals, cash crops, and other resources. As a result, there were few **incentives** to promote democratic institutions or stable long-term property rights systems. The differing initial institutions helped shape economic growth over the years and, because of the broad persistence of those institutions, continue to shape the political and legal character and the standard of living in these nations today.

## INSTITUTIONAL CHANGE TODAY

Recent events also illustrate that the effects of political and legal institutions can be drastically accelerated—in either direction. Consider China, which in 1979 began to change its institutions in two key ways. First, China began to experiment with private property rights for a few of its citizens, under narrow circumstances. Second, the Chinese government began to clear away obstacles to foreign investment, making China a more secure place for Western companies to do business. Although the institutional changes have been modest, their combined effects have been substantial. Over the years since, economic growth in China has accelerated, averaging almost 7 percent per year. And if that doesn't sound like much, keep in mind that it has been enough over that period to raise real per capita income in China by a factor of 8.

For an example of the potential *destructive* impact of institutional change, we need to look no further than Zimbabwe. When that country won its independence from Britain in 1980, it was one of the most prosperous nations in Africa. Soon after taking power as Zimbabwe's first (and so far only) president, Robert Mugabe began disassembling that nation's rule of law, tearing apart the institutions that had helped it grow rich. He reduced the security of property rights in land and eventually confiscated those rights altogether. Mugabe has also gradually taken control of the prices of most goods and services in his nation and even controls the price of its national currency, at least the price at which Zimbabweans are allowed to trade it. Moreover, the Mugabe government has confiscated large stocks of food and much of anything of value that might be exported out of or imported into Zimbabwe. In short, anything that is produced or saved has become subject to confiscation, so the incentives to do either are—to put it mildly—reduced.

As a result, between 1980 and 1996, real per capita income in Zimbabwe fell by one-third, and since 1996, it has fallen by an additional third. Eighty percent of the workforce is unemployed, investment is nonexistent, and the annual inflation rate reached an astonishing 231 million percent. (In 2009 Zimbabwe gave up on having its own currency, and now uses American dollars and South African rand.) The fruit of decades of labor and capital investment has been destroyed because the institutions that made that progress possible have been eliminated. It is a lesson we ignore at our peril.

# Discussion Questions

1. Go to a source such as the CIA Factbook or the World Bank and collect per capita income and population data for each of the nations listed in Table 5–1. Compare the average per capita income of the common law countries with the average per capita income of the civil law countries. Based on the discussion in the chapter, identify at least two other factors that you think are important to take into account when assessing whether the differences you observe are likely due to the systems of the countries.

2. Most international attempts to aid people living in low-income nations have come in one of two forms: (i) gifts of consumer goods (such as food) and (ii) assistance in constructing or obtaining capital goods (such as tractors, dams, or roads). Based on what you have learned in this chapter, how likely are such efforts to *permanently* raise the standard of living in such countries? Explain.

3. Both Louisiana and Quebec have systems of local law (state and provincial, respectively) that are heavily influenced by their common French heritage, which includes civil law. What do you predict is true about per capita income in Louisiana compared to the other U.S. states, and per capita income in Quebec compared to the other Canadian provinces? Is this prediction confirmed by the facts (which can be readily ascertained with a few quick Web searches)? Identify at least two other factors that you think are important to take into account when assessing whether the differences you observe are likely due to the influence of civil law institutions.

4. Consider two countries, A and B, which have identical *physical* endowments of a key natural resource. In country A, any profits that are made from extracting that resource are subject to confiscation by the government, while in country B, there is no such risk. How does the risk of expropriation affect the *economic* endowment of the two nations? In which nation are people richer?

5. In light of your answer to question 4, how do you explain the fact that in some countries there is widespread political support for government policies that expropriate resources from some groups for the purpose of handing them out to other groups?

6. If the crucial factor determining a country's low standard of living is the adverse set of legal and cultural institutions it possesses, can you offer suggestions for how the other nations of the world might help in permanently raising that country's standard of living?

# PART TWO

# Globalization and International Trade

# CHAPTER 6

# The Opposition to Globalization

The last 20 years has been a time of great change on the international trade front. The North American Free Trade Agreement (NAFTA), for example, substantially reduced **trade barriers** among citizens of Canada, the United States, and Mexico. On a global scale, the Uruguay Round of the General Agreement on Tariffs and Trade (GATT) was ratified by 117 nations including the United States. Under the terms of this agreement, the **World Trade Organization (WTO),** whose membership now numbers more than 150, replaced GATT, and **tariffs** were cut worldwide. Agricultural **subsidies** were also reduced, and patent protections were extended. The WTO has also established arbitration boards to settle international disputes over trade issues.

## THE GAINS FROM TRADE

Many economists believe that both NAFTA and the agreements reached during the Uruguay Round were victories not only for free trade and **globalization** (the integration of national economies into an international economy) but also for the citizens of the participating nations. Nevertheless, many noneconomists, particularly politicians, opposed these agreements, so it is important to understand what is beneficial about NAFTA, the Uruguay Round, the WTO, and free trade and globalization.

Voluntary trade creates new **wealth.** In voluntary trade, both parties in an exchange gain. They give up something of lesser value to them in return for something of greater value to them. In this sense, exchanges are always unequal. But it is this unequal nature of exchange that is the source of the increased **productivity** and higher wealth that occur whenever trade takes place. When we engage in exchange, what we give up is worth less than what we get—if this were not true, we would not have traded. What is true for us is also true for our trading partner, meaning that the partner is better off, too. (Of course, sometimes after an exchange, you may believe that you were mistaken about the value of what you just received—this is called *buyer's remorse*, but it does not affect our discussion.)

Free trade encourages individuals to employ their abilities in the most productive manner possible and to exchange the fruits of their efforts. The **gains from trade** arise from one of the fundamental ideas in economics: A nation gains from doing what it can do best *relative to other nations*, that is, by specializing in those endeavors in which it has a **comparative advantage.** Trade encourages individuals and nations to discover ways to specialize so that they can become more productive and enjoy higher incomes. Increased productivity and the subsequent increase in the rate of **economic growth** are exactly what the signatories of the Uruguay Round and NAFTA sought—and are obtaining—by reducing trade barriers and thus increasing globalization.

## KEEPING THE COMPETITION OUT

Despite the enormous gains from exchange, some people (sometimes a great many of them) routinely oppose free trade, particularly in the case of international trade. This opposition comes in many guises, but they all basically come down to one: When our borders are open to trade with other nations, this exposes some individuals and businesses in our nation to more **competition.** Most firms and workers hate competition, and who can blame them? After all, if a firm can keep competitors out, its **profits** are sure to stay the same or even rise. Also, if workers can prevent competition from other sources, they can enjoy higher wages and perhaps a larger selection of jobs. So the real source of most opposition to globalization is that the opponents of trade dislike the competition that comes with it. This position is not immoral or unethical, but it is not altruistic or noble, either. It is based on self-interest, pure and simple.

Opposition to globalization is nothing new, by the way. In the twentieth century, it culminated most famously in the Smoot–Hawley Tariff Act of 1930. This federal statute was a classic example of **protectionism**—an effort to protect a subset of U.S. producers at the expense of consumers and other producers. It included tariff schedules for over twenty thousand products, raising taxes on affected imports by an average of 52 percent.

The Smoot–Hawley Tariff Act encouraged so-called *beggar-thy-neighbor* policies by the rest of the world. Such policies are an attempt to improve (a portion of) one's domestic economy at the expense of foreign countries' economies. In this case, tariffs were imposed to discourage imports in the hope that domestic import-competing industries would benefit. France, the Netherlands, Switzerland, and the United Kingdom soon adopted beggar-thy-neighbor policies to counter the American ones. The result was a massive reduction in international trade. According to many economists, this caused a worldwide worsening of the Great Depression.

Opponents of globalization sometimes claim that beggar-thy-neighbor policies really do benefit the United States by protecting import-competing industries. In general, this claim is not correct. It is true that *some* Americans benefit from such policies, but two large groups of Americans lose. First, the purchasers of imports and import-competing goods suffer from the higher prices and reduced selection of goods and suppliers caused by tariffs and import **quotas.** Second, the decline in imports caused by protectionism also causes a decline in *exports,* thereby harming firms and workers in these industries. This result follows directly from one of the fundamental propositions in international trade: *In the long run, imports are paid for by exports.* This proposition simply states that when one country buys goods and services from the rest of the world (imports), the rest of the world eventually wants goods from that country (exports) in exchange. Given this fundamental proposition, a corollary becomes obvious: *Any restriction on imports leads to a reduction in exports.* Thus, any extra business for import-competing industries gained as a result of tariffs or quotas means at least as much business *lost* for exporting industries.

## THE ARGUMENTS AGAINST GLOBALIZATION

Opponents of globalization often raise a variety of objections in their efforts to reduce it. For example, it is sometimes claimed that foreign companies engage in **dumping,** which is selling their goods in the United States "below cost." The first question to ask when such charges are made is, below *whose* cost? Clearly, if the foreign firm is selling in the United States, it must be offering the good for sale at a price that is at or below the costs of U.S. firms. Otherwise it could not induce Americans to buy it. But the ability of individuals or firms to obtain goods at lower cost is one of the *benefits* of free trade, not one of its harmful aspects.

What about claims that import sales are taking place at prices below the foreign company's costs? This amounts to arguing that the owners of the foreign company are voluntarily giving some of their wealth to us, namely, the difference between their costs and the (lower) price they charge us. It is possible, though unlikely, that they might wish to do this, perhaps because this could be the cheapest way of getting us to try a product that we would not otherwise purchase. But even supposing it is true, why would we want to refuse this gift? As a nation, we are richer if we accept it. Moreover, it is a gift that will be offered for only a short time. There is no point in selling at prices below cost unless the seller hopes to soon raise the price profitably above cost!

Another argument sometimes raised against globalization is that the goods are produced abroad using "unfair" labor practices (such as the use of child labor) or production processes that do not meet U.S. environmental standards. Such charges are sometimes true. But we must remember two things here. First, although we may find the use of child labor (or perhaps 60-hour workweeks with no overtime pay) objectionable, such practices were at one time commonplace in the United States. They were common here for the same reason they are currently practiced abroad. The people involved were (or are) too poor to do otherwise. Some families in developing nations cannot survive unless all family members contribute. As unfortunate as this situation is, if we insist on imposing our values and attitudes—shaped in part by our high wealth—on peoples whose wealth is far lower than ours, we run the risk of making them worse off even as we think we are helping them.

Similar considerations apply to environmental standards. Individuals' and nations' willingness to pay for environmental quality is very much shaped by their wealth. Environmental quality is a **normal good.** This means that people who are rich (such as Americans) want to consume more of it per capita than people who are poor. Insisting that other nations meet environmental standards that we find acceptable is much like insisting that they wear the clothes we wear, use the modes of transportation we prefer, and consume the foods we like. The few people who can afford it will indeed be living in the style to which we are accustomed, but most people in developing countries will not be able to afford anything like that style.

There is one important exception to this argument. When foreign air or water pollution is generated near enough to our borders (e.g., in Mexico or Canada) to cause harm to Americans, good public policy presumably dictates that we seek to treat that pollution as though it were being generated inside our borders.

Our point is not that foreign labor or environmental standards are, or should be, irrelevant to Americans. Instead, our point is that achieving high standards of either is costly, and trade restrictions are unlikely to be the most efficient or effective way to achieve them. Just as important, labor standards and environmental standards are all too often raised as smokescreens to hide the real motive: keeping the competition out.

## WHY ARE ANTITRADE MEASURES PASSED?

If globalization is beneficial and restrictions on trade are generally harmful, how does legislation such as the Smoot–Hawley Tariff Act and other restrictions on international trade ever get passed? The explanation is that because foreign competition often affects a narrow and specific import-competing industry, such as textiles, shoes, or automobiles, trade restrictions are crafted to benefit a narrow, well-defined group of economic agents. For example, limits on imports of Japanese automobiles in the 1980s chiefly benefited workers and owners of the Big Three automakers in this country: General Motors, Ford, and Chrysler. Similarly, long-standing quotas that limit imports of sugar benefit the owners of a handful of large U.S. sugar producers. Because of the concentrated benefits that accrue when Congress votes in favor of trade restrictions, sufficient funds can be raised in those industries to aggressively lobby members of Congress to impose those restrictions.

The eventual reduction in exports that must follow is normally spread throughout all export industries. Consequently, no specific group of workers, managers, or shareholders in export industries will be motivated to contribute funds to lobby Congress to reduce international trade restrictions. Further, although consumers of imports and import-competing goods lose due to trade restrictions, they, too, are typically a diffuse group of individuals, none of whom will be greatly affected individually by any particular import restriction. This simultaneous existence of concentrated benefits and diffuse costs led Mark Twain to observe long ago that the free traders win the arguments but the **protectionists** win the votes.

Of course, the protectionists don't win *all* the votes—after all, about one-seventh of the U.S. economy is based on international trade. Despite the opposition to free trade that comes from many quarters, its benefits to the economy as a whole are so great that it is unthinkable that we might do away with international trade altogether. Both economic theory and empirical evidence clearly indicate that on balance, Americans will be better off with freer trade achieved through such developments as NAFTA and the WTO.

# FOR CRITICAL ANALYSIS

1. For a number of years, Japanese automakers voluntarily limited the number of cars they exported to the United States. What effect do you think this had on Japanese imports of U.S. cars and U.S. exports of goods and services *other than* automobiles?

2. Until a few years ago, U.S. cars exported to Japan had the driver controls on the left side (as in the United States). The Japanese, however, drive on the left side of the road, so Japanese cars sold in Japan have the driver controls on the right side. Suppose the Japanese tried to sell their cars in the United States with the driver controls on the right side. What impact would this likely have on their sales in this country? Do you think the unwillingness of U.S. carmakers to put the driver controls on the "correct" side for exports to Japan had any effect on their sales of cars in that country?

3. Keeping in mind the key propositions of globalization outlined in this chapter, what is the likely impact of international trade restrictions on the following variables in the United States: employment, the **unemployment rate, real GDP,** and the **price level**? Explain your responses.

4. During the late 1980s and early 1990s, American automobile manufacturers greatly increased the quality of the cars they produced relative to the quality of the cars produced in other nations. What effect do you think this had on American imports of Japanese cars, Japanese imports of American cars, and American exports of goods and services other than automobiles?

5. The U.S. government subsidizes the export of U.S.-manufactured commercial aircraft. What effect do you think this policy has on American imports of foreign goods and American exports of products other than commercial aircraft? Explain.

6. Who bears the costs and enjoys the benefits of the subsidies mentioned in the previous question?

# CHAPTER 7

# The $750,000 Job

In even-numbered years, particularly years evenly divisible by four, politicians of all persuasions are apt to give long-winded speeches about the need to protect U.S. jobs from the evils of **globalization.** To accomplish this goal, we are encouraged to "buy American." If further encouragement is needed, we are told that if we do not voluntarily reduce the amount of imported goods we purchase, the government will impose (or make more onerous) **tariffs** (taxes) on imported goods or **quotas** (quantity restrictions) that physically limit imports. The objective of this exercise is to "save U.S. jobs."

Unlike African elephants or blue whales, U.S. jobs are in no danger of becoming extinct. There are virtually an unlimited number of potential jobs in the U.S. economy, and there always will be. Some of these jobs are not very pleasant, and many others do not pay very well, but there will always be employment of some sort as long as there is **scarcity.** So when a steelworker making $72,000 per year says that imports of foreign steel should be reduced to save his job, what he really means is this: He wants to be protected from **competition** so that he can continue his present employment at the same or a higher salary rather than move to a different job that has less desirable working conditions or pays less. There is nothing wrong with the steelworker's goal (better working conditions and higher pay), but it has nothing to do with "saving jobs."

## THE GAINS FROM GLOBALIZATION

In any discussion of the consequences of international trade restrictions, it is essential to remember two facts. First, *we pay for imports with exports.* It is true that in the short run, we can sell off **assets** or borrow from abroad if we happen to import more goods and services than we export. But we have only a finite amount of assets to sell, and foreigners will not wait forever for us to pay our bills. Ultimately, our accounts can be settled only if we *provide* (export) goods and services to the trading partners from whom we *purchase* (import) goods and services. Trade, after all, involves a quid pro quo (literally, "something for something").

The second point to remember is that *voluntary trade is mutually beneficial to the trading partners.* If we restrict international trade, we reduce those benefits, both for our trading partners and for ourselves. One way these reduced benefits are manifested is in the form of curtailed employment opportunities for workers. The reasoning is simple. Other countries will buy our goods only if they can market theirs because they, too, have to export goods to pay for their imports. Thus, any U.S. restrictions on imports to this country—via tariffs, quotas, or other means—ultimately cause a reduction in our exports because other countries will be unable to pay for our goods. This implies that import restrictions must inevitably decrease the size of our export sector. So imposing trade restrictions to save jobs in import-competing industries has the effect of costing jobs in export industries. Most studies have shown that the net effect seems to be reduced employment overall.

## The Adverse Effects of Trade Restrictions

Just as important, import restrictions impose costs on U.S. consumers as a whole. By reducing competition from abroad, quotas, tariffs, and other trade restraints push up the prices of foreign goods and enable U.S. producers to hike their own prices. Perhaps the best-documented example of this effect is found in the automobile industry, where "voluntary" restrictions on Japanese imports were in place for more than a decade.

Due in part to the enhanced quality of imported cars, sales of domestically produced automobiles fell from nine million units in 1978 to an average of six million units per year between 1980 and 1982. Profits of U.S. automakers plummeted as well, and some incurred substantial losses. The automobile manufacturers' and autoworkers' unions demanded protection from import competition. Politicians from automobile-producing states rallied to their cause. The result was a "voluntary" agreement by Japanese car companies (the most important competitors of U.S. firms) to restrict their U.S. sales to 1.68 million units per year. This agreement—which amounted to a quota, even though it never officially bore that name—began in April 1981 and continued well into the 1990s in various forms.

Robert W. Crandall, an economist with the Brookings Institution, estimated how much this voluntary trade restriction cost U.S. consumers in higher car prices. According to his estimates, the reduced supply of Japanese cars pushed their prices up by $2,000 per car, measured in 2011 dollars. The higher prices of Japanese imports in turn enabled domestic producers to hike their prices an average of $800 per car. The total tab in the first full year of the program was over $8 billion. Crandall also estimated that about twenty-six thousand jobs in automobile-related industries were protected by the voluntary import restrictions. Dividing $8 billion by twenty-six thousand jobs yields a cost to consumers of more than $300,000 *per year* for every job preserved in the automobile industry. U.S. consumers could have saved nearly $5 billion on their car purchases each year if instead of implicitly agreeing to import restrictions, they had simply given $100,000 in cash to every autoworker whose job was protected by the voluntary import restraints.

The same types of calculations have been made for other industries. Tariffs in the apparel industry were increased between 1977 and 1981, preserving the jobs of about 116,000 U.S. apparel workers at a cost of $45,000 per job each year. The cost of **protectionism** has been even higher in other industries. Jobs preserved in the glassware industry due to trade restrictions cost $200,000 apiece each year. In the maritime industry, the yearly cost of trade restriction is $290,000 per job. In the steel industry, the cost of protecting a job has been estimated at an astounding $750,000 per year. If free trade were permitted, each steelworker losing a job could be given a cash payment of half that amount each year, and consumers would still save a lot of **wealth.**

## THE REAL IMPACT ON JOBS

What is more, none of these cost studies has attempted to estimate the ultimate impact of import restrictions on the flow of exports, the number of workers who lose their jobs in the export sector, and thus total employment in the economy.

Remember that imports pay for exports and that our imports are the exports of our trading partners. So when imports to the United States are restricted, our trading partners will necessarily buy less of what *we* produce. The resulting decline in export sales means less employment in exporting industries. And the total reduction in trade leads to less employment for workers such as stevedores (who load and unload ships) and truck drivers (who carry goods to and from ports). On both counts—the overall cut in trade and the accompanying fall in exports—protectionism leads to employment declines that might not be obvious immediately.

Some years ago, Congress tried to pass a "domestic-content" bill for automobiles. The legislation would have required that cars sold in the United States have a minimum percentage of their components manufactured and assembled in this country. Proponents of the legislation argued that it would have protected 300,000 jobs in the U.S. automobile manufacturing and auto parts supply industries. Yet the legislation's supporters failed to recognize the negative impact of the bill on trade in general and its ultimate impact on U.S. export industries. A U.S. Department of Labor study did recognize these impacts, estimating that the domestic-content legislation would have cost more jobs in trade-related and export industries than it protected in import-competing businesses. Congress ultimately decided not to impose a domestic-content requirement for cars sold in the United States.

## THE LONG-RUN FAILURE OF IMPORT CONTROLS

In principle, trade restrictions are imposed to provide economic help to specific industries and to increase employment in those industries. Ironically, the long-term effects may be just the opposite. Researchers at the **World Trade Organization (WTO)** examined employment in three industries that have been heavily protected throughout the world: textiles, clothing, and iron and steel. Despite stringent **protectionist** measures, employment in these industries actually declined during the period of protection, in some cases dramatically. In textiles, employment fell 22 percent in the United States and 46 percent in the European Common Market (the predecessor of the **European Union**). Employment losses in the clothing industry ranged from 18 percent in the United States to 56 percent in Sweden. Losses in the iron and steel industry ranged from 10 percent in Canada to 54 percent in the United States. In short, the WTO researchers found that restrictions on free trade were no guarantee against employment losses, even in the industries supposedly being protected.

The evidence seems clear: The cost of protecting jobs in the short run is enormous, and in the long run, it appears that jobs cannot be protected, especially if one considers all aspects of protectionism. Free trade is a tough platform on which to run for office, but it is likely to be the one that will yield the most general benefits if implemented. Of course, this does not mean that politicians will embrace it. So we end up "saving jobs" at an annual cost of $750,000 each.

## For Critical Analysis

1. If it would be cheaper to give each steelworker $375,000 per year in cash than impose restrictions on steel imports, why do we have the import restrictions rather than the cash payments?

2. Most U.S. imports and exports travel through our seaports at some point. How do you predict that members of Congress from coastal states would vote on proposals to restrict international trade? What other information would you want to know in making such a prediction?

3. Who gains and who loses from import restrictions? In answering, you should consider both consumers and producers in both the country that imposes the restrictions and in the other countries affected by them. Also, be sure to take into account the effects of import restrictions on *export* industries.

4. When you go shopping for a new computer, is your real objective to "import" a computer into your apartment, or is it to "export" cash from your wallet? What does this tell you about the true object of international trade—is it imports or exports?

5. Some U.S. policy is designed to subsidize exports and thus increase employment in export industries. What effect does such policy have on our imports of foreign goods and thus on employment in industries that compete with imports?

6. What motivates politicians to impose trade restrictions?

# CHAPTER 8

# The Trade Deficit

The idea is not new. Indeed, it goes back centuries: Selling to foreigners is better than buying from them. That is, exports are good and imports are bad. Today, reading between the lines of the press coverage about international trade reveals that political and public thinking is not much different than it was three hundred years ago. The **mercantilists** who ruled public policy during the sixteenth through eighteenth centuries felt that the only proper objective of international trade was to expand exports without expanding imports. Their goal was to acquire large amounts of the gold that served as the money of their era. The mercantilists felt that a **trade surplus** (an excess of goods and service exports over imports) was the only way a nation could gain from trade. This same idea is expressed by modern-day patriots who reason, "If I buy a Sony laptop computer from Japan, I have the laptop and Japan has the money. On the other hand, if I buy a Dell laptop in the United States, I have the laptop and the United States has the money. I should therefore 'buy American.'" This sort of reasoning leads to the conclusion that the persistent international **trade deficit** that the United States experiences year after year is bad for America. Let's see if this conclusion makes any sense.

## MODERN-DAY MERCANTILISTS

During any given month, you cannot fail to see headlines about our continuing (or growing) trade deficit. Even if you are not quite sure how to calculate our international trade deficit, you might guess that the problem seems to be that we are importing more than we are exporting.

**Table 8–1** Exports and Imports of Goods (Billions of Dollars)

| Year | Exports | Imports | Deficit |
|------|---------|---------|---------|
| 2000 | 772.0 | −1,224.4 | −452.4 |
| 2001 | 718.7 | −1,145.9 | −427.2 |
| 2002 | 682.4 | −1,164.7 | −482.3 |
| 2003 | 713.4 | −1,260.7 | −547.3 |
| 2004 | 807.5 | −1,472.9 | −665.4 |
| 2005 | 894.6 | −1,677.4 | −782.8 |
| 2006 | 1,023.1 | −1,861.4 | −838.3 |
| 2007 | 1,160.4 | −1,983.1 | −823.2 |
| 2008 | 1,304.9 | −2,139.5 | −834.7 |
| 2009 | 1,068.5 | −1,575.4 | −506.9 |
| 2010 | 1,288.7 | −1935.7 | −647.1 |

*Source:* U.S. Department of Commerce, Bureau of Economic Analysis.

*Note:* Sums may not add to totals due to rounding.

To understand the actual numbers reported in the press, you must understand that there are several components of trade deficits. The most obvious part consists of merchandise exports and imports. This is the number that receives the most coverage in the press. Table 8–1 shows the merchandise (goods) trade deficit for the United States for a recent ten-year period.

It looks pretty bad, doesn't it? It seems as if we've become addicted to imports. But merchandise is not the only thing that we buy and sell abroad. Increasingly, service exports and imports are a major component of international trade, at least in the United States. (Some of the types of services we export involve accounting, legal research, investment advice, travel and transportation, and medical research.) For these and other service items, even mercantilists would be happy to know that the United States consistently exports more than it imports, as you can see in Table 8–2, which shows the *net* balance of trade for the various categories of services.

## The Link Between Imports And Exports

Obviously, a comparison of the two tables still shows a substantial trade deficit, no matter how many times you look at the numbers. Should residents of the United States be worried? Before we can answer this question, we must look at some basic propositions about the relationship between imports and exports.

**Table 8–2** Net Exports of Services (Billions of Dollars)

| Year | Net Service Exports |
|------|---------------------|
| 2000 | 74.9 |
| 2001 | 64.4 |
| 2002 | 61.2 |
| 2003 | 52.4 |
| 2004 | 54.1 |
| 2005 | 66.0 |
| 2006 | 85.0 |
| 2007 | 119.1 |
| 2008 | 135.9 |
| 2009 | 132.0 |
| 2010 | 151.3 |

*Source:* U.S. Department of Commerce, Bureau of Economic Analysis.

We begin by considering how we pay for the foreign goods and services that we import. Countries do not ship goods to the United States simply to hold pieces of paper in exchange. Businesses in the rest of the world ship us goods and services because they want goods and services in exchange. That means only one thing, then: *In the long run, we pay for imports with exports. So in the long run, imports must equal exports.* The short run is a different story, of course. Imports can be paid for by the sale of real and financial **assets,** such as land, **shares of stock,** and **bonds,** or through an extension of credit from other countries. But in the long run, foreigners eventually want goods and services in return for the goods and services they send us. **Consumption** is, after all, the ultimate objective of production.

Because imports are paid for with exports in the long run, any attempt to reduce this country's trade deficit by restricting imports must also affect exports. In fact, a direct corollary of our first proposition must be that *any restrictions on imports must ultimately lead to a reduction in exports.* Thus, every time politicians call for a reduction in our trade deficit, they are implicitly calling for a reduction in exports, at least in the long run.

It is possible that politicians don't understand this, but even if they did, they might still call for restricting imports. After all, it is easy for the domestic firms that lose business to foreign competition to claim that every dollar of imports represents a lost dollar of sales for them—implying a corresponding reduction in U.S. employment. In contrast, the tens of thousands of exporters of U.S. goods and services probably won't ever be able to put an exact value on their reduced sales and employment due to proposed and actual import restrictions. Hence, the people with "evidence" about the supposed harms of imports will always outnumber those businesses who lose export sales when international trade is restricted.

## A Renegade View of Imports?

Many discussions about international trade have to do with the supposed "unfairness" of imports. Somehow, it is argued, when goods come in from a foreign land, the result is unfair to the firms and workers who must compete with those imports. To see how such reasoning is no reasoning at all, one need only consider a simple example.

Assume that you have just discovered a way to produce textiles at one-tenth the cost of your closest competitors, who are located in South Carolina. You set up your base of operations in Florida and start selling your textiles at lower prices than your South Carolina competitors do. Your workers are appreciative of their jobs, and your **shareholders** are appreciative of their profits. To be sure, the textile owners and employees in South Carolina may not be happy, but there is nothing legally they can do about it. This, of course, is the essence of unfettered trade among the fifty states: Production takes place where costs are lowest and consumers benefit from the lower prices that result.

Now let's assume that you build the same facility in Florida, but instead of actually producing the textiles yourself, you secretly have them brought from South Africa to sell, as before, at lower prices than those at which the South Carolina firms can profitably produce. If everyone continues to believe that you are producing the textiles on your own, there will be no problems. But if anybody finds out that you are importing the textiles, the political wrath of members of Congress from South Carolina will descend on you. They will try to prohibit the importation of "cheap" textiles from South Africa or put a high tax, or **tariff,** on those textiles.

Is there really any difference between these two "production processes"? The first one involves the use of some textile machinery within the United States, while the second involves having a ship and some trucks pick up the textiles and drop them off at the "factory" in Florida. Are they really any different? We think not. Such is the conclusion when using positive economic analysis. Once the world of politics gets involved, however, the domestic production process is favored and the production process that involves imports is frowned upon.

## THE OTHER SIDE OF TRADE DEFICITS

Most discussions of the trade deficit are further flawed by the fact that they completely ignore the mirror image of the deficit. In the short run, when exports of goods and services don't match up, dollar for dollar, with imports, the trading partners involved must obviously make arrangements for short-run methods to pay for the difference. For example, when the United States is importing more goods and services than it is exporting, we must be selling real and financial assets to our trading partners. For example, we might be borrowing from abroad (selling bonds) or selling shares of stock in U.S. corporations. (In the late 1990s, we also sold real estate, such as golf courses and office buildings.)

Now, at first blush, this sounds like we are "mortgaging the future," selling assets and borrowing funds in order to consume more now. But there is a different way to look at this: America is the safest, most productive place in the world to invest. *If the rest of the world is to be able to invest in the United States, we must run a trade deficit.* This proposition is a simple matter of arithmetic.

When, say, a South Korean automobile company builds a factory in the United States, there is an inflow of funds from South Korea to the United States. When foreign residents buy U.S. government securities, there is an inflow of funds from other countries to the United States. These investments are usually called *private capital flows,* and they include private land purchases, acquisitions of corporate stock shares, and purchases of government bonds. Virtually every year for at least thirty years, foreign residents have invested more in the United States than U.S. residents have invested abroad. This net inflow of capital funds from abroad is called a **capital account surplus.**

As a glance at Figure 8–1 reveals, this net inflow of investment funds into the United States nearly mirrors the trade deficit that the United States experiences each year. That is, when the current account trade deficit is small, the capital account surplus is small, and when the current account deficit is large, so is the capital account surplus. Is this just a coincidence? Certainly not. Think about it. If a foreign resident wants to buy stock in a U.S. company, that foreign resident must obtain dollars to pay for the stock. While it is true that the foreign resident simply goes to the foreign exchange market to do so, these dollars must somehow get supplied to the foreign exchange market. That supply of dollars must in turn come from the excess of U.S. goods and services imports over exports each year. In other words, *our international trade deficit supplies the dollars in foreign exchange markets necessary for foreigners to invest in the United States.* If Americans did not import more goods and services than they export, foreign residents could not invest in the United States.

**Figure 8–1** The Relationship between the Current Account and the Capital Account.

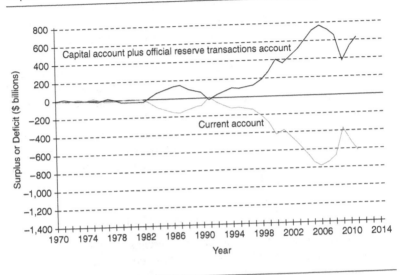

*Sources:* International Monetary Fund; *Economic Indicators*

## The Sweep of History

Contrary to what you might think from reading the newspapers, although the United States has been running a trade deficit for the past thirty-five years, this is not the first time we have run such a deficit over a long period of time. Indeed, from the Civil War to World War I, the United States ran a trade deficit year after year, borrowing funds and selling corporate stock all around the world. Were the consequences disastrous? Hardly. We used the funds we obtained from abroad to build railroads and steel mills and much of the rest of our industrial base, as well as to settle the West. We benefited from having access to low-cost finance (which we used to purchase key goods from abroad), and foreigners benefited from risk-adjusted rates of return that were higher than they could obtain in their home countries.

Beginning in World War I, this pattern reversed itself. Americans began lending money to Europeans to help them finance their war expenditures and then after the war lent them funds to rebuild. This pattern of American lending abroad continued through World War II and on until the late 1970s. All the while, we were running a trade surplus, exporting more goods and services than we were importing. Foreign residents were financing their purchases from us by borrowing and by selling us shares of stock in their corporations. They benefited by getting access to lower-cost finance and goods than they otherwise could have obtained. We benefited by selling our goods at a better price than we could get at home and also by earning a higher net rate of return than we could have obtained if we had invested only in domestic assets.

You can now see that the trade deficits of recent decades are a return to the pattern of the late nineteenth and early twentieth centuries. The United States is once again the nation offering the highest risk-adjusted return, so foreigners invest here. There is one key difference between now and one hundred years ago, however. Back then, virtually all of the borrowing was being done by the private sector, so one could be reasonably certain that it was going to turn out to yield net benefits. Today, much of the borrowing is being done by the U.S. government. Will this turn out to yield net benefits? Only time will tell.

## For Critical Analysis

1. Why can't competing producers in different states prevent "imports" into their own state? (*Hint:* To what document written over two hundred years ago are the states still subject?)

2. How does the concept of "buy local" relate to concerns about trade deficits on an international basis?

3. Does it matter to you where the product you are buying has been manufactured? Why or why not?

4. What would have been the likely consequences for the development of the American economy between the Civil War and World War I if Congress has sought to reduce imports by, say, imposing high import tariffs? Explain.

5. In the three decades after World War II, Europe rebuilt from the war by borrowing from the United States and also by running a trade deficit with us. What would have happened to the rebuilding effort if European politicians had sought to reduce their trade deficit with the United States by imposing high import tariffs on American goods? Explain.

6. Some politicians express concern about our trade deficit with specific nations. For example, twenty years ago they worried about our trade deficit with Japan. More recently they have expressed concern over our trade deficit with China. Is there any reason to believe that a trade deficit with any particular nation is of any particular importance? If South Carolina runs a trade deficit with Texas, is this cause for concern in either state? Explain.

# CHAPTER 9

# The Value of
# the Dollar

When the euro was introduced in 1999, you could purchase one for $1.18. Three years later, when euro banknotes and coins began circulating as the monetary unit of most of the **European Union (EU),** the market price of the euro had fallen to $0.90. Since then, the euro's price has fluctuated between $0.86 and $1.70. This pattern of fluctuating prices is not unique to the euro. In a world of **flexible exchange rates,** the prices at which different **currencies** trade for each other are determined by the forces of world **demand** and **supply.** Thus, if the demand for euros rises, its price will rise, and if its demand falls, so too will its price. And what is true for the euro is just as true for the British pound sterling, the Japanese yen, and our very own U.S. dollar. As we shall see, these changes in market forces, and the resulting changes in **exchange rates,** play a key role in determining patterns of international trade.

## SOME TERMINOLOGY

Although we referred to the dollar price of the euro, we could just as well have talked of the euro price of the dollar. Thus, if it takes $1.25 to purchase a euro, it must also be true that a dollar buys less than a euro. In fact, it buys exactly 1/1.25 euros in this example. That is, the euro price of the dollar is €0.80 (where € is the symbol for the euro). The exchange rate between the two currencies can be expressed either way, although in America people usually refer to the exchange rate as the dollar price of foreign currency, and so too shall we. In this example, the exchange rate between the dollar and the euro is thus $1.25.

You will also hear some people, especially journalists and politicians, talk about a "stronger" or "weaker" dollar, accompanied by

53

pronouncements that one or the other condition is good for America. When people say the dollar has gotten "stronger," what they mean is that one dollar will buy more units of foreign currency than it used to. Hence, a reduction in the exchange rate from, say, $1.25 to $1.20 per euro amounts to a stronger dollar. Conversely, if the dollar price of the euro rises from $1.25 to $1.35, this would mean that the dollar was weaker because one dollar would buy fewer euros.

## GOOD NEWS OR BAD?

Is a weaker dollar good news or bad? Like most value judgments (notice the words *good* and *bad*), the answer is in the eye of the beholder. Suppose the price of the euro rises from $1.25 to $1.50. We say that the dollar has gotten weaker relative to the euro because people must pay more dollars for each euro. Because American consumers must eventually come up with euros if they want to buy French wine or Italian pasta, when the euro becomes more expensive, European goods become more expensive for American consumers.[1] So from the perspective of American consumers, a weak dollar is bad news.

But producers in America may have a different view of the world. For example, automobile manufacturers with plants in America compete with manufacturers that have European facilities. When the dollar price of the euro rises, so does the dollar price of cars made in Europe. This induces some American consumers to "buy American," which is surely good news for the companies that receive their business. Similarly, recall that the *rise* in the price of the euro is equivalent to a *fall* in the price of the dollar. Such a move in the exchange rate makes American-made goods cheaper abroad. As a result, foreign consumers are also more likely to "buy American," again good news for the companies from whom they purchase. Thus, a weaker dollar encourages exports and discourages imports, but whether that is "good" or "bad" news is clearly a matter on which people might reasonably disagree.

Now, what about the consequences of a "stronger" dollar? When the dollar can buy more euros, this means it can also buy more European goods. This clearly benefits American consumers, so we conclude that they like a strong dollar. American producers, however, will have a different take on matters. They will lose business from American customers, who are now more likely to "buy European." In addition, people in the EU will now find American goods more expensive

---

1 Of course, consumers typically don't physically obtain the euros themselves, but the importers who bring the goods in on their behalf must certainly do so.

because the dollar is now more expensive. So they will buy fewer American goods and make more purchases at home. Thus, we conclude that a stronger dollar will encourage imports into America and discourage exports from America. Presumably, American consumers and producers will have much different opinions on whether this is good news or bad.

## PURCHASING POWER PARITY

Of course, exchange rates don't just move around without cause. There are four well-established forces that play key roles in making them what they are. The first of these, which is by far the most important long-run determinant of exchange rates, is called **purchasing power parity (PPP)**. This principle simply states that the relative values of different currencies must ultimately reflect their **purchasing power** in their home countries.

To see how this works, let's consider the United States and Switzerland, which uses the Swiss franc as its currency. Over the past fifty years, the exchange rate between these two currencies has varied between roughly $0.25 and $1.15, that is, by a factor of more than four. In the 1960s, for example, the exchange rate was near the bottom end of that range, but it has followed a persistent rise until quite recently, albeit with some ups and downs along the way. The reason the Swiss franc rose in value relative to the U.S. dollar is simple: Typically, the **inflation** rate in Switzerland has been much lower than that in the United States. The amount of goods that American dollars would buy generally has been shrinking, so the Swiss demand for dollars has fallen, even as Americans have tried to unload their depreciating dollars for Swiss francs. Together these forces helped push the value of the Swiss franc up, and so the exchange rate rose, to $0.40, then $0.70, and then even above $1.00.

This process applies across all countries. When the **price level** rises in country A relative to the price level in country B, people in both nations will switch some of their purchases of goods from country A to country B. This will push down the value of A's currency and push up the value of B's currency. In fact, this tendency is so strong that it will continue until "parity" is reached. If A's price level *rises* 20 percent relative to B's price level, then A's currency ultimately will *fall* in value by 20 percent relative to B's currency. It may take a while for this adjustment to work out, and it may be temporarily masked by some of the forces we shall talk about next, but eventually it will happen.

## INTEREST RATES

One key reason for wishing to acquire the currency of another nation is that you want to acquire goods produced in that nation. But there is another reason: You may wish to invest or to lend funds in that nation. For example, suppose you wanted to purchase **bonds** issued by a Canadian corporation. These would be denominated in Canadian dollars (C$), so you would first have to obtain those Canadian dollars before you could purchase the bonds. Given this, it should be apparent that one of the factors influencing your demand for Canadian dollars is the rate of return, or interest rate, on **investments** in Canada, compared to the interest rate on investments elsewhere. The simplest way of putting this is that if interest rates in Canada rise relative to interest rates in the United States, investors will want to move funds from the United States into Canada. That is, there will be a drop in the demand for U.S. dollars and a rise in the demand for Canadian dollars, and so the exchange rate will rise—you will have to give up more U.S. dollars to obtain one Canadian dollar. The U.S. dollar will have become "weaker" against the Canadian currency.

Note that the interest rates of which we speak are **real interest rates,** that is, adjusted for any expected inflation. If interest rates rise in Canada because of an increase in the expected inflation rate there, this hardly makes them more attractive to American, European, or Chinese investors. It simply neutralizes the effects of the higher expected inflation. Similarly, we must be careful to compare interest rates on obligations that have the same **default risk.** If the interest rate is high on bonds issued by a Canadian company that is in danger of **bankruptcy,** that higher interest rate simply compensates **bondholders** for the added default risk they face. It doesn't make those bonds unusually attractive to investors in the United States or elsewhere.

But as long as we are careful to adjust for expected inflation and risk, interest rate differentials can sometimes be quite useful in understanding events. For example, during the late nineteenth century, inflation- and risk-adjusted interest rates were higher in the United States than they were in Britain because America was rebuilding from the Civil War, settling the West, and industrializing at a rapid rate. All of these factors made America a productive place in which to invest. The higher rate of return in America made it attractive for British investors to lend funds to American firms, which in turn meant a higher demand for American dollars. As a result, the American dollar was more valuable on world markets than it otherwise would have been.

## HARD CURRENCY

If you've ever visited a developing nation or a formerly Communist country, you may have heard people refer to "hard currency." You may even have had them insist you pay for your purchases not with the local currency but with American dollars or euros or even Swiss francs. The reasoning behind this insistence is simple.

In such countries, whatever the *current* state of economic and political affairs, the *future* state of both is often filled with great uncertainty. Perhaps the current government's political support is not too secure. Or there may be the simmering threat of a military-backed coup. Or maybe there is a suspicion that the national government won't be able to finance its future spending with conventional taxes. Should any of these eventualities be realized, the likely result is that the government will resort to printing money as a means of financing its activities, causing future high inflation that will devastate the purchasing power of the local currency. And because the exact timing and magnitude of this outcome are highly uncertain, so is the expected future value of the local currency.

To reduce their risk, people thus try to hold currencies whose value is unlikely to be subject to political vagaries—and these are currencies issued by strong democratic governments, such as those in the United States and the EU. This increases the demand for such currencies and thus tends to set their values in world markets higher than they otherwise would be. The reference to "hard currency" stems from the notion that the purchasing power of such currencies is as stable as a rock—which it is, compared to the local monies that people are trying to avoid holding.

## BOEING AND THE BEATLES

The final key factor that helps determine exchange rates is quite simply the relative attractiveness of the goods produced in various nations. Consider the Boeing Corporation, long regarded as the maker of some of the best commercial jet planes in existence. Airlines all over the world purchase billions of dollars' worth of Boeing aircraft every year. To do this, they must acquire U.S. dollars, and their demand for dollars makes the value of the dollar on world markets higher than it otherwise would be.

Of course, the residents of foreign countries have been known to produce some nice products themselves. Many people feel that the best wines come from France, the best ties from Italy, and so forth. And then there are the Beatles, perhaps the most prolific and popular rock group ever, at least measured by worldwide sales of music. When the Beatles hit the music scene in the 1960s, millions of Americans wanted to acquire recordings of their songs. To do so, they first had to acquire pounds sterling (the money used in Britain). This increased the demand for pounds sterling and thus caused the dollar price of the pound to rise in foreign exchange markets. So the next time you are paying to download music of the British rock group Coldplay, you will know that your decision to buy their music has pushed the dollar price of the pound sterling up, even if just by the tiniest of amounts.

## FOR CRITICAL ANALYSIS

1. Although the United Kingdom is a member of the EU, it does not use the euro as its monetary unit. Instead it uses the pound sterling. If the United Kingdom decided to switch from the pound to the euro, how might this decision affect the value of the euro in foreign exchange markets?

2. In an effort to discourage drug smugglers from using U.S. currency in major drug deals, the U.S. government refuses to issue currency in denominations greater than $100. How does this policy decision affect the demand for dollars and thus the exchange rate between the dollar and other currencies, such as the euro (which comes in denominations as big as €500)?

3. Sometimes national governments decide that they don't want their currencies to be any lower in value than they currently are. Explain how, if a country wants to raise the value of its currency in foreign exchange markets, it might use the following tools to do so:

    (a) Altering the rate of growth in its money supply, thus changing the current and expected inflation rate

    (b) Limiting the ability of citizens to invest in foreign nations

    (c) Imposing **tariffs or quotas** on imports

    (d) Subsidizing exports by domestic firms

4. From shortly after World War II to the early 1970s, the United States (like many countries) was on a system of fixed exchange rates. That is, the U.S. government pledged to take whatever actions were necessary to keep the value of the dollar fixed relative to other

currencies. Consider the emergence of the Beatles in the 1960s. What would the U.S. government have to do to prevent the value of the dollar from changing as a result? Alternatively, consider the introduction of the popular Boeing 707 in the 1950s. What would the U.S. government have to do to prevent the value of the dollar from changing as a result?

5. Why do politicians worry about whether the dollar is "strong" or "weak"?

6. What do you think happened to the value of the U.S. dollar when BMW (a German company) moved an important part of its manufacturing facilities to the United States some years ago? Explain.

# CHAPTER 10

# The Lion, the Dragon, and the Future

For decades after the Communists' rise to power in 1949, China was best known for poverty and repression, and its aggression came mostly on the military front. But in recent years, *economic* aggression has become the byword. Although both poverty and repression are still the norm, both are changing for the better. China, it seems, is trying to learn from capitalism, even if not converting to it.

## THE AWAKENING OF CHINA

China's economic offensive began thirty years ago in its southeastern province of Guangdong. The Chinese leadership decided to use this province as a test case, to see if capitalist **direct foreign investment** could stimulate **economic growth** in a way that could be politically controlled. The experience was deemed a success—economic growth soared amid political stability. What the government learned from the experience helped it smooth the 1997 transition of Hong Kong from British to Chinese control. Most important in terms of China's long-term economic aspirations, many foreign investors came to view the Guangdong experiment as solid evidence that they could invest in China without fear that the Communist government would confiscate their capital. The result: Foreign investment in China soared.

There are two powerful forces that are attracting economic investment to China: **demand** and **supply.** On the demand side, almost 1.4 billion people live there, some 20 percent of the world's population. Although **per capita income** is still low by world standards, it has been increasing by more than 6 percent per year, after adjusting for inflation. At that rate, the standard of living for the Chinese people—and hence their **purchasing power** in world markets—is doubling every decade or so. China is already the world's largest cell-phone market, and China will soon account for 25 percent of the world's purchases of personal computers. Indeed, China now spends over $150 billion per year on information technology and services. By 2030, the Chinese economy will likely have eclipsed the United States' and become the world's largest.

With its huge population, China also offers attractions on the supply side. Highly skilled workers have been plentiful in the Chinese labor market with hundreds of thousands of engineering graduates each year. In many cities, the fact that the Chinese workforce is generally well educated and often English-speaking has helped make the country attractive to foreign employers. Collaborative scientific ventures between Chinese researchers and U.S. firms are becoming increasingly common. A research team at Beijing University played a role in deciphering the genetic makeup of rice, for example. American computer hardware and software firms Intel, IBM, Oracle, and Microsoft have shifted some key components of their research to China in recent years. Indeed, American firms of all types are setting up operations in China. Chinese firms, meanwhile, are proving to be formidable competitors both at home and abroad.

## CONCERNS IN OTHER NATIONS

The situation has become critical in Japan, where wages are much higher than in China but whose technological lead over China is gradually eroding. "Are we to become a vassal of the Chinese dynasty again?" asked one Japanese official, clearly concerned that his nation's manufacturing firms were having trouble competing with Chinese firms. Eventually, Japanese firms will adjust to the growing economic presence of China, but the transition may be unpleasant.

Americans are more concerned about the likely impact on the U.S. economy of China's capitalist ambitions. Will the dragon consume American firms and jobs as it grows? The short answer is no. The long answer has two elements. To this point, a key element of China's competitiveness has been the low wages there. Even though American and European firms operating in China choose to pay their workers more than state-owned enterprises pay, this has still yielded considerable savings. As recently as ten years ago, unskilled and semiskilled labor in China cost only 25 percent as much as in Europe. Moreover, in the past, foreign firms have been able to hire engineers for salaries that are only 10–20 percent of the cost of hiring engineers in the West.

## MARKETS IN CHINA

Labor markets in China are changing rapidly, however. Between 2000 and 2010, average real wages rose 60 percent, with bigger increases among higher-skilled workers. Many firms were unable to hire as many workers as they would have liked, and most firms had to upgrade their fringe benefits and other on-the-job amenities just to retain existing workers. Wages are still well below American and European levels, but the gap has closed, thereby cutting the competitive advantage of many Chinese firms. The recent worldwide recession has altered labor market conditions in China as it has elsewhere. But it is unlikely to impede China's march to economic superpower status.

Higher wages in China will also translate into higher demand for goods produced by American and European firms. China, like all nations, must in the long run import goods equal in value to those it exports (unless China intends to give its exports away, which so far no one is claiming). This means that just as China has become a potent supplier of many goods and services, it is at the same time becoming a potent demander of still other goods and services.

Thus far, the Chinese demand for goods has not been as visible in American markets because American firms tend to produce goods and services designed for higher-income consumers, and China has relatively few of those. In the meantime, the demand-side influence of the Chinese economy is already showing up, albeit in odd places. To take one example, right now China's most important import from the United States is trash. Ranging from used newspapers to scrap steel, Chinese companies buy billions of dollars' worth of the stuff every year to use as raw materials in the goods they produce. In addition to yielding profits (and employment) in these U.S. export industries, this exportation of U.S. trash reduces the burden on U.S. landfills and, by pushing up the prices of recyclable scrap, encourages more recycling in the United States.

Eventually, of course, we'd like to be sending China more than our rubbish, and that time is coming. As China's economy grows, so will the number of affluent Chinese, and with 1.4 billion potential candidates, that ultimately means *plenty* of consumers for America's high-end goods. Thus, the long-run effects of China's growth will mean a different American economy—we'll be producing and consuming different mixes of goods and services—but America will also be a richer nation. Voluntary exchange creates wealth, and the Chinese dragon is big enough to create a lot of wealth.

# THE LION OF INDIA

To China's southwest, another giant is stirring. Around 1990, the lion of India began to throw off the self-imposed shackles of nearly a half century of markets largely closed to international **competition.** The central government, for example, began opening state-owned companies to competition from private-sector rivals. FedEx and United Parcel Service (UPS) have made huge inroads on the Indian postal service, and numerous foreign firms are now competing with the state-owned telephone service, which had long been a complete **monopoly.**

Entry into the Indian market brought familiarity with its workforce, many of whose members are fluent in English. The technical capabilities of graduates of top Indian universities, combined with their English skills and low wages, made them perfect staffers for a proliferation of call centers that have opened throughout India. Tens of thousands of technical and customer relations jobs that used to go to Middle America are now held by the growing middle class in India. It was in many respects this very movement that brought **outsourcing** into the American consciousness.

But India, too, is struggling with growth. The talent pool at the top is thin: Only a dozen or so of India's seventeen thousand universities and colleges can compete with America's best, and the wages of graduates of these top schools are soaring. Moreover, India suffers from overwhelming infrastructure problems: Much of its road system is either overcrowded or in disrepair, and its port facilities are in desperate need of modernization. For the time being, such transportation problems are likely to keep India from becoming a major manufacturing powerhouse. India has also been hampered by its huge and seemingly permanent government bureaucracy. For example, despite the fact that the postal service there has lost more than half of its business to newcomers such as FedEx and UPS, none of the 550,000 postal service employees can be fired.

# CAPITALISM VERSUS COMMUNISM

At least India is a democracy, and its legal system, inherited from the British, who ruled there for so long, is in close conformity with the legal systems of most developed nations. Matters are rather different in China. As noted in Chapter 5, political and legal **institutions** are crucial foundations for sustained economic growth. Despite the advances China has made over the past thirty years, its wealth-creating future may be clouded unless it can successfully deal with two fundamental institutional issues.

First, there is the matter of resolving the tension inherent when a Communist dictatorship tries to use capitalism as the engine of economic growth. Capitalism thrives best in an environment of freedom and itself creates an awareness of and appreciation for the benefits of that freedom. Yet freedom is antithetical to the ideological and political tenets of the Communist government of China. Will the government be tempted to confiscate the fruits of capitalist success to support itself? Or will growing pressure for more political freedom force the government to repress the capitalist system to protect itself? Either route would likely bring economic growth in China to a swift halt.

The second potential long-run problem faced by China lies in that nation's cultural attitude toward **intellectual property.** In a land in which imitation is viewed as the sincerest form of flattery, it is routine to use the ideas of others in one's own pursuits. As a result, patent and copyright laws in China are far weaker than in Western nations. Moreover, actions elsewhere considered to be commercial theft (such as software piracy) are largely tolerated in China. If foreign firms find that they cannot protect their economic **assets** in the Chinese market, foreign investment will suffer accordingly, and so will the growing dragon that depends on it so heavily.

## DISCUSSION QUESTIONS

1. Currently, AIDS is spreading rapidly in China and India. If the governments of these nations fail to stop the spread of AIDS, what are the likely consequences for future economic growth in China and India?

2. In 1989, a massive protest against political repression in China was halted by the government's massacre of more than 150 individuals at Tiananmen Square in Beijing. What impact do you think that episode had on foreign investment and growth in China during the years immediately thereafter?

3. Most of the advances in institutions in China have come in the cities rather than in the countryside. Indeed, local officials in farming villages actively redistribute wealth among villagers to keep the distribution of income among local farmers roughly equal. Thus, a farmer's success or failure with his crops has little impact on his family's standard of living. Given these facts, where do you think the economic growth in China has occurred over the past thirty years, in the cities or on the farms? Explain.

4. Explain how the following factors will influence India's ability to succeed in a highly competitive, rapidly changing global marketplace: (a) an educational system that is largely state-operated and that emphasizes job security for teachers and professors; (b) a transportation infrastructure that is largely antiquated and in disrepair; and (c) a political system that is adept at protecting favored constituents from competition and handing out favors that have concentrated benefits and widely dispersed costs.

5. How does protection of rights to intellectual property help promote innovation?

6. What are the central threats to future economic growth in China and India?

# PART THREE
# Supply and Demand

# CHAPTER 11

# Sex, Booze, and Drugs

Before 1914, cocaine was legal in this country; today it is not. Alcoholic beverages are legal in the United States today; from 1920 to 1933, they were not. Prostitution is legal in Nevada today; in the other forty-nine states, it is not.[1] All these goods—sex, booze, and drugs—have at least one thing in common: The consumption of each brings together a willing seller with a willing buyer, creating an act of mutually beneficial exchange (at least in the opinion of the parties involved). Partly because of this property, attempts to proscribe the consumption of these goods have met with less than spectacular success and have yielded some peculiar patterns of production, distribution, and usage. Let's see why.

## SUPPLY-SIDE ENFORCEMENT

When the government seeks to prevent voluntary exchange, it must generally decide whether to go after the seller or the buyer. In most cases—and certainly where sex, booze, and drugs are concerned—the government targets sellers because this is where the authorities get the most benefit from their enforcement dollars. A cocaine dealer, even a small retail pusher, often supplies dozens or even hundreds of users each day, as did speakeasies (illegal saloons) during Prohibition; a hooker typically services three to ten "tricks" per day. By incarcerating the supplier, the police can prevent several, or even several hundred, transactions from taking place, which is usually much more cost-effective than going after the buyers one by one. It is not that the police ignore the

---

1 These statements are not entirely correct. Even today, cocaine may be obtained legally by prescription from a physician. Prostitution in Nevada is legal only in counties that have chosen to permit it. Finally, some counties in the United States remain "dry," prohibiting the sale of beer, wine, and distilled spirits.

consumers of illegal goods; indeed, sting operations, in which the police pose as illicit sellers, often make the headlines. Nevertheless, most enforcement efforts focus on the supply side, and so shall we.

Law enforcement activities directed against the suppliers of illegal goods increase the suppliers' operating costs. The risks of fines, jail sentences, and possibly even violence become part of the costs of doing business and must be taken into account by existing and potential suppliers. Some entrepreneurs will leave the business, turning their talents to other activities; others will resort to clandestine (and costly) means to hide their operations from the police; still others will restrict the circle of buyers with whom they are willing to deal to minimize the chances that a customer is a cop. Across the board, the costs of operation are higher, and at any given price, less of the product will be available. There is a reduction in supply, and the result is a higher price for the good.

This increase in price is, in a sense, exactly what the enforcement officials are after, for the consumers of sex, booze, and drugs behave according to the **law of demand:** The higher the price of a good, the lower the amount consumed. So the immediate impact of the enforcement efforts against sellers is to reduce the consumption of the illegal good by buyers. There are, however, some other effects.

## Violence Emerges

First, because the good in question is illegal, people who have a **comparative advantage** in conducting illegal activities will be attracted to the business of supplying (and perhaps demanding) the good. Some may have an existing criminal record and are relatively unconcerned about adding to it. Others may have developed skills in evading detection and prosecution while engaged in other criminal activities. Some may simply look at the illegal activity as another means of thumbing their noses at society. The general point is that when an activity is made illegal, people who are good at being criminals are attracted to that activity.

Illegal contracts are usually not enforceable through legal channels (and even if they were, few suppliers of illegal goods would be foolish enough to complain to the police about not being paid for their products). So buyers and sellers of illegal goods must frequently resort to private methods of contract enforcement, which often entails violence.[2] Hence, people who are relatively good at violence are attracted to illegal

---

2 Fundamentally, violence—such as involuntary incarceration—also plays a key role in the government's enforcement of legal contracts. We often do not think of it as violence, of course, because it is usually cushioned by constitutional safeguards and procedural rules.

activities and have greater **incentives** to employ their talents. This is one reason why the murder rate in America rose to record levels during Prohibition and then dropped sharply when liquor was again made legal. It also helps explain why the number of drug-related murders soared during the 1980s and why drive-by shootings became commonplace in many drug-infested cities. The Thompson submachine gun of the 1930s and the MAC-10 machine gun of the 1980s were just low-cost means of contract enforcement.

## USAGE CHANGES

The attempts of law enforcement officials to drive sellers of illegal goods out of business have another effect. Based on recent wholesale prices, $50,000 worth of pure heroin weighs about 1 pound; $50,000 worth of marijuana weighs about 50 pounds. As any drug smuggler can tell you, hiding 1 pound of contraband is a lot easier than hiding 50 pounds. Thus, to avoid detection and prosecution, suppliers of the illegal good have an incentive to deal in the more valuable versions of their product, which for drugs and booze mean the more potent versions. Bootleggers during Prohibition concentrated on hard liquor rather than on beer and wine; even today, moonshine typically has roughly twice the alcohol content of legal hard liquor such as bourbon, scotch, or vodka. After narcotics became illegal in this country in 1914, importers switched from the milder opium to its more valuable, more potent, and more addictive derivative, heroin.

The move to the more potent versions of illegal commodities is enhanced by enforcement activities directed against users. Not only do users, like suppliers, find it easier (cheaper) to hide the more potent versions, but there is also a change in relative prices due to user penalties. Typically, the law has lower penalties for using an illegal substance than for distributing it. Within each category (use or sale), however, there is commonly the same penalty regardless of value per unit. For example, during Prohibition, a bottle of wine and a bottle of more expensive, more potent hard liquor were equally illegal. Today, the possession of 1 gram of 90 percent pure cocaine brings the same penalty as the possession of 1 gram of 10 percent pure cocaine. Given the physical quantities, there is a fixed cost (the legal penalty) associated with being caught, regardless of value per unit (and thus potency) of the substance. Hence, the structure of legal penalties raises the relative price of less potent versions, encouraging users to substitute more potent versions—heroin instead of opium, hashish instead of marijuana, and hard liquor instead of beer.

Penalties against users also encourage a change in the nature of usage. Prior to 1914, cocaine was legal in this country and was used openly as a mild stimulant, much as people today use caffeine. (Cocaine was even an ingredient in the original formulation of Coca-Cola.) This type of usage—small, regular doses over long time intervals—becomes relatively more expensive when the substance is made illegal. Extensive usage (small doses spread over time) is more likely to be detected by the authorities than intensive usage (a large dose consumed at once), simply because possession time is longer and the drug must be accessed more frequently. Thus, when a substance is made illegal, there is an incentive for consumers to switch toward usage that is more intensive. Rather than ingesting cocaine orally in the form of a highly diluted liquid solution, as was commonly done before 1914, people switched to snorting or injecting it. During Prohibition, people dispensed with cocktails before dinner each night; instead, on the less frequent occasions when they drank, they more often drank to get drunk. The same phenomenon is observed today. People under the age of 21 consume alcoholic beverages less frequently than people over the age of 21. But when they do drink, they are more likely to drink to get drunk.

## INFORMATION COSTS RISE

Not surprisingly, the suppliers of illegal commodities are reluctant to advertise their wares openly; the police are as capable of reading billboards and watching TV as potential customers are. Suppliers are also reluctant to establish easily recognized identities and regular places and hours of business because to do so raises the chance of being caught by the police. Information about the price and quality of products being sold goes underground, often with unfortunate effects for consumers.

With legal goods, consumers have several means of obtaining information. They can learn from friends, advertisements, and personal experience. When goods are legal, they can be trademarked for identification. The trademark cannot legally be copied, and the courts protect it. Given such easily identified brands, consumers can be made aware of the quality and price of each. If their experience does not meet expectations, they can assure themselves of no further contact with the unsatisfactory product by never buying that brand again.

When a general class of products becomes illegal, there are fewer ways to obtain information. Brand names are no longer protected by law, so falsification of well-known brands ensues. When products do not meet expectations, it is more difficult (costly) for consumers to punish suppliers. Frequently, the result is degradation of and uncertainty about product quality. The consequences for consumers of the illegal goods are often unpleasant and sometimes fatal.

## DANGEROUS SEX

Consider prostitution. In Nevada counties where prostitution is legal, the prostitutes are required to register with the local authorities, and they generally conduct their business in well-established bordellos. These establishments advertise openly and rely heavily on repeat business. Health officials test the prostitutes weekly for venereal disease and monthly for AIDS. Contrast this with other areas of the country, where prostitution is illegal. Suppliers are generally streetwalkers because a fixed, physical location is too easy for the police to detect and raid. They change locations frequently to reduce harassment by police. Repeat business is reported to be minimal; frequently, customers have never seen the prostitute before and never will again.

The difference in outcomes is striking. In Nevada, the spread of venereal disease by legal prostitutes is estimated to be almost nonexistent; to date, none of the registered prostitutes in Nevada has tested positive for AIDS. By contrast, in some major cities outside Nevada, the incidence of venereal disease among prostitutes is estimated to be near 100 percent. In Miami, one study found that 19 percent of all incarcerated prostitutes tested positive for AIDS; in Newark, New Jersey, 52 percent of the prostitutes tested were infected with the AIDS virus, and about half of the prostitutes in Washington, DC, and New York City are also believed to be carrying the AIDS virus. Because of the lack of reliable information in markets for illegal goods, customers frequently do not know exactly what they are getting; as a result, they sometimes get more than they bargained for.

## DEADLY DRUGS AND BAD BOOZE

Consider alcohol and drugs. Today, alcoholic beverages are heavily advertised to establish their brand names and are carried by reputable dealers. Customers can readily punish suppliers for any deviation from the expected potency or quality by withdrawing their business, telling their friends, or even bringing a lawsuit. Similar circumstances prevailed before 1914 in this country for the hundreds of products containing opium or cocaine.

During Prohibition, consumers of alcohol often did not know exactly what they were buying or where to find the supplier the next day if they were dissatisfied. Fly-by-night operators sometimes adulterated liquor with far more lethal methyl alcohol. In tiny concentrations, this made watered-down booze taste like it had more kick, but in only slightly higher concentrations, the methyl alcohol blinded or even killed the unsuspecting consumer. Even in "reputable" speakeasies (those likely to be in business at the same location the next day), bottles bearing the labels of high-priced foreign whiskeys were refilled repeatedly with locally (and illegally) produced rotgut until their labels wore off.

In the 1970s, more than one purchaser of what was reputed to be high-potency Panama Red or Acapulco gold marijuana ended up with low-potency pot heavily loaded with stems, seeds, and maybe even oregano. Buyers of cocaine must worry about not only how much the product has been cut along the distribution chain but also what has been used to cut it. In recent years, the purity of cocaine at the retail level has ranged between 10 and 95 percent; for heroin, the degree of purity has ranged from 5 to 50 percent. Cutting agents can turn out to be any of various sugars, local anesthetics, or amphetamines; on occasion, rat poison has been used. We noted earlier that the legal penalties for the users of illegal goods encourage them to use more potent forms and to use them more intensively. These facts and the uncertain quality and potency of the illegal products yield a deadly combination. During Prohibition, the death rate from acute alcohol poisoning (due to overdose) was more than thirty times higher than today. In 1927 alone, twelve thousand people died from acute alcohol poisoning, and many thousands more were blinded or killed by contaminated booze. Today, about four thousand people per year die as a direct result of consuming either cocaine or heroin. Of that total, it is estimated, roughly 80 percent die from either an overdose caused by an unexpectedly potent product or an adverse reaction to the material used to cut the drug. Clearly, caveat emptor ("let the buyer beware") is a warning to be taken seriously if one is consuming an illegal product.

## SUCCESS IS LIMITED

We noted at the beginning of this chapter that one of the effects of making a good illegal is to raise its price. One might well ask, by how much? During the early 1990s, the federal government was spending about $2 billion per year in its efforts to stop the importation of cocaine from Colombia. One study concluded that these efforts had hiked the price of cocaine by 4 percent relative to what it would have been had the federal government done nothing to interdict cocaine imports. The study estimated that the cost of raising the price of cocaine an additional 2 percent would be $1 billion per year. More recently, Nobel Laureate Gary Becker and his colleagues have estimated that America's war on drugs costs at least $100 billion per year. And the results? The prices of heroin and cocaine are at record-low levels.

The government's efforts to halt imports of marijuana have had some success, presumably because that product is easier to detect than cocaine. Nevertheless, suppliers have responded by cultivating marijuana domestically instead of importing it or by bringing it in across the relatively open U.S.-Canadian border rather than from elsewhere. The net effect has been an estimated tenfold increase in potency due to the superior farming techniques available in this country and Canada, as well as the use of genetic bioengineering to improve strains.

A few years ago, most states and the federal government began restricting sales of cold medicines containing pseudoephedrine because that ingredient was widely used for making the illegal stimulant methamphetamine in home laboratories. The restrictions succeeded in sharply curtailing home production of "meth." They also led to a huge increase in imports of a far more potent version of meth from Mexico. Overall, it is estimated that neither consumption of nor addiction to methamphetamine was reduced by the restrictions. But overdoses from the drug rose sharply because of the greater purity of the imports.

Consider also the government's efforts to eliminate the consumption of alcohol during the 1920s and 1930s. They failed so badly that the Eighteenth Amendment, which put Prohibition in place, was the first (and so far the only) constitutional amendment ever to be repealed. As for prostitution, it is reputed to be "the oldest profession" and by all accounts continues to flourish today, even in Newark and Miami.

The government's inability to halt the consumption of sex, booze, or drugs does not mean that those efforts have failed. Indeed, the impact of these efforts is manifested in their consequences, ranging from tainted drugs and alcohol to disease-ridden prostitutes. The message instead is that when the government attempts to prevent mutually beneficial exchange, even its best efforts are unlikely to meet with spectacular success.

## DISCUSSION QUESTIONS

1. From an economic perspective, is it possible for laws restricting dangerous or destructive activity to be *too* strict? Explain.

2. In recent years several states have passed so-called medical marijuana laws. Typically, these laws permit individuals to lawfully purchase marijuana from licensed stores, provided they have letter from their doctor recommending its use. Use the reasoning in this chapter to predict how the characteristics of medical marijuana will differ from illegal marijuana. Focus specifically on price, quality, variety, and consistency (or predictability).

3. The federal government currently taxes alcohol on the basis of the 100-proof gallon. (Alcohol that is 100 proof is 50 percent pure ethyl alcohol; most hard liquor sold is 80 proof, or 40 percent ethyl alcohol, whereas wine is usually about 24 proof, and most beer is 6–10 proof.) How would alcohol consumption patterns change if the government taxed alcohol strictly on the basis of volume rather than also taking its potency into account?

4. During Prohibition, some speakeasy operators paid bribes to ensure that the police did not raid them. Would you expect the quality of the liquor served in such speakeasies to be higher or lower than in those that did not pay bribes? Would you expect to find differences (e.g., with regard to income levels) among the customers patronizing the two types of speakeasies?

5. The markets for prostitution in Nevada and New Jersey have two important differences: (1) prostitutes in New Jersey face higher costs because of government efforts to prosecute them and (2) customers in New Jersey face higher risks of contracting diseases from prostitutes because the illegal nature of the business makes reliable information about product quality much more costly to obtain. Given these facts, in which state would you expect the price of prostitution services to be higher? Which state would have the higher amount of services consumed (adjusted for population differences)? Explain your answer.

6. According to the Surgeon General of the United States, nicotine is the most addictive drug known to humanity, and cigarette smoking kills perhaps 300,000–400,000 people per year in the United States. Why isn't tobacco illegal in America?

# CHAPTER 12

# Kidneys for Sale

This year, more than eight thousand Americans will die waiting for an organ transplant. They will not die because physicians are unable to transplant organs or because their health insurance does not cover the cost of the transplant. They will die because since 1984, it has been against federal law to pay for human organs.[1] It is lawful to pay a man for his sperm, a woman for her eggs, and members of either gender for their blood. It is even lawful to donate an organ or to receive one as a gift. And it is certainly legal to pay the surgeons who perform the transplants. It is even lawful for hospitals to make a profit on organ transplants performed in their operating rooms. But it is against the law for you to sell a cornea, a kidney, or a lobe of your liver; it is even unlawful for your loved ones to benefit from the harvesting of any of your organs after your death. And thus eight thousand people die every year, waiting in vain for someone to donate an organ to them.

## An Overview of Organ Transplants

The transplantation of human body parts is not new. The first cornea was successfully transplanted in Austria in 1905. The first successful kidney transplant (between identical twins) was conducted in Boston in 1954. Since then, successful transplants of the pancreas, liver, heart, lung, hand, and even face have been performed. Indeed, there are now thirty-seven different organs and types of human tissues that can be transplanted. None of this is cheap. In the United States, a kidney transplant costs about $250,000 on average, a liver transplant

---

1 This legislation was originally introduced by Rep. Al Gore (D., Tenn.), who went on to become vice president of the United States (1993–2001).

runs $520,000, and a heart transplant costs an average of $650,000. But there are services that arrange for international transplants (performed, for example, in India or China) of any of these organs at less than half the price. None of these figures include payment for the organ itself because such payments are illegal in the United States and in most other countries.

These astronomical sums are obviously out of the reach of most people. In fact, however, transplants done in the United States are generally not paid for directly by the recipients. For a person under the age of 65 with health insurance, private insurance pays for the transplant. For anyone 65 or older, the federal Medicare system pays for the transplant. And for people under 65 with neither private insurance nor the wealth to pay by themselves, transplants are paid for by the Medicaid system, which is financed jointly by the federal government and the states. (Neither private insurance plans nor Medicare or Medicaid will pay for international transplants, which are generally chosen only by relatively affluent people who are unwilling to wait—or to die waiting.)

## THE CASE OF KIDNEYS

Now, to begin our inquiry into the economics of organ transplants, let's consider the case of kidneys. We start here because the technical features of the transplant process have become relatively routine and because we each are born with two kidneys but can get by quite well with only one. In fact, thanks to the technique known as dialysis, humans can actually survive for years without functioning kidneys. In 2011, over ninety thousand people were awaiting kidney transplants in the United States. That same year, ten thousand Americans received transplants from deceased strangers. Another six thousand received a transplant from a living donor (recall that "extra" kidney we each have), usually a close friend or relative. Tragically, more than five thousand of the people waiting for a kidney either died or were dropped from the list because they had become too sick to qualify for a transplant. Another three thousand died that year waiting for a liver, heart, lung, or other critical organ. Could they be saved, if it were as lawful to pay for kidneys as it is to pay for the surgeons who transplant them? Or would a market for kidneys ultimately become a black market, relying on "donated" organs removed from unwilling victims by unscrupulous brokers motivated by cash rather than kindness? That is precisely the nexus of the debate over whether we should permit people (or the relatives of just-deceased donors) to be remunerated for lifesaving organ donations.

First things first: Surely we cannot object to a market for organs because the act of donating a kidney or the lobe of a liver is potentially hazardous to the donor. After all, we currently permit people to undergo such risks under the current system with *no* monetary compensation. If it is safe enough to allow friends or family to donate without payment, why is it too risky for someone to give up a kidney or part of his or her liver in return for money?

## THE CASE OF IRAN

There are, of course, many other contentious issues. To start exploring them, let's look first at a nation where it *is* legal to pay people for human organs: Iran, which just happens to have the highest living-donor rate in the world, at twenty-three donations per million people. Monetary compensation for organs in Iran has been lawful there since 1988, and in the ensuing decade, Iran eliminated the *entire* backlog of kidney transplant patients, something no other nation has achieved.

Under the Iranian system, a person awaiting a kidney must first seek a suitable, willing donor in his or her family. If none is forthcoming, the person must wait up to six months for a suitable deceased donor. At that point, the potential recipient can apply to the national transplant association for a kidney from a willing donor who is paid for the kidney. The donor receives from the government $1,200 plus a year of fully paid health insurance and a payment of $2,300–$4,500 from the recipient (or a charity, if the recipient is poor). Donor and recipient are also free to agree to an additional cash payment, although in most cases, the sums already mentioned are sufficient to get the job done. There are still purely altruistic donors in Iran, as well as cadaveric donations from the recently deceased. But it is the payment for organs that has permitted essentially all who seek kidney donations in Iran to get them, and the Iranian system has done so *without* leading to "back alley" donations or to people who are unable to afford a transplant because of the high cost of the organs themselves. Meanwhile, the system has saved the lives of thousands of Iranians.

## THE FEAR OF INVOLUNTARY DONATIONS

Many people worry about a system of payment for human transplant because of the possibility that it would yield *involuntary* donors. That is, if there is a market for organs, some unscrupulous brokers might be tempted by profits to knock people over the head and harvest their organs for sale at the highest price. Yet it is generally agreed that the Iranian system has worked for more than 20 years without a hint of any such activities. Perhaps this should not be too surprising, given the medical techniques that have been developed to ensure that the tissue match between organ and recipient is close enough to make transplant feasible. These and other DNA tests can now quickly ascertain with substantial certainty that "organ A" came from voluntary "donor A" rather than from involuntary "donor B."

Indeed, apart from gruesome works of fiction, most of the horror stories about the hazards of allowing markets for human organs are stories about behavior caused by the *lack* of a market for organs. In China, for example, many "transplant tourists" in the past received organs taken from the bodies of the thousands of prisoners who are executed there every year. China insisted that the prisoners' organs were used only with their "consent," a claim that many human rights groups have disputed. But on one point all agree: There were no payments to the prisoners or their surviving relatives. The organs were simply taken (a practice now supposedly halted).

In both the United States and Britain, there have been highly publicized cases of what amount to "body snatching"—removal of organs and other body parts from the recently deceased. Some of these cases involved body parts used in research, while other body parts were intended for sale at a profit. In each of these cases, removal was done without the prior consent of the deceased or the postmortem consent of relatives. But this amounts to theft; it is singularly horrifying, but we must remember that it is theft. Consider another form of stealing: Every year many thousands of senior citizens are defrauded of their hard-earned retirement funds by unscrupulous individuals who masquerade as "financial advisers." Should we make it illegal for anyone to pay for investment advice—or should we devote our efforts to prosecuting and incarcerating the perpetrators of such crimes?

In Pakistan and the Philippines, there were small-scale markets for transplant organs until recently, although Pakistan has now banned the trade in human organs and transplants for non-Filipinos have been outlawed in that nation. In both countries, there were anecdotes of donors who sold kidneys for $2,000–$3,000 (about a year's worth of per capita income in either nation), but who later came to regret the transaction because of adverse long-term health effects. But this would be a potential issue even with unpaid donors, and in any nation such as the United States, donors in a market for organs would surely receive at least as much medical and psychological counseling as volunteer donors receive now.

## THE COSTS OF PAYING FOR ORGANS

Now, what about the added expense of allowing payments for donated organs? Would this break the budgets of Medicare or Medicaid or empty the coffers of the private insurance companies that pay for the bulk of transplants? In the case of kidneys, we have enough information from elsewhere to say the answer is probably not. In Iran, where per capita income is about $12,000 per year, payments to donors smaller than this amount have been sufficient to clear the market for kidneys. In Pakistan and the Philippines, payments equivalent to a year's worth of per capita income were enough to support a substantial transplant tourist market in both countries.

At almost $50,000 per year, average per capita income in the United States is clearly much higher than in any of these nations, suggesting that payments for kidneys would also have to be much larger to induce a substantial increase in the number of donations. But experts have estimated that even if the payment for a kidney were as much as $100,000, private and public insurance systems (which, as we have noted, pay for almost all of the transplants in the United States) could actually *save* money on many transplants because dialysis (at $70,000 per year) and the other treatments associated with chronic kidney disease are so expensive.

It is true that allowing payments for human organs would almost surely increase the number of transplants each year—indeed, this is the very point. Payments would bring forth more organs, and this would in turn reduce deaths among people waiting for transplants. A payment system would have added costs associated with it: There would be more transplant operations (at $250,000 each for kidneys, for example, plus another, say, $100,000 for each of the organs themselves). Suppose that the payments for kidneys enabled an additional five thousand transplants per year (assuming that the U.S. system would be as successful as the Iranian system in eliminating the excess demand for kidneys). That would yield added costs nationwide of about $1.75 billion (five thousand transplants estimated at $350,000 each).

And there is a second cost: Paying for organs would cause a reduction in the number of altruistic donations. How many fewer there would be we cannot know for sure, but let us make two assumptions to be on the safe side. First, we assume that there would be *no* altruistic donations from living donors under a payment system. Second, we assume that the relatives of all deceased donors would insist on payment. Together these assumptions imply there would be an added expense of $100,000 on each of the sixteen thousand kidney transplants performed under the current system. The added cost here would be $1.6 billion per year, which, when added to the $1.75 billion cost of the new transplants, yields a total added annual cost of $3.35 billion for the organ payment system.

## THE BENEFITS OF PAYING FOR ORGANS

In return for this sum, we would surely recoup some savings from the dialysis system because at least five thousand people per year would no longer be on dialysis at $70,000 per year—they would instead have a kidney to do that work for them. Moreover, the current three- to four-year delay on kidney transplants would be sharply reduced, generating additional savings. But far more important, we would be saving the lives of five thousand people every year, at a cost per life saved of but $600,000—and this number does not count any of the savings from reduced dialysis treatments.

All these calculations seem a callous way to view a human life. But by the standards of medical care of today, allowing payments for human organs is almost surely a safe and remarkably cheap way to alleviate needless suffering and save thousands of lives every year. And once this is clear, aren't the truly callous people those who would deprive human beings of that opportunity?

## DISCUSSION QUESTIONS

1. For the purposes of this question, assume that allowing payment for kidney donations would cause us to spend another $3.5 billion on kidney transplants. (This is slightly above the estimate provided in the text.) Also assume that permitting such payments saves the lives of five thousand patients who would otherwise die waiting for a kidney? How much must we value a human life for it to make economic sense to permit payments for kidneys? How much is that number reduced if each of the five thousand also ends up spending 18 months less on dialysis? Show all of your calculations.

2. Per capita income varies substantially across the country. If there was a free market in which payments for kidneys was permitted within the United States, would you expect there to be different prices in different parts of the country? In which areas of the countries would you expect the most organs to be offered for donation? Keeping in mind that insurance, either private or public, pays for essentially all transplants, would these same areas also be the chief "exporting" areas? Explain.

3. Why might the owners of the private insurance companies that pay for most organ transplants be in favor of a system that prohibits paying for a donated organ? Should the taxpayers of the United States, who ultimately cover the cost of Medicare and Medicaid transplants, similarly be opposed to paying for donated organs?

4. If payment for organs drives up the financial costs of transplants, is it possible that private insurance companies, and even Medicare and Medicaid, might tighten their standards for transplants so as to reduce the number of transplants each year? If they do, who would gain and who would lose compared to the current system?

5. The average waiting time on transplant lists is three to four years for kidneys (although this is expected to rise sharply, due to the rising incidence of diabetes, a major cause of kidney damage). Many of these people waiting must undergo dialysis, at a cost of $70,000 per year, paid for by private insurance, Medicare, or Medicaid. Suppose that if payment for organs were permitted, the transplant waiting time was shortened by three years, and that for the average patient, the result was 18 months less on dialysis. At what price for a kidney would a system of paying for organs be a "break-even" proposition for insurers? Show all calculations and explain your reasoning.

6. The United States currently has an "opt-in" system for organ donations from the deceased: People must explicitly choose postmortem donation ahead of time (as when they obtain their driver's licenses). Many other nations have "opt-out" systems: A desire to donate postmortem is presumed to exist unless an individual explicitly chooses ahead of time *not* to permit donation. How—if at all—would a shift to an opt-out system likely change the supply of cadaveric (postmortem) donations?

# CHAPTER 13

# Are We Running Out of Water?

If you believe the headlines, humans are about to die of thirst. A few samples should be enough to convince you:

"A World of Thirst" (*U.S. News & World Report*)

"Water Shortages May Lead to War" (*Financial Times*)

"Drying Up" (*The Economist*)

"Water Shortages Could Leave World in Dire Straits" (*USA Today*)

The world, it seems, is running out of water.

But how can this be true? After all, about 71 percent of the earth's surface is covered in water. Lake Michigan alone contains more water than the world's population uses in two years. Even more to the point, the earth is a closed system. Using water does not destroy water. Whether we drink it, flush it, irrigate with it, or even let it evaporate, it comes back to us eventually, just as clean and pure as the raindrops of a spring shower. In fact, every three weeks, enough rain falls to satisfy the water uses of the entire world's population for a year. So what, exactly, is the problem?

## The Ultimate Renewable Resource

Water is the ultimate renewable resource: The act of using it begins the process that returns it to us. But—and this is the crux—water is also *scarce*. That is, having the amount of clean water we want, where we want it, when we want it there is not free. We must sacrifice other resources to accomplish this. And as the level of economic activity grows, the demand for water grows, and so the costs of consuming water also grow.

In this sense, water is no different from any other **scarce good.** If we want more of it, we must sacrifice more of other things to achieve that goal. But what makes water seem different is that unlike, say, broccoli, if we do entirely without it, disastrous things happen in a relatively short period of time. If water gets sufficiently scarce, people may start doing some pretty unpleasant things to each other to ensure that they, rather than their neighbors or enemies, are the ones who end up with it. But before we see if this is really something we should worry about, we had better start by learning a little more about water.

## WATER, WATER EVERYWHERE

Of the enormous amount of water on the earth's surface, about 97.2 percent is ocean water, which is too saline under normal circumstances to drink or use for irrigation. Another 2.15 percent is polar ice, which is certainly not a very convenient source. Of the remaining 0.65 percent, about 0.62 percent is underground in aquifers and similar geological structures. This groundwater takes hundreds of years to recharge and so is not really a sustainable source of freshwater over the relevant time span. That leaves us with rain.

Fortunately, it rains a lot, and despite the headlines, on a *worldwide* basis, the amount of rainfall doesn't vary much from year to year. About two-thirds of the rain falls on the world's oceans, where almost no one lives. But even so, and even taking into account evaporation and the fact that much of the rain over land quickly runs off into the oceans before it can be captured, there is still a lot of usable rainfall every year. Indeed, there is enough every day to yield 5,700 liters per person—about six times as much as the average person actually consumes in all uses.

Of course, Mother Nature is not particularly evenhanded in the distribution of this usable rainfall. For example, China gets only 5 percent of it, despite having 20 percent of the world's population. Brazil, Canada, and Russia, which together have 6 percent of the world's population, receive 29 percent of the usable rainfall. And although the United States does pretty well on average, picking up 5 percent of the rain and having about 5 percent of the world's population, there are plenty of differences within our borders. Massive amounts of rain fall in southeastern Alaska and on the mountain slopes of Hawaii, while very little falls in Southern California. But the fact that people routinely choose to locate themselves in places where it does not rain highlights one of the fundamental points of this chapter: Water is an **economic good**, and the distribution and consumption of water are fundamentally economic problems, ones that can be solved in markets, just as other economic problems (such as the provision of food, shelter, and clothing) are solved in markets. To focus clearly on this point, let's examine some of the myths that have grown up around water in recent years:

*Myth 1: The planet is drying up.* As we have suggested earlier, there is nothing to worry about here. The cheapest (and completely sustainable) source of clean freshwater is rainfall, and roughly 113,000 cubic kilometers (3 quadrillion gallons) of the stuff falls every year on land areas around the world, year in and year out. Although small amounts of this are temporarily stored in plants and animals while they are alive, all of it eventually either recharges groundwater or evaporates, forms clouds, and precipitates—all 113,000 cubic kilometers, year after year. Sometimes, more is in Brazil and less in Sudan, and sometimes more of it inconveniently runs off in floods. But because the earth is a closed system, all of that water stays with us.

*Myth 2: We can save water by flushing less and using less in agriculture.* Remember the closed system? That applies to toilets and alfalfa, too. Flushing the toilet does not send the water to the moon. It just sends it through the sewer system to a water treatment plant and eventually into aquifers under the ground or back down on our heads in the form of raindrops. So-called low-flow toilets (and showers) have no effect on the amount of water in existence. (Because they may slightly reduce the amount of water running through water and sewer systems, they may conserve a bit on the amount of resources used in these systems. But there are offsets. Such devices are routinely more costly to produce than regular toilets or shower heads, and they occupy people's time—because of double flushes and longer showers. On balance, besides not "saving" water, there is thus no evidence that such devices conserve resources at all.)

Even agriculture, notorious for consuming an enormous amount of (usually subsidized) water around the world, does not destroy the stuff. Most of the water used by agriculture evaporates or runs off into rivers or soaks into underground aquifers. A small amount is temporarily stored in the crops, but this, soon enough, is consumed by animals or humans and simply returns to the same system that delivers 113,000 cubic kilometers of water onto our heads every year. There is no doubt that all of this use of water in agriculture is costly because it could be used elsewhere. Moreover, agricultural use of water is generally subsidized by taxpayers. Making farmers pay full market value for water would reduce agricultural use and raise our collective wealth by improving the allocation of resources. But it would not alter the amount of water available.

Having said this, agricultural use of water does present two important economic issues. First, as we just noted, government policies around the world routinely cause water for agriculture to be heavily subsidized. Farmers often pay as little as $10 to $20 per acre-foot (about 325,000 gallons) for water that costs anywhere from $500 to $1,000 per acre to provide to them. Because of this huge subsidy, farmers are no doubt richer, but the losses to society are much greater, meaning that our overall wealth is lower. (For an explanation of why we get such subsidies despite this, see Chapters 20.)

Second, we not only subsidize water use for agriculture, but also routinely forbid farmers to sell or lease their water to other users, especially nonagricultural users. This is a particular problem in the relatively arid American West, where farmers effectively own most of the rights to surface and groundwater but must "use it or lose it"—if they don't put it to beneficial use on their crops, they lose their rights to it. But often this water would be much more productively "used" if it were left in the streams to help support the spawning and other essential life activities of downstream species, such as trout or salmon. Laws are slowly changing to recognize environmental uses as being "beneficial" uses, but existing restrictions on the use of water still yield lower overall wealth for us.

*Myth 3: Water is different from other goods.* Many people seem to think that because it is essential to life, water is somehow different from other goods—or at least that it should be treated differently in some very specific ways. Let's first get rid of the notion that water doesn't obey the laws of demand and supply. In fact, although the demand for water in some uses is relatively inelastic, usage of water in *all* uses responds as predicted by the law of demand—when the price of water goes up, people use less of it. Similarly, although getting water from where it is to where people would like it to be is costly, the law of supply still holds true—when the price of water rises, suppliers of water provide more of it to consumers. Sometimes this process is as simple as diverting a stream or capturing rainfall. Sometimes it is as complicated as using reverse osmosis to convert seawater into freshwater. But even if the production technique is as esoteric as recycling urine into fresh, drinkable water (as is done on the international space station), the fact remains that when water becomes more valuable, people are incredibly ingenious in finding ways to make sure it is available.

*Myth 4: Price controls on water protect low-income consumers.* Some people claim that water should *not* be treated like other goods, specifically arguing that both the price of water received by suppliers and the price paid by consumers should be kept down by government decree. This, it is said, will protect people, especially those who are poor, from high water prices and will prevent suppliers from earning "excessive" profits. After all, some 1.1 billion people around the world currently do not have ready access to clean water, which makes an inviting target for anyone who might become a monopoly supplier to substantial numbers of these people.

It is true that governments can reduce the profits of the suppliers of water (or anything else) by limiting the prices they charge. But in reality, this does not protect consumers, particularly not the poorest consumers. Price controls on water *reduce* the amount supplied and, especially for the poor, generally make consumers worse off. They end up with less water than if prices were allowed to reach equilibrium levels, and they are forced to undergo nonprice rationing schemes (ranging from limited hours of service to getting no clean water at all). In fact, if we examine places around the world where the poor have little or no access to clean water, we find that government efforts to "protect" people from potential suppliers of water are in fact a key source of this lack of access. In Brazil, for example, government limits on private water rates forced a major international water project company to cease operations there, reducing the supply of clean water. In India, the widespread insistence by many local governments that water be provided free of charge has effectively stalled most efforts to improve water distribution in that country. And in China, government price controls have discouraged water utilities from developing new water supplies and from upgrading water distribution systems. As we see in detail in Chapter 15, government controls on prices make goods *more* scarce, not less, and it is generally the disadvantaged members of society who suffer the most as a result.

**Myth 5: The ocean is too salty to drink.** As a practical matter, prolonged consumption of saltwater by species not specifically adapted for it is highly deleterious. But the technology for desalination of seawater is advancing rapidly, and the cost of desalination is falling just as rapidly—more than 95 percent over the past 20 years. In relatively arid parts of the earth (including Southern California) desalination has become price-competitive with other sources of supply, and large-scale desalination plants are in operation around the world.

The process yields highly concentrated brine as a by-product. To avoid damage to ocean species that are sensitive to excess salinity, this brine must be dealt with carefully (dispersed widely) when it is returned to the sea. Nevertheless, this is simply a matter of routine care. Moreover, if local conditions make wide dispersal impractical or expensive, the brine can be evaporated, and the resulting solid materials then either used or disposed of in ordinary landfills. The upshot is that with continued technological progress in desalination, water from the ocean will likely become cheaper than collecting rainfall in large portions of the world. Far from running out of water, people everywhere will then find themselves able to secure it as easily as, well, turning on the tap.

# DISCUSSION QUESTIONS

1. How much water do people "need"? Is your answer the same if you have to pay their water bills?

2. Evaluate the following: "Although taxpayers foot the bill for federal water sold to farmers at subsidized prices, they also eat the crops grown with that water. Because the crops are cheaper due to the subsidized water, taxpayers get back exactly what they put in, and so there is no waste from having subsidized water for farmers." Would you give the author of this quote an A or an F in economics? Explain.

3. During the droughts that periodically plague California, farmers in that state are able to purchase subsidized water to irrigate their crops, at the same time that many California homeowners have to pay large fines if they water their lawns. Can you suggest an explanation for this difference in the treatment of two different groups of citizens in the state of California?

4. If allocating water through nonprice means generally harms society, can you suggest why governments often do this?

5. Consider two otherwise identical communities; call them P and N. Suppose that in P, all homes, apartments, and businesses have meters that record the usage of water. In addition, the users of the water must pay more when they use more water. Thus, water is priced like most other goods. In community N, there are no meters and the local supplier of water charges everyone in the community a fixed amount per person, per month for their water service. Thus, using another gallon costs the user nothing additional. In which community will per capita water use be higher? Explain, using the relevant principles of economics.

6. Referring back to the facts of the previous question: Suppose you knew that in one community water is supplied by a privately owned company, while in the other community water is supplied by the local government. In which community do you predict that water is supplied by the privately owned company? Explain.

# CHAPTER 14

# The (Dis)incentives of Higher Taxes

Politicians always seem to be looking for additional ways to raise tax revenues. And most often, politicians talk (and even act) as though their taxing decisions have no effect on the quantity supplied or the quantity demanded of whatever good or service they wish to tax. Indeed, there is a saying among economists that politicians believe all demand curves and supply curves are **perfectly inelastic.** In such a world, higher taxes would have no effect on either quantity demanded or quantity supplied. What a wonderful world that would be—for politicians.

## THE LUXURY TAX

In the real world, however, changes in taxes cause changes in **relative prices,** and individuals in their roles as consumers, savers, investors, and workers react to these relative price changes. Consider a truly telling example: the luxury tax enacted by Congress in 1991. Members of Congress were looking for additional revenues to reduce the federal budget deficit. What better way to raise these hoped-for revenues than with new taxes on the purchases of high-priced luxury items, such as big boats, expensive cars, furs, planes, and jewelry. After all, rich people don't really care how much they pay, right? That is why we call them rich. So Congress passed a 10 percent luxury surcharge tax on boats priced over $100,000, cars over $30,000, aircraft over $250,000, and furs and jewelry over $10,000.

The federal government estimated that it would rake in $9 billion in extra revenues over the following five-year period. Yet just a few years later, the luxury tax was quietly eliminated. Why? Because the actual take for the federal government was almost *nothing.*

Rich people, strange as it may seem, react to relative price changes, too. For high-priced new boats, for example, they had alternatives. Some bought used luxury boats instead of new ones. Others decided not to trade in their older luxury boats for new ones. Still others bought their new boats in other countries and never brought them back to the United States to be taxed. The moral of the story for politicians is that the laws of supply and demand apply to everyone, rich and poor, young and old, whatever their description might be.

## STATIC VERSUS DYNAMIC ANALYSIS

The discrepancy between the fantasyland of politics and the reality of human behavior can be traced in part to the fact that politicians routinely engage in **static analysis.** They assume that people's behavior is static (unchanging), no matter how the constraints they face—such as higher taxes—might change. If the politicians who had pushed for the luxury tax had used **dynamic analysis,** they would have correctly anticipated that consumers (even rich ones) were going to change their buying decisions when faced with the new taxes.

Dynamic analysis takes into account the fact that the impact of the tax *rate* on tax *revenue* actually collected depends crucially on the **elasticity** of the relevant demand or supply curves. That is, even a high *rate* (measured in tax per item, or as a percentage of the value of the item) can yield relatively little *revenue* (total dollars collected) if consumers are highly responsive to the tax-inclusive price of the good. For example, in the case of the luxury tax, the **elasticity of demand** for new, high-end boats was relatively high: When the tax per boat went up, the quantity demanded fell so far that tax collections were negligible.

## INCOME TAXES AND LABOR SUPPLY

Now let's shift from the demand side of this taxing issue to the supply side. Does quantity supplied react to changing relative prices? Yes, but you might not know it from listening to politicians. The first modern federal personal income tax was imposed in 1916. The highest rate was 15 percent. Eventually, the top federal personal marginal income tax rate reached an astounding 91 percent, during the years 1951–1964. This marginal tax rate was cut to 70 percent in 1965. In 1980, it was lowered to 50 percent. For much of the 1980s and since, the highest federal marginal income tax rate has ranged from 31 percent to about 40 percent.

Often politicians (and even some members of the general public) believe that the income tax rates paid by America's richest individuals do not matter to them because they are so rich that even after paying taxes, they are still very rich. The underlying "theory" behind such a belief is that the supply of labor is completely unresponsive to the net after-tax price received by the providers of labor. Stated another way, if you were to draw the **supply curve** of labor, it would be a nearly vertical line for each individual at some fixed number of work hours per year. Supposedly, then, the **elasticity of supply** of labor is low.

To be sure, you might know somebody who loves work so much that she or he will work with the same intensity and for the same number of hours per year no matter what the income tax rate is. But changes occur at the margin in economics (meaning in the real world). If there are *some* individuals who respond to higher federal marginal tax rates by working less, then the overall supply curve of labor is going to be upward-sloping even for the ultrarich—just like all other supply curves for goods and services.

## THE EVIDENCE IS CLEAR

The data seem to confirm our economic predictions. In 1980, the top marginal income tax rate was 70 percent. The highest 1 percent of income-earning Americans paid 19 percent of all federal personal income taxes in that year. In 2007, when the top tax rate was 35 percent, the richest 1 percent paid more than double that share. How can this be explained? The answer is relatively straightforward: Lower marginal income tax rates create an incentive for people to work more and harder because the rewards of doing so are greater. Also, in their role as risk-taking entrepreneurs, individuals are almost always going to be willing to take bigger risks if they know that success will yield greater net after-tax increases in their incomes.

Data from Europe suggest that exactly the same incentives are at work across a broad spectrum of income earners. Researchers have found that a tax increase of just over 12 percentage points induces the average adult in Europe to reduce work effort by over 120 hours per year—the equivalent of almost four weeks' work. Such a tax change also causes a sharp reduction in the number of people who work at all and causes many others to join the underground economy. Overall, then, higher tax rates cause lower output and higher unemployment and also induce marked increases in efforts devoted to tax evasion.

## INCENTIVES APPLY TO EVERYONE

It is also true that what we have been talking about applies even among people who are at the very bottom of the income distribution. In many countries today, and in many circumstances in the United States, poorer individuals receive benefits from the government. These benefits can be in the form of food stamps, subsidized housing, subsidized health care or health insurance, and direct cash payments (often referred to as "welfare"). Those who receive such government benefits typically pay no income taxes on these benefits. In the case of the United States, they may even receive an **Earned Income Tax Credit,** which is a type of **negative tax** or **tax credit.**

If such individuals were to accept a job (or a higher-paying job, if they are already employed), two things will normally occur. The first is that they will lose some or all of their government benefits. The second is that they may have to start paying federal (and perhaps state) personal income taxes. They understand that the loss of a benefit is the equivalent of being taxed more. And when they also have to pay explicit taxes, they know that the result is effectively double taxation.

## A LESSON FROM IRELAND

Just as at the top end of the income ladder, the quantity of labor supplied by people at the lower end is affected by changes in the marginal income tax rates they face. If taking a good job and getting off the welfare rolls means losing benefits plus paying income taxes, the person on welfare has less incentive to accept a job. A good case in point is Ireland, which for most of the past twenty years was the fastest-growing economy in Europe. Twenty-five years ago, its economy was a disaster, one of the poorest among European countries. One of the problems was that individuals on welfare faced an effective (implicit) marginal income tax rate of about 120 percent if they got off the dole and went back to work. Obviously, they weren't directly taxed at 120 percent, but with the actual income tax that did apply, combined with the loss in welfare benefits, the *implicit* marginal tax rate was indeed 120 percent. Stated differently, their available spendable income would drop by about 20 percent if they went back to work! Needless to say, large numbers of poorer Irish stayed on the welfare roles until the program was completely overhauled.

Interestingly enough, this overhaul of the incentives facing low-income individuals was accompanied by an overhaul of the tax rates (and thus incentives) facing high-income corporations, with much the same results. In the 1990s, the Irish slashed the corporate profits tax to 12.5 percent, the lowest in Europe and only about one-third as high as the U.S. rate of 35 percent. Beginning in 2004, the Irish government also began offering a 20 percent tax credit for company spending on research and development, offering high-tech firms an opportunity to cut their taxes by starting up and expanding operations in Ireland. Almost immediately, Ireland became a magnet for new investment and for successful companies that didn't want to hand over one-third or more of their profits to the tax collector.

The combination of lower corporate tax rates and tax breaks on research and development induced hundreds of multinational corporations to begin operations in Ireland. They brought with them hundreds of thousands of new jobs (and this to a nation of only four million residents), and Ireland quickly became number one among the European Union's fifteen original members in being home to companies that conduct research and development. And tax revenues of the Irish government? Well, despite the drastic cut in tax rates, tax revenues actually soared to levels never seen before. Indeed, measured as a share of gross domestic product, Ireland soon collected 50 percent more tax revenues out of corporate profits than America did, despite Ireland's lower tax rate.

The lesson of our story is simple. It is true that "nothing in life is certain but death and taxes." But it is equally true that higher tax rates don't always mean higher tax revenues. And that is a lesson that politicians can ignore only at their own peril.

## DISCUSSION QUESTIONS

1. Suppose the government spends more this year than it collects in taxes, borrowing the difference. Assuming that the government will repay its debts, what does this imply about what must happen to taxes in the *future*? How might people adjust their behavior to account for this predicted change in taxes?

2. Consider three scenarios. In each, your neighbor offers to pay $500 if you will clear brush out of his backyard this week.

   Scenario 1: If you decline the offer, you can collect $200 in unemployment benefits this week. If you accept the offer, you get to keep the entire $500, without having to pay taxes on it.

   Scenario 2: If you decline the offer, you can collect $100 in unemployment benefits this week. If you accept the offer, you must pay $100 in income taxes out of your earnings from work.

   Scenario 3: If you decline the offer, you collect no unemployment benefits. If you accept the offer, you must pay $200 in income taxes out of your earnings from work.

   What is the net monetary gain from working in each of these three scenarios? How, if at all, do your incentives change between scenarios? Explain, briefly.

3. If you found yourself in the 91 percent federal personal income tax bracket in 1951, how great would have been your incentive to find legal loopholes to reduce your federal tax liabilities? If you found yourself in the lowest federal personal income tax bracket of, say, 15 percent, would your incentive to find loopholes to reduce your tax bill be the same? Explain.

4. Explain how the incentive effects of each of the following hypothetical taxes would cause people to change their behavior. Be sure to explain what people are likely to do *less* of and what they are likely to do *more* of in response to each tax:

   (a) A $1,000,000-per-story tax on all office buildings more than two stories tall

   (b) A $2,000-per-car tax on all red (and only red) cars

   (c) A $100-per-book tax on all *new* college textbooks

5. Suppose that federal marginal personal income tax rates will rise significantly over the next 10 years. Explain the ways in which individuals at all levels of income can react over time, not just immediately after taxes are raised. How will the size of the response differ, say, a year after the rise in tax rates compared to a week after the increase? Is it possible that some people will actually change their behavior *before* the higher tax rates go into effect? Explain.

6. How does a country's tax structure affect who decides to immigrate into the nation or emigrate out of the nation? Contrast, for example, nations A and B. Assume that nation A applies a 20 percent tax on every dollar of income earned by an individual. Nation B applies a 10 percent tax on the first $40,000 per year of income and a 40 percent tax on all income above $40,000 per year earned by an individual. Start by computing the tax bill in each country that must be paid by a person earning $40,000 per year and the tax bill that must be paid by a person earning $100,000 per year. Then consider the more general issue: If the language, culture, and climate of the two nations are similar, and if a person can choose to live on one side or the other of a river separating the two nations, who is more likely to choose to live in A and who is more likely to choose to live in B? To what extent does your reasoning apply if an ocean, rather than a river, separates the two countries? Does it apply if the language, culture, or climate in the two nations differs? Explain.

# CHAPTER 15

# Bankrupt Landlords, from Sea to Shining Sea

Take a tour of Santa Monica, a beachfront enclave of Los Angeles, and you will find a city of bizarre contrasts. Pick a street at random, and you may find run-down rental units sitting in disrepair next to homes costing $800,000. Try another street, and you may see abandoned apartment buildings adjacent to luxury car dealerships and trendy shops that sell high-fashion clothing to Hollywood stars. Sound strange? Not in Santa Monica—known locally as the People's Republic of Santa Monica— where stringent rent-control laws once routinely forced property owners to leave their buildings empty and decaying rather than even bothering to sell them.

Three thousand miles to the east, rent-control laws in New York City—known locally as the Big Apple—have forced landlords to abandon housing units because the laws imposed on owners huge financial losses. Largely as a result of such abandonments, the city government of New York owns thousands of derelict housing units—empty, except for rats and small-time cocaine dealers. Meanwhile, because the controls also discourage new construction, the city faces a housing gap of 200,000 rental units—apartments that could easily be filled at current controlled rental rates if the units were in habitable condition.

From coast to coast, stories like these are commonplace in the two hundred or so American cities and towns that practice some form of **rent control**—a system in which the local government tells building owners how much they can charge for rent. Time and again, the stories are the same: poorly maintained rental units, abandoned apartment buildings, tenants trapped by housing gridlock in apartments no longer suitable for them, bureaucracies bloated with rent-control enforcers, and even homeless families that can find no one who will rent to them. Time and again, the reason for the stories is the same: legal limits on the rent that people may pay for a place to live.

## A BRIEF HISTORY OF RENT CONTROLS

Our story begins in 1943, when the federal government imposed rent control as a temporary wartime measure. Although the federal program ended a few years after the war, New York City continued the controls on its own. Under New York's controls, a landlord generally could not raise rents on apartments as long as the tenants continued to renew their leases. Rent controls in Santa Monica are more recent. They were spurred by the inflation of the 1970s, which, combined with California's rapid population growth, pushed housing prices and rents to record levels. In 1979, the city of Santa Monica (where 80 percent of the residents were renters) ordered rents rolled back to the levels of the year before and stipulated that future rents could go up by only two-thirds as much as any increase in the overall price level. In both New York and Santa Monica, the objective of rent controls has been to keep rents below the levels that would be observed in freely competitive markets. Achieving this goal required that both cities impose extensive regulations to prevent landlord and tenant from evading the controls—regulations that are costly to enforce and that distort the normal operation of the market.

It is worth noting that the rent-control systems in New York and Santa Monica are slowly yielding to decontrol. For a number of years, some apartments in New York have been subject only to "rent stabilization" regulations, which are somewhat less stringent than absolute rent controls. In addition, New York apartments renting for over $2,000 per month are deregulated when a lease ends. In Santa Monica, the state of California mandated that as of 1999, rent for newly vacant apartments could increase. Even so, in both cities, much of the rental market is dominated by rent controls. Accordingly, in this chapter we focus on the consequences of those controls.

## THE ADVERSE EFFECTS OF RENT CONTROLS

In general, the unfettered movement of rental prices in a freely competitive housing market performs three vital functions: (1) it allocates existing scarce housing among competing claimants; (2) it promotes the efficient maintenance of existing housing and stimulates the production of new housing, where appropriate; and (3) it rations usage of housing by demanders, thereby preventing waste of scarce housing. Rent control prevents rental prices from effectively performing these functions. Let's see how.

**Rent control discourages the construction of new rental units.** Developers and mortgage lenders are reluctant to get involved in building new rental properties because controls artificially depress the most important long-run determinant of profitability—rents. Thus, in one recent year, eleven thousand new housing units were built in Dallas, a city with a 16 percent rental vacancy rate but no rent-control statute. In that same year, only two thousand units were built in San Francisco, a city with a 1.6 percent vacancy rate but stringent rent-control laws. In New York City, the only rental units being built are either exempt from controls or heavily subsidized by the government. Private construction of new apartments in Santa Monica also dried up under controls, even though new office space and commercial developments—both exempt from rent control—were built at a record pace.

*Rent control leads to the deterioration of the existing supply of rental housing.* When rental prices are held below free market levels, property owners cannot recover through higher rents the costs of maintenance, repairs, and capital improvements. Thus, such activities are sharply curtailed. Eventually, taxes, utilities, and the expenses of the most rudimentary repairs—such as replacing broken windows—exceed the depressed rental receipts; as a result, the buildings are abandoned. In New York, some owners have resorted to arson, hoping to collect the insurance on their empty rent-controlled buildings before the city claims them for back taxes. Under rent controls in Santa Monica, the city insisted that owners wishing to convert empty apartment buildings to other uses had to build new rental units to replace the units they no longer rented. At a cost of up to $50,000 per apartment, it is little wonder that few owners were willing to bear the burden, choosing instead to leave the buildings empty and graffiti-scarred.

*Rent control impedes the process of rationing scarce housing.* One consequence of this is that tenant mobility is sharply restricted. Even when a family's demand for living space changes—due, for example, to a new baby or a teenager's departure for college—there can be substantial costs in giving up a rent-controlled unit. In New York City, landlords often charge "key money" (a large up-front cash payment) before a new tenant is allowed to move in. The high cost of moving means that large families often stay in cramped quarters while small families or even single persons reside in large apartments. In New York, this phenomenon of nonmobility came to be known as *housing gridlock.* It is estimated that more than 20 percent of renters in New York City live in apartments that are bigger or smaller than they would otherwise occupy. In Santa Monica, many homeowners rented out portions of their houses in response to soaring prices in the 1970s and then found themselves trapped by their tenants, whom they could not evict even if they wanted to sell their homes and move to a retirement community.

## EFFORTS TO EVADE CONTROLS

Not surprisingly, the distortions produced by rent control lead to efforts by both landlords and tenants to evade the rules. This in turn leads to the growth of cumbersome and expensive government bureaucracies whose job is to enforce the controls. In New York, where rents can be raised when tenancy changes hands, landlords have an incentive to make life unpleasant for tenants or to evict them on the slightest pretense. The city has responded by making evictions extremely costly for landlords. Even if a tenant blatantly and repeatedly violates the terms of a lease, the tenant cannot be evicted if the violations are corrected within a "reasonable" time period. If the violations are not corrected—despite several trips to court by the owners and their attorneys—eviction requires a tedious and expensive judicial proceeding. For their part, tenants routinely try to sublet all or part of their rent-controlled apartments at prices substantially above the rent they pay the owner. Because both the city and the landlords try to prohibit subletting, the parties often end up in the city's housing courts, an entire judicial system developed chiefly to deal with disputes over rent-controlled apartments.

Strict controls on monthly rents force landlords to use other means to discriminate among prospective tenants. Simply to ensure that the rent check comes every month, many landlords rent only to well-heeled professionals. As one commentator put it, "There is no disputing that Santa Monica became younger, whiter, and richer under rent control." The same pattern occurred under the rent-control laws of Berkeley, California, and Cambridge, Massachusetts.

## BUREAUCRACIES FLOURISH

There is little doubt the bureaucracies that evolve to administer rent-control laws are cumbersome and expensive. Between 1988 and 1993, New York City spent $5.1 billion rehabilitating housing confiscated from private landlords. Even so, derelict buildings continued piling up at a record rate. The overflow and appeals from the city's housing courts clog the rest of New York's judicial system, impeding the prosecution of violent criminals and drug dealers. In Santa Monica, the Rent Control Board began with an annual budget of $745,000 and a staff of twenty people. By the early 1990s, the staff had tripled in size, and the budget was pushing $5 million. Who picked up the tab? The landlords did, of course, with an annual special assessment of $200 per unit levied on them. And even though the 1999 state-mandated changes in the law meant that apartment rents in Santa Monica can be increased when a new tenant moves in, the new rent is then controlled by the city for the duration of the tenancy. Indeed, the Rent Control Board conveniently maintains a Web site where one can go to learn the maximum allowable rent on any of the tens of thousands of rent-controlled residences in Santa Monica.

## THE LOSERS FROM RENT CONTROLS

Ironically, the big losers from rent control—in addition to landlords—are often low-income individuals, especially single mothers. Indeed, many observers believe that one significant cause of homelessness in cities such as New York and Los Angeles is rent control. Poor individuals often cannot assure the discriminating landlord that their rent will be paid on time—or paid at all—each month. Because controlled rents are generally well below free market levels, there is little incentive for apartment owners to take a chance on low-income individuals as tenants. This is especially true if the prospective tenant's chief source of income is a welfare check. Indeed, a significant number of the tenants appearing in New York's housing courts have been low-income mothers who, due to emergency expenses or delayed welfare checks, have missed rent payments. Often their appeals end in evictions and residence in temporary public shelters or on the streets. Prior to the state-mandated easing of controls, some apartment owners in Santa Monica who used to rent one- and two-room units to welfare recipients and other low-income individuals simply abandoned their buildings, leaving them vacant rather than trying to collect artificially depressed rents that failed to cover operating costs. The disgusted owner of one empty and decaying eighteen-unit building had a friend spray-paint his feelings on the wall: "I want to tear this mess down, but Big Brother won't let me." Perhaps because the owner had escaped from a concentration camp in search of freedom in the United States, the friend added a personalized touch: a drawing of a large hammer and sickle, symbol of the former Soviet Union.

## DAMAGE AROUND THE WORLD

It is worth noting that the ravages of rent controls are not confined to the United States. In Mumbai, India, rents are still set at the levels that prevailed back in 1940. A two-bedroom apartment near the center of the city may have a controlled rent of as little as $8.50 per month. (Nearby, free market rents for an apartment of the same size can be as much as $3,000 per month.) Not surprisingly, landlords have let their rent-controlled buildings decay, and collapsing apartments have become a regular feature of life in this city of twelve million people. Over the past 10 years, about ninety people have been killed in the collapse of more than fifty rent-controlled buildings. The city government estimates that perhaps one hundred more apartment buildings are on the verge of collapse.

Even Communist nations are not exempt from rent controls. In a heavily publicized news conference several years ago, the foreign minister of Vietnam, Nguyen Co Thach, declared that a "romantic conception of socialism" had destroyed his country's economy after the Vietnam War. Thach stated that rent control had artificially encouraged demand and discouraged supply and that all of the housing in Hanoi had fallen into disrepair as a result. Thach concluded by noting, "The Americans couldn't destroy Hanoi, but we have destroyed our city by very low rents. We realized it was stupid and that we must change policy."

Apparently, this same thinking was what induced the state of California to compel changes in Santa Monica's rent-control ordinance. The result of that policy change was an almost immediate jump in rents on newly vacant apartments, as well as a noticeable rise in the vacancy rate—exactly the results we would expect. Interestingly enough, however, prospective new tenants were less enthusiastic about the newly available apartments than many landlords had expected. The reason? Twenty years of rent controls had produced many years of reduced upkeep and hence apartments that were less than pristine. As one renter noted, "The trouble is, most of this area ... [is] basically falling apart." And another complained, "I don't want to move into a place that's depressing, with old brown carpet that smells like chicken soup." Higher rents are changing both the ambience and the aroma of Santa Monica apartments—but only at the same rate that the market is allowed to perform its functions.

## DISCUSSION QUESTIONS

1. Why do you think governments frequently attempt to control apartment rents but not house prices?

2. What determines the size of the key-money payments that landlords demand (and tenants offer) for the right to rent a controlled apartment?

3. Who, other than the owners of rental units, loses as a result of rent controls? Who gains from rent controls? What effect would the

imposition of rent controls have on the market price of an existing single-family house? What effect would rent controls have on the value of vacant land?

4. Why do the owners of rental units reduce their maintenance expenditures on the units when rent controls are imposed? Does their decision have anything to do with whether they can afford those expenditures?

5. Because rent controls reduce the rental price below the market clearing price, the quantity of rental units on the market must decline. What does this imply *must* happen to the full cost of renting an apartment including "key money," harassment by the landlord, and so forth? Explain.

6. How does the percentage of voters who are renters (as opposed to owners) affect the incentives for politicians to propose rent controls? Does this incentive depend on the likelihood that renters are less likely to vote in local elections than are owners of apartments and houses? Why do you suppose renters are less likely to vote in local elections? Explain.

# CHAPTER 16

# The Effects of the Minimum Wage

Ask workers if they would like a raise, and the answer is likely to be a resounding yes. But ask them if they would like to be fired or have their hours of work reduced, and they would probably tell you no. The effects of the minimum wage are centered on exactly these points.

Proponents of the **minimum wage**—the lowest hourly wage firms may legally pay their workers—argue that low-income workers are underpaid and therefore unable to support themselves or their families. The minimum wage, they say, raises earnings at the bottom of the wage distribution, with little disruption to workers or businesses. Opponents claim that most low-wage workers are low-skilled youths without families to support. The minimum wage, they say, merely enriches a few teenagers at the far greater expense of many others, who can't get jobs. Most important, opponents argue, many individuals at the bottom of the economic ladder lack the skills needed for employers to hire them at the federal minimum. Willing to work but unable to find jobs, these people never learn the basic job skills needed to move up the economic ladder to higher-paying jobs. The issues are clear—but what are the facts?

## BACKGROUND

The federal minimum wage was instituted in 1938 as a provision of the Fair Labor Standards Act. It was originally set at 25 cents per hour, about 40 percent of the average manufacturing wage at the time. Over the next forty years, the legal minimum was raised periodically, roughly in accord with the movement of market wages throughout the economy. Typically, its level has averaged between 40 and 50 percent of average manufacturing wages. In response to the high inflation of the late 1970s, the minimum wage was hiked seven times between 1974 and 1981, reaching $3.35 per hour—about 42 percent of manufacturing wages. President Ronald Reagan vowed to keep a lid on the minimum wage, and by the time he left office, the minimum's unchanged level left it at 31 percent of average wages. Legislation passed in 1989 raised the minimum to $3.80 in 1990 and $4.25 in 1991. Five years later, Congress raised it in two steps to $5.15 per hour. Over the period 2007–2009, the minimum was hiked in three steps to its current level of $7.25 per hour.

About half a million workers earn the minimum wage; another 1.5 million or so are paid even less because the law doesn't cover them. Supporters of the minimum wage claim that it prevents exploitation of employees and helps people earn enough to support their families and themselves. Even so, at $7.25 per hour, a full-time worker earns only about two-thirds of what the government considers enough to keep a family of four out of poverty. In fact, to get a family of four with one wage earner up to the poverty line, the minimum wage would have to be above $11.00 per hour.

Yet opponents of the minimum wage argue that such calculations are irrelevant. For example, two-thirds of the workers earning the minimum wage are single, and they earn enough to put them 30 percent above the poverty cutoff. Moreover, about half of these single workers are teenagers, most of whom have no financial obligations, except perhaps clothing and automobile-related expenditures. Thus, opponents argue that the minimum wage chiefly benefits upper middle class teens who are least in need of assistance at the same time that it costs the jobs of thousands of disadvantaged minority youths.

## RECENT EVIDENCE

The debate over the minimum wage intensified a few years ago when research suggested that a change in the New Jersey minimum wage had no adverse short-run impact on employment. Further research by other scholars focusing on Canada reveals more clearly what actually happens when the minimum wage is hiked. In Canada, there are important differences in minimum wages both over time and across different provinces. These differences enabled researchers to distinguish between the short- and long-run effects of changes in minimum wages. The short-run effects are indeed negligible, as implied by the New Jersey study. But the Canadian research shows that in the long run, the adverse effects of a higher minimum wage are quite substantial. In the short run, it is true that firms do not cut their workforce by much in response to a higher minimum. But over time, the higher costs due to a higher minimum wage force smaller firms out of business, and it is here that the drop in employment shows up clearly.

The Canadian results are consistent with the overwhelming bulk of the U.S. evidence on this issue, which points to a negative impact of the minimum wage on employment. After all, the number of workers demanded, like the quantity demanded for all goods, responds to price: The higher the price, the lower the number desired. There remains, however, debate over how many jobs are lost due to the minimum wage. For example, when the minimum wage was raised from $3.35 to $4.25, credible estimates of the number of potential job losses ranged to 400,000. When the minimum was hiked to $5.15, researchers suggested that at least 200,000 jobs were at stake. More recently, economists have estimated that the latest increase in the federal minimum wage to $7.25 from $6.55 caused 300,000 people to lose their jobs. With a workforce of over 155 million persons, numbers like these may not sound very large. But most of the people who don't have jobs as a result of the minimum wage are teenagers; they comprise less than five percent of the workforce but bear almost all the burden of foregone employment alternatives.

## THE BIG LOSERS

Significantly, the youths most likely to lose work due to the minimum wage are disadvantaged teenagers, chiefly minorities. On average, these teens enter the workforce with the fewest job skills and the greatest need for on-the-job training. Until and unless these disadvantaged teenagers can acquire these skills, they are the most likely to be unemployed as a result of the minimum wage—and thus least likely to have the opportunity to move up the economic ladder. With a teen unemployment rate triple the overall rate and unemployment among black youngsters of 40 percent and more, critics argue that the minimum wage is a major impediment to long-term labor market success for minority youth.

Indeed, the minimum wage has an aspect that its supporters are not inclined to discuss: It can make employers more likely to discriminate on the basis of gender or race. When wages are set by market forces, employers who would discriminate face a reduced, and thus more expensive, pool of workers. But when the government mandates an above-market wage, the result is a surplus of low-skilled workers. It thus becomes easier and cheaper to discriminate. As former U.S. Treasury secretary Lawrence Summers noted, the minimum wage "removes the economic penalty to the employer. He can choose the one who's white with blond hair."

Critics of the minimum wage also note that it makes firms less willing to train workers lacking basic skills. Instead, companies may choose to hire only experienced workers whose abilities justify the higher wage. Firms are also likely to become less generous with fringe benefits in an effort to hold down labor costs. The prospect of more discrimination, less job training for low-skilled workers, and fewer fringe benefits for entry-level workers leaves many observers uncomfortable. As the economist Jacob Mincer noted, the minimum wage means "a loss of opportunity" for the hard-core unemployed.

## LIVING WAGES?

Despite these adverse effects of the minimum wage, many state and local governments believe that people with jobs should be paid a wage on which they can "afford to live." In fact, some states and localities mandate that minimum wages (sometimes called "living wages") be even higher, at levels ranging up to almost $10 an hour in Santa Fe, New Mexico, and San Francisco, California. (Both amounts are adjusted up to reflect inflation each year.) In some cases, as in Baltimore, Maryland, the local minimum wage applies only to workers at firms that do business with the relevant government entity. But in the case of the Santa Fe and San Francisco minimum wages and all state-determined minimums, the law applies to all but a few firms that are declared exempt because of their very small size or their industry (such as agriculture).

When politicians decide to raise the minimum wage, it is only after heated battles often lasting months. Given the stakes involved—an improved standard of living for some and a loss of job opportunities for others—it is not surprising that discussions of the minimum wage soon turn to controversy. As one former high-level U.S. Department of Labor official said, "When it comes to the minimum wage, there are no easy positions to take. Either you are in favor of more jobs, less discrimination, and more on-the-job training, or you support better wages for workers. Whatever stance you choose, you are bound to get clobbered by the opposition." When Congress and the president face this issue, one or both usually feel the same way.

## DISCUSSION QUESTIONS

1. Are teenagers better off when a higher minimum wage enables some to earn higher wages but causes others to lose their jobs?

2. Are there methods other than a higher minimum wage that could raise the incomes of low-wage workers without reducing employment among minority youngsters?

3. Why do you think organized labor groups, such as unions, are supporters of a higher minimum wage, even though all their members earn much more than the minimum wage?

4. Is it possible that a higher minimum wage could ever *increase* employment?

5. Even without a minimum wage, the unemployment rate would almost surely be higher among teenagers than among adults. Suggest at least two reasons why this is so.

6. Why is it teenagers (rather than members of any other age group) who are most likely to lose their jobs (or get turned down for employment) when the minimum wage is raised?

# PART FOUR

# Markets and Government

# CHAPTER 17

# Patent Trolls and Seed Monopolies

Nathan Myhrvold is a patent troll. Monsanto Corporation is a seed monopoly. Or so their critics claim. Myhrvold, formerly the chief technical officer at Microsoft, founded Intellectual Ventures, which creates and invests in inventions. Monsanto, which got its start by creating the artificial sweetener saccharin, is now the world's leader in creating genetically modified (GM) seeds for agriculture. Whatever their history, however, both Myhrvold's company and Monsanto regularly make headlines because of the many patents they each own.

## The Nature of Patents

A **patent** is a set of exclusive rights granted by a national government to an inventor for a limited period in return for a public disclosure of the invention.[1] The notion of a patent dates back at least 2,500 years to the Greek city of Sybaris. Patents have been a part of the history of the United States since our nation's inception. Article 1, section 8, clause 8 of the U.S. Constitution specifically authorizes Congress to issue exclusive rights to new ideas, and the Patent Act of 1790 laid out the first rules for doing so in this country. (Thomas Jefferson, in his role as Secretary of State from 1790 to 1793, was our first Patent Commissioner.) Originally, patents in the United States were issued for 14 years. In the nineteenth century this was raised to 17 years, and in 1994 it was upped to 20 years. During the period of the patent, the inventor has exclusive rights to the commercial use of the patented item, but the inventor must publicly disclose all of the details of the patented item.

---

1 **Copyrights** and **trademarks** are similar to patents. The former grant exclusive rights to authors or creators of books (such as this one), songs, or other original works. The latter protect distinctive signs or indicators used by businesses to identify their products or services to consumers. (A famous example is McDonald's "Golden Arches.")

Devising new ideas is an uncertain, costly business. For people to undertake this risky investment, they must have some reasonable expectation of a reward if they are successful. A patent increases the chance of reward by granting the inventor a **monopoly** on the use of his or her new idea. For the duration of the patent, its owner has the exclusive rights to the patented process, design, or good. Anyone else who wants to use the design or process or manufacture the product must compensate the patent's owner.

## THE COSTS AND BENEFITS OF PATENTS

The advantages of patents are twofold. First, they ensure inventors (such as the famous Thomas Edison) that they can lawfully protect, and thus profit, from the commercial value of their ideas. Second, because the inventor is required to publicly reveal all elements of his or her idea, other people have the opportunity to be inspired by it and perhaps create other useful products. On both counts, patents tend to foster invention (the creation of new ideas) and innovation (the successful commercial application of new ideas).

But patents may come at a cost. Because the patent owner has a monopoly on the patented item, the owner can charge a monopoly price for the item, which may be well above the price that would be observed if the product were supplied by many competing firms. Hence, the output of the patented item is less than if it were supplied competitively. This in turn implies that the total **gains from trade** associated with the product are lower than they would be if anyone were free to sell it.

This, then, is the **trade-off** of having patents. We get more inventions because the profits are higher for inventors. But we enjoy smaller gains from trade on each individual invention because of the monopoly pricing of them. As a matter of logic, it seems possible that offering patent protection might either raise or lower the total gains from trade arising from inventions.

## PATENTS AS PROPERTY RIGHTS

There is another way to think of patents, however. Imagine you own a piece of land that is hilly and covered with scrub trees, weeds, and rocks. In its current condition, it is useful for almost nothing. Now imagine that you clear the weeds, trees, and rocks from the site, and rent a bulldozer to level out the worst of the hilly areas, so that now the property is something on which a residence or business might easily be constructed.

Given that you own the land, you can sell or lease it for "whatever the market will bear." You would likely be surprised if anyone objected to your "monopoly" over this piece of land—and quite upset if someone argued that you should not be allowed to profit from all of your hard work on the property.

Well, a patent can be viewed as nothing more than a **property right** that entitles the inventor to profit from the hard work and expense that he or she puts into creating the invention. It is true that you (the hypothetical landowner) and the inventor each have a "monopoly" over the item you own. But neither of you will be able to charge a price much above the competitive level unless the item in question is appreciably different from or superior to other items in the market. And even in this case, nothing prevents other people from continuing to do what they were doing before the land was cleared or the invention was created. Hence, it is difficult to see what damage to society can come from granting patent rights.

In contrast, it is easy to understand the damage that is done when property rights (such as patents) are either nonexistent or are costly to enforce or transfer. In particular, economic growth is diminished, and in the long run we are poorer as a result. In the absence of patent protection, the damage arises because there is less investment in the creation of new ideas.

## ALTERNATIVES TO PATENTS

Patents have not always existed, and they do not exist in all nations today. Yet in their absence, there is still innovation. How does this occur? There are two important ways that inventors can profit from their ideas, even without patent protection.

The first method is simply by getting a product to the market first. Even if competitors are free to copy a product, it will still take them time to do. Until they do so, the inventor will have a monopoly on the item, and hence be able to charge a monopoly price and thereby profit. This method is an important source of profits for fashion designers, whose new creations each year are quickly copied by imitators—but often not before the designers have profited handsomely by being the first to market.

A second and more long-lived way to profit in the absence of a patent is by keeping the essence of an invention secret. **Trade secrets** have long been an important means of protecting **intellectual property.** A famous example of this is the formula for Coca-Cola. When he first concocted the beverage back in 1886, John Pemberton did not seek to patent it and, as far as anyone knows, the formula may not even be something that *could* be patented. But Pemberton and all successive owners of the formula have managed to keep it secret, and thus despite the lack of patent protection the profits have kept rolling in.

Of course, both of these alternatives to patents have significant drawbacks. Being first to market often yields significant profits for a short period of time, perhaps only weeks or months. Long-term profitability in such a setting requires that the innovator keep coming up with one new—and profitable—idea after another, time after time. Few people are able to maintain such a pace of creative endeavor over long periods. As the Coca-Cola example suggests, it is sometimes possible for trade secrets to help avoid this problem, but they present their own problem. If the formula for Coca-Cola is ever revealed, there is nothing to prevent another company from imitating the original, grabbing business by cutting prices, and eliminating Coca-Cola's profits.

## PATENT TROLLS

Let's now return to the cast of characters that started our story. As the term "patent troll" is commonly used, it is taken to mean an individual or firm that enforces its patents in a manner that is seen as unduly aggressive or opportunistic. Often the trolls don't actually manufacture anything. They just hold portfolios of patents and collect payments from firms that want to use them—or that simply don't want to be sued by the troll for supposed patent infringement.

But it is difficult to see the difference between a patent troll and, say, computer giants HP and IBM. Both of these companies earn hundreds of millions of dollars from their patents every year, and both of them aggressively enforce their patents. Moreover, in today's world of sophisticated computer and communication systems, it is hard to imagine a setting in which companies didn't cooperate one way or another in their use of patents. Modern electronic devices typically rely on dozens of patented ideas that may have been created by just as many inventors. Each of the patents individually might be almost worthless, yet when combined in a single product may yield something of great value.

Bringing together the owners of many different patents and getting them to agree to act in a common purpose can be a costly, sensitive business. Whether or not they manufacture anything, there is thus a potentially important economic role for companies such as Nathan Myhrvold's firm. Such "patent aggregators" (as they are also known) bring together portfolios of patents and negotiate agreements between patent holders whose inventions are worth far more when combined with other patents than when separate.

## SEED MONOPOLIES

What then of our seed monopoly? Monsanto, which for many years focused its business on industrial chemicals, now directs much of its attention to creating genetically modified (GM) seeds. The company's original interest in this line of work came about because of a potent weed killer called Roundup, which the company began selling in 1976. Because Roundup can also kill the plants it is designed to protect against weeds, farmers were limited in when and how they could use the herbicide. Monsanto thus began developing and patenting GM seeds for crops, such as soy beans, which would be resistant to the Roundup. This strategy succeeded so well that sales of "Roundup Ready" seeds now account for 40 percent of the company's revenues.

Just as importantly, the company learned a great deal about the process of genetic modification, and began looking for other ways to apply it. One result was patented GM corn that is resistant to most of the insects that normally attack it. The superiority of Monsanto's genetic innovations is such that Monsanto's patented genes are now being inserted into roughly 95 percent of all soybeans and 80 percent of all corn sold in the United States.

With market share numbers like these, it is no surprise that Monsanto has been pricing its seeds accordingly. Indeed, over the past decade, the company has raised the average price of its seeds by about 80 percent in inflation-adjusted terms. Some farmers have said they wished Monsanto charged less for their seeds. No surprise there. But the biggest complainers about Monsanto, it turns out, are Monsanto's *competitors,* who argue that the company is engaged in "unfair competition."

Let's consider the implications of such competitor complaints. If Monsanto seeds were, say, 50 percent superior to those of other firms and it raised its prices by 80 percent, then farmers would indeed be harmed by Monsanto's patent monopoly. But competitors would benefit because Monsanto would effectively be pricing itself out of the market. Now imagine that Monsanto seeds are, say, 100 percent better than those of competitors and it chooses to raise its prices by "only" 80 percent. In this case, competitors will indeed be harmed (Monsanto is outcompeting them on quality-adjusted price), but only because Monsanto is *benefiting* the farmers who buy its seed. Our inference from this is that the loud complaints from Monsanto's competitors are the surest sign yet that Monsanto's seed monopoly is actually making farmers better off, not worse off.

## LOOK OUT FOR MOTHER NATURE

In an ironic twist, Monsanto's Roundup Ready crops are so successful that they have become the dominant variety for many crops. This has helped Monsanto's Roundup remain the most heavily used herbicide in the United States. But the heavy use of Roundup has provoked natural selection in favor of weeds that are relatively resistant to the herbicide. In the long run, this resistance may destroy the value of Monsanto's monopoly of both Roundup and Roundup Ready seeds. And while there is no evidence yet that insects are adapting to Monsanto's insect-repelling corn, don't count Mother Nature out here just yet, either.

## DISCUSSION QUESTIONS

1. Suppose property rights to new buildings were limited to 20 years. How would this affect the incentive to invest in new buildings?

2. What is it about innovations that make them more likely to be subject to monopoly pricing than are, say, new buildings?

3. It is possible to produce GM "terminator seeds" that yield healthy crops that are sterile. The crops are perfectly suitable for consumption, but farmers cannot use the seeds from the crops to grow another generation of crops. What is the potential advantage to Monsanto in using "terminator seeds"?

4. Referring back to question 3, what is the potential *disadvantage* to Monsanto from using terminator seeds?

5. If patents are best thought of as strengthening property rights, what are the other legal and institutional characteristics you would expect to see in nations with strong patent laws?

6. New pharmaceutical drugs are protected by patents. When the patents expire, other firms are free to produce chemically identical versions of the brand name, formerly patented drug. These are referred to as "generic" versions of the drug. What do you predict will be the price of these generic drugs, compared to the price of the branded drug while it was on patent? What do you predict will happen to the price of the branded drug when its patent ends and the production of generic drugs begins? Explain.

# CHAPTER 18

# Mortgage Meltdown

Between 1995 and 2010, the U.S. housing market went on the wildest ride in its history. Over the years 1995–2005, median real (inflation-adjusted) house prices soared 60 percent nationwide and then crashed, falling 40 percent in just four years. Over the same period, the proportion of Americans who owned homes, normally a variable that changes quite slowly, leapt from 64 percent to 69 percent and then quickly dropped back to 66 percent. Meanwhile, the number of new houses built each year soared from 1.4 million to 2.2 million and then plummeted to below 500,000 per year.

## THE HOUSING MARKET COLLAPSES

But what really got people's attention—and created huge pressures on financial markets here and abroad—was the fact that just as quickly as people had snapped up houses during the boom years of 1995–2005, they simply *abandoned* their houses beginning in 2006, refusing to make any more payments on their mortgages. In a typical year, about 0.3 percent of homeowners (fewer than one out of three hundred) stop making mortgage payments each year and thus have their houses go into **foreclosure**, a process in which the borrower must give up ownership in a home because of a failure to meet payment obligations. The foreclosure rate doubled to 0.6 percent in 2006, doubled again in 2007, and rose yet again in 2008. In some hard-hit states, such as Nevada, foreclosures exploded to more than *ten times* the normal nationwide rate.

Across the country, people were literally walking away from their homes, leaving them in the hands of banks and other lenders. These lenders then took huge financial losses when forced to sell the abandoned properties in a market in which house prices were already falling.

The result was further downward pressure on prices, which gave more owners the incentive to walk away from their homes, which raised foreclosures, and so forth. Within just a few years, the housing market was more depressed than it had been any time since, well, the Great Depression of the 1930s.

## The Role of Congress

What happened? To answer this, we need to examine why, over this fifteen-year period, the housing market first exploded and then imploded, causing financial chaos on a worldwide scale. Although numerous factors played a role, the principal culprit was none other than our own Congress. Operating under a banner promoting "affordable housing," Congress first amended key mortgage-lending legislation and then put considerable implicit and explicit pressure on government-sponsored mortgage agencies to make more loans to potential home buyers. These actions encouraged mortgage lenders to dramatically reduce the financial standards expected of home buyers who wished to obtain mortgages. These lower standards enabled many more people to obtain mortgage funding, increasing the demand for housing and leading to the housing boom of 1995–2005. But these same lower standards meant that people in weaker financial shape were heavily represented among home buyers, which in turn played a central role in the housing crash and mortgage meltdown of 2006–2010. To see how this evolved, we are going to have to do some digging in the history books.

## A Brief History of Mortgage Legislation

Prior to World War II, most home mortgages were of short duration, such as one or two years (as opposed to fifteen to thirty years, which is common now). During the Great Depression, many risk-weary lenders refused to renew mortgages when they came due. The state of the economy was such that most borrowers were unable to pay the balance immediately, and so their homes were foreclosed. In response, the U.S. government in 1934 created the Federal Housing Administration (FHA) to guarantee some home mortgages from default and in 1938 created the Federal National Mortgage Association (FNMA, known as Fannie Mae) to purchase mortgages from the FHA, enabling the latter to guarantee still more mortgages. In 1968, Congress authorized Fannie Mae to buy mortgages from virtually all lenders, and in 1970, Congress created Freddie Mac (the Federal Home Mortgage Loan Corporation) to offer competition to Fannie Mae. Both Fannie Mae and Freddie Mac are referred to as "government-sponsored enterprises" (GSEs); both are technically independent of the federal government, but both are subject to congressional oversight and, it turns out, to political pressure to do what Congress wants them to do.

The next key congressional action came in 1977 when the Community Reinvestment Act (CRA) was passed, a law that required banks to lend in all neighborhoods of the geographic areas where they operated, even areas where risks were likely to be much higher than the banks would normally undertake. In 1995, the CRA was amended so that banks were, in effect, *compelled* to ignore their lending standards when making loans in low-income and minority neighborhoods or else face the wrath of government regulators. Not long thereafter, Congress began putting considerable pressure on Fannie Mae and Freddie Mac to buy up the low-quality mortgages being made under the CRA, in the hopes that this would encourage lenders to make still more low-quality loans. And indeed it did. The banks soon recognized that with the two GSEs standing ready to take the worst of their mortgages off their hands, they could earn hefty fees for originating the mortgages and then dump the risks of default off onto Fannie Mae and Freddie Mac. At this point, many potential lenders, including banks, savings and loans, and mortgage brokers, concluded that if Fannie Mae and Freddie Mac were happy to buy up risky mortgages at the drop of a hat, so to speak, then it was OK to hold on to some of the risky mortgages they were making. After all, these mortgages (called subprime mortgages) fattened profits with their above-average interest rates, and if the market turned sour, the GSEs would presumably stand ready to take them off lenders' hands.

## Regulatory Pressure

Thus, we see that it was regulatory and legislative pressure from the federal government (spearheaded by Congress) that pushed mortgage lenders to cut their lending standards in truly remarkable ways. For example, lenders have historically insisted on down payments ranging from 5 to 20 percent on home loans. This gives borrowers an incentive to keep making monthly payments (or else they lose their down payment on foreclosure), and it provides a cushion for the lender (to ensure it gets all its money back on foreclosure). Under pressure from federal regulators, however, lenders were induced to cut required down payments and even to make so-called piggyback loans, giving borrowers a *second* mortgage on top of the first whose sole function was to provide cash for the down payment. In effect, down payments were driven to zero or close thereto.

But there was more. Federal regulators pushed banks to:

- Ignore mortgage applicants' credit histories if they were less than stellar
- Forgo confirmation of applicants' current or past employment or income levels
- Permit applicants to have lower than normal income-to-loan ratios
- Count as part of income such sources as unemployment insurance and welfare payments, despite the temporary nature of such payments.

Banks that had never before offered loans under such conditions soon made them routinely, pushed by the requirements of the CRA and pulled by the willingness of Fannie Mae and Freddie Mac to acquire the loans as soon as the ink was dry. And because the GSEs were so active in making the market for loans, many lenders felt comfortable in making and holding on to such loans, even buying more loans from other lenders.

Congress's avowed intention in this process was to "help promote affordable housing," especially for low-income and minority individuals. Congress claimed to be particularly interested in making home owner-ship possible for people who had been renters all their lives. And indeed, low-income and minority individuals were for the first time able to own their homes—at least for a while. But once banks became comfortable with making and disposing of high-risk loans, they quickly became ame-nable to making such loans to anyone who showed up, first-time buyer or not. And if the loan was to buy a house in a low-income or minor-ity neighborhood, it became that much more attractive, because of the possibility that it would keep the bean-counting regulators happy. Thus, beginning in the late 1990s and accelerating rapidly in 2002 (when the house price trajectory shot up), speculators—people buying a second or third house in the hopes of selling it quickly for a profit—became an in-creasingly important part of the market. Indeed, it is now estimated that one-quarter of all borrowers over this period were making speculative purchases of this sort.

## THE ROLE OF ADJUSTABLE-RATE MORTGAGES

Not surprisingly, speculators wanted to make low down payments and to obtain **adjustable-rate mortgages (ARMs)**. The ARMs offered slighter lower initial interest rates and payments (because borrowers absorbed the risk of higher rates in the future). They also gave lenders the flexibility to offer low "teaser" interest rates (and thus ultra low payments) during the first few years of the mortgage. Such mortgages were considerably riskier for borrowers because of the hazard of higher payments later, when the mortgages "popped" (automatically adjusted their interest rates to full long-run levels). But by then, of course, speculators hoped to have sold for a profit and paid off the mortgage. The spread of ARMs, especially those with low teaser rates, was accelerated by people who bought homes hoping to refinance at a low fixed rate later, after rising home prices built equity for them in their houses.

All went well until 2005, when many of the early ARMs began to pop (with payments adjusting upward sharply). Some borrowers found that they were unable to make the higher payments and were thus forced to sell their homes. This slowed the rise in house prices by 2006, making housing less attractive as an investment, which in turn reduced the speculative demand and put further downward pressure on prices. In markets such as Arizona, California, Florida, and Nevada, where speculative activity had been the greatest, house prices started to *fall*, and growing numbers of individuals (especially those who put up low or no down payments) found themselves "upside down," owing more on their mortgages than their houses were worth. By the middle of 2006, the prudent financial course for such people was to stop making payments (especially on ARMs that had popped) and to simply walk away when the lender began foreclosure proceedings.

## The Evidence on Adjustable-Rate Mortgages

Many accounts of this process in the popular press have claimed that it is exclusively high-risk, subprime mortgages that are at the root of the crisis. This sounds sensible enough, because subprime mortgages have always had relatively high foreclosure rates; indeed, the subprime foreclosure rate has historically been about eight times as high as the rate on prime mortgages (1.6 percent per year versus 0.2 percent per year). Hence, subprime mortgages now, as in normal times, are disproportionately represented among foreclosures. But a closer look at the data also reveals that foreclosures on *both* types of mortgages shot upward in the middle of 2006, with foreclosures on subprime mortgages soon reaching 4 percent and those on prime mortgages hitting 0.5 percent. Thus, it appears that both types of borrowers began to get in trouble at the same time; not just subprime mortgages were affected.

The data also reveal that it is chiefly borrowers who obtained ARMs who have been at the root of the meltdown. Prior to 2006, foreclosures on ARMs and on fixed-rate mortgages were occurring at about the same rate.

But beginning in early 2006, even as the foreclosure rate on fixed-rate mortgages hardly budged, the rate on ARMs exploded: on prime ARMs, the rate leapt by a factor of 5, while the foreclosure rate on subprime ARMs tripled. Moreover, it was on ARMs that foreclosures started up first (at the very beginning of 2006). Forced sales on these homes started the downward pressure on house prices, which gave more owners the incentive to walk away from their homes, which raised foreclosures, and so forth. Soon enough, the entire market had begun to implode.

## THE LASTING DAMAGE

By the time you read this, we expect (and hope!) that the housing market will have shown signs of recovery. But we also hope that the lesson of this episode will not be forgotten. The road to the mortgage meltdown of 2006–2010 was paved by our very own U.S. Congress, which sought to subvert the market to achieve its political goals. The methods used are perhaps little different than those Congress usually employs when it hopes to achieve politically popular social objectives. But the very real difference of this episode is the enormous social cost that it has brought on Americans of all races and all income levels. Literally millions of Americans had their hopes of home ownership first artificially raised and then cruelly dashed. The financial losses and emotional stresses inflicted on individuals, the blighted neighborhoods littered with abandoned houses, and the turmoil felt throughout the states most affected are all costs that will imprint the American scene for years to come.

## DISCUSSION QUESTIONS

1. It seems likely that members of Congress, even the strongest supporters of the CRA and those who put the most pressure on the GSEs to buy high-risk mortgages, will likely escape being held responsible for any part of the mortgage meltdown. Can you suggest why?

2. Many large lenders, along with Fannie Mae and Freddie Mac, obtained funding for their activities by selling bonds that offered as collateral the mortgages that were made using those funds. These bonds are often referred to as "mortgage-backed securities." Many billions of dollars of these mortgage-backed securities were purchased by citizens and governments of foreign lands. Explain how this fact helped the financial crisis in America spread to other nations.

3. In light of the fact that foreclosure rates have been much higher on ARMs than on fixed-rate mortgages, what do you predict will

happen in the future to the proportion of mortgages that are of each type? Explain.

4. In effect, the CRA and the actions of Fannie Mae and Freddie Mac acted to subsidize home purchases by people who otherwise would not have purchased houses. All subsidies must be financed by taxes, implicit or explicit, on someone. Who is paying the "taxes" in this case? Explain.

5. Suppose you ranked states from highest to lowest based on their foreclosure rates over the years 2006–2010. In what states do you predict that prices rose the most from 1995 to 2005? In what states do you predict that prices fell the most from 2006 to 2010? Explain your reasoning.

6. Would you expect housing price volatility (the combination of rise and fall) over the period 1995–2010 to be greatest in urban housing markets or rural housing markets? Would you expect such volatility to be highest in areas with lots of immigration from other states and emigration to other states, or little immigration and emigration of this type? Explain you reasoning in each case.

# CHAPTER 19

# Greenhouse Economics

The sky may not be falling, but it is getting warmer—maybe. The consequences will not be catastrophic, but they will be costly—maybe. We can reverse the process but should not spend very much to do so right now—maybe. Such is the state of the debate over the greenhouse effect—the apparent tendency of carbon dioxide ($CO_2$) and other gases to accumulate in the atmosphere, acting like a blanket that traps radiated heat, thereby increasing the earth's temperature. Before turning to the economics of the problem, let's take a brief look at the physical processes involved.

Certain gases in the atmosphere, chiefly water vapor and $CO_2$, trap heat radiating from the earth's surface. If they did not, the earth's average temperature would be roughly 0°F instead of just over 59°F, and everything would be frozen solid. Human activity helps create some so-called greenhouse gases, including $CO_2$ (mainly from combustion of fossil fuels) and methane (from landfills and livestock). We have the potential, unmatched in any other species, to profoundly alter our ecosystem.

There seems little doubt that humankind has been producing these gases at a record rate and that they are steadily accumulating in the atmosphere. Airborne concentrations of $CO_2$, for example, are increasing at the rate of about 0.5 percent per year. Over the past fifty years, the amount of $CO_2$ in the atmosphere has risen a total of about 25 percent. Laboratory analysis of glacial ice dating back at least 160,000 years indicates that global temperatures and $CO_2$ levels in the atmosphere do, in fact, tend to move together, suggesting that the impact of today's rising $CO_2$ levels may be higher global temperatures in the future. Indeed, the National Academy of Sciences (NAS) has suggested that by the middle of the twenty-first century, greenhouse gases could be double the levels they were in 1860 and that global temperatures could rise by 2–9°F.[1] The possible consequences of such a temperature increase include:

- A rise in the average sea level, inundating coastal areas, including much of Florida
- The spread of algal blooms capable of deoxygenating major bodies of water, such as Chesapeake Bay
- The conversion of much of the Midwestern wheat and corn belt into a hot, arid dust bowl

## THE RESPONSE TO NEGATIVE EXTERNALITIES

When an individual drives a car or heats a house, greenhouse gases are produced. In economic terms, this creates a classic **negative externality.** Most of the **costs** (in this case, those arising from global warming) are borne by individuals *other than* the one making the decision about how many miles to drive. Because the driver enjoys all the benefits of the activity but suffers only a part of the cost, that individual engages in more than the economically efficient amount of the activity. In this sense, the problem of greenhouse gases parallels the problem that occurs when someone smokes a cigarette in an enclosed space or litters the countryside with fast food wrappers. If we are to get individuals to reduce production of greenhouse gases to the efficient rate, we must somehow induce them to act *as though* they bear all the costs of their actions. The two most widely accepted means of doing this are government regulation and taxation, both of which have been proposed to deal with greenhouse gases.

The 1988 Toronto Conference on the Changing Atmosphere, attended by representatives from forty-eight nations, favored the regulation route. The conference recommended a mandatory cut in $CO_2$ emissions by 2005 to 80 percent of their 1988 level—a move that would have required a major reduction in worldwide economic output. The 1997 Kyoto conference on climate change, attended by representatives from 160 nations, made more specific but also more modest proposals. Overall, attendees agreed that by 2012, thirty-eight

---

1 This may not sound like much, but it does not take much to alter the world as we know it. The global average temperature at the height of the last ice age eighteen thousand years ago—when Canada and most of Europe were covered with ice—was 51°F, a mere 8°F or so cooler than today.

developed nations should cut greenhouse emissions by 5 percent relative to 1990 levels.[2] Developing nations, including China and India (the two most populous nations in the world), would be exempt from emissions cuts. On the taxation front, one prominent U.S. politician has proposed a tax of $100 per ton on the carbon emitted by fuels. It is estimated that such a tax would raise the price of coal by $70 per ton and elevate the price of oil by $8 per barrel. These proposals, and others like them, clearly have the potential to reduce the buildup of greenhouse gases but only at substantial costs. It thus makes some sense to ask: What are we likely to get for our money?

## SOME FACTS OF LIFE

Perhaps surprisingly, the answer to this question is not obvious. Consider the raw facts of the matter. On average over the past century, greenhouse gases have been rising, and so has the average global temperature. Yet most of the temperature rise occurred before 1940, whereas most of the increase in greenhouse gases occurred after 1940. In fact, global average temperatures fell about 0.5°F between 1940 and 1970. This cooling actually led a number of prominent scientists during the 1970s to forecast a coming ice age!

Between 1975 and 2000, the upward march of global temperatures resumed, accompanied by rising concentrations of greenhouse gases. At the same time, however, sunspot and other solar activity rose considerably, and the sun became brighter than in a thousand years. Then temperatures started falling, accompanied by diminished solar activity. Many scientists believe that the sun has thus contributed to the earth's temperature fluctuations. Debate remains, however, over how big this contribution has been.

Let us suppose for the moment that barring a significant reduction in greenhouse gas emissions, global warming is under way and that more is on the way. What can we expect? It appears that the answer is a "good news, bad news" story.

## GOOD NEWS, BAD NEWS

The bad news is this: The likely rise in sea level by one to three feet will inundate significant portions of our existing coastline. The expected decline in precipitation in key regions will necessitate more widespread use of irrigation. The higher average temperatures will compel more widespread

---

2  This agreement has not been adhered to. In fact, emissions among this group of nations are *higher* than they were in 1990.

use of air conditioning, along with the associated higher consumption of energy to power it. The blazing heat in southern latitudes may make these areas too uncomfortable for all but the most heat-loving souls.

The good news is that the technology for coping with changes such as these is well known and the costs of coping are surprisingly small (on a scale measured in hundreds of billions of dollars, of course). Moreover, many of the impacts that loom large at the individual level will represent much smaller costs at a societal level. For example, although higher average temperatures could prove disastrous for farmers in southern climes, the extra warmth could be an enormous windfall farther north, where year-round farming might become feasible. Similarly, the loss of shoreline due to rising sea levels would partly just be a migration of coastline inland—current beachfront property owners would suffer, but their inland neighbors would gain.[3]

None of these changes are free, of course, and there remain significant uncertainties about how global warming might affect species other than *Homo sapiens*. It is estimated, for example, that temperate forests can "migrate" only at a rate of about sixty miles per century, not fast enough to match the speed at which warming is expected to occur. Similarly, the anticipated rise in the sea level could wipe out between 30 and 70 percent of today's coastal wetlands. Whether new wetlands would develop along our new coastline and what might happen to species that occupy existing wetlands are questions that have not yet been resolved.

Yet the very uncertainties that surround the possible warming of the planet suggest that policy prescriptions of the sort that have been proposed—such as the cut in worldwide $CO_2$ emissions agreed to at Kyoto—may be too much, too soon. Caution seems particularly wise because the exclusion of China, India, and other developing nations from any emissions cuts could result in huge costs for developed nations but little or no reduction in worldwide greenhouse gases. Some sense of the damage that can be wrought by ignoring such counsel and rushing into a politically popular response to a complex environmental issue is well illustrated by another atmospheric problem: smog.

## GASOLINE AND SMOG

Gasoline is a major source of the hydrocarbons in urban air, but its contribution to smog plummeted because cars now run much cleaner than their predecessors. In the 1970s, cars spewed about

---

3 There would be a net loss of land area and thus a net economic loss. Nevertheless, the net loss of land would be chiefly in the form of less valuable inland property.

nine grams of hydrocarbons per mile. Emissions controls brought this down to about 1.5 grams per mile by 1995. The cost of this reduction is estimated to be approximately $1,000 for each ton of hydrocarbon emissions prevented—a number that many experts believe to be well below the benefits of the cleaner air that resulted. Despite the improvements in air quality, smog is still a problem in many major cities. Additional federal regulations aimed primarily at the nine smoggiest urban areas, including New York, Chicago, and Los Angeles, went into effect in 1995. Meeting these standards meant that gasoline had to be reformulated at a cost of about 6 cents per gallon. This brought the cost of removing each additional ton of hydrocarbons to about $10,000—ten times the per-ton cost of removing the first 95 percent from urban air.

Over the past fifteen years, new Environmental Protection Agency (EPA) rules for reformulated gasoline (RFG) have added even more to the cost of gasoline and have had other (presumably unintended) adverse consequences. For example, initially, the RFG standards could be met only with the addition to gasoline of ethanol or methyl tertiary butyl ether (MTBE). Because ethanol was considerably more expensive than MTBE, refiners used MTBE. But after a few years, it appeared that leakage of MTBE from storage tanks was contaminating groundwater and that the substance was highly carcinogenic. Numerous states banned its use on the grounds that whatever it did to improve air quality, its adverse effects elsewhere were likely far more damaging. (The EPA has since allowed refiners more flexibility in meeting the RFG standards.)

Overall, EPA rules on RFG have led to a "patchwork quilt" of regulations across the country: Some dirty-air locations must use one type of gas, while others, with cleaner air, can use different gas. The presence of multiple EPA standards across the country has left supplies of gasoline vulnerable to disruption because fuel often cannot be transshipped from one area to another to meet temporary **shortages.** This fact has contributed substantially to large spikes in the price of gasoline in major Midwestern cities, such as Milwaukee and Chicago, every time there has been even a minor supply disruption.

Overall, the costs of EPA-mandated gasoline reformulation are huge, even though the EPA has never shown that RFG is necessary to meet its air quality standards. The potential benefits of RFG appear to be small compared to the costs, yet we are stuck with this EPA mandate because few politicians want to be accused of being in favor of smog.

## THE TAKE AWAY

There is no doubt that atmospheric concentrations of greenhouse gases are rising and that human actions are playing a role. It is probable that as a result, the global average temperature is rising. If temperatures rise significantly, the costs will be large, but the consequences are likely to be manageable. Given the nature of the problem, private action, taken on the individual level, will not yield the optimal outcome for society. Thus, the potential gains from government action, in the form of environmental regulations or taxation, may be substantial. But the key word here is *potential* because government action, no matter how well intentioned, does not automatically yield benefits that exceed the costs. As we seek solutions to the potential problems associated with greenhouse gases, we must be sure that the consequences of action are not worse than those of first examining the problem further. If we forget this message, greenhouse economics may turn into bad economics—and worse policy.

## DISCUSSION QUESTIONS

1. Why will voluntary actions, undertaken at the individual level, be unlikely to bring about significant reductions in greenhouse gases such as $CO_2$?

2. Does the fact that the $CO_2$ produced in one nation results in adverse effects on other nations have any bearing on the likelihood that $CO_2$ emissions will be reduced to the optimal level? Would the problem be easier to solve if all the costs and benefits were concentrated within a single country? Within a single elevator or office?

3. The policy approach to greenhouse gases will almost certainly involve limits on emissions rather than taxes on emissions. Can you suggest why limits rather than taxes are likely to be used?

4. It costs about $100,000 per acre to create wetlands. How reasonable is this number as an estimate of what wetlands are worth?

5. Suppose the United States decides to discourage $CO_2$ emissions by imposing a tax on $CO_2$ emissions. How large should the tax be?

6. Human-caused (anthropogenic) emissions of $CO_2$ are only about 3 percent of *total* $CO_2$ emissions each year. (Oceans are the biggest emitters.) Why is so much attention directed at anthropogenic emissions of $CO_2$?

# CHAPTER 20

# Ethanol Madness

Henry Ford built his first automobile in 1896 to run on pure ethanol. If Congress has its way, the cars of the future will be built the same way. But what made good economic sense in the late nineteenth century doesn't necessarily make economic sense in the early twenty-first century—although it does make for good politics. Indeed, the ethanol story is a classic illustration of how good politics routinely trumps good economics to yield bad policies.

## ETHANOL MANDATES AND SUBSIDIES

Ethanol is made in the Midwest just like moonshine whiskey is made in Appalachia. Corn and water are mixed into a mash, enzymes turn starch to sugar, yeast is added, and heat ferments the brew. Once this is distilled, the liquid portion is ethanol and the solids are used as a high-protein animal food. The high-proof ethanol is combustible but yields far less energy per gallon than gasoline does. Despite this inefficiency, federal law requires that ethanol be added to gasoline, in increasing amounts through 2022. This requirement is supposed to conserve resources and improve the environment. It does neither. Instead, it lines the pockets of American corn farmers and ethanol makers and incidentally enriches some Brazilian sugarcane farmers along the way.

Federal law has both encouraged and subsidized ethanol as a so-called alternative fuel for more than thirty years. But it was not until 2005 that ethanol really achieved national prominence. The use mandates of the Energy Policy Act, combined with surging gas prices and an existing 51-cent-per-gallon federal ethanol subsidy, created a boom in ethanol production. Soon ethanol refineries were springing up all over the Midwest, and imports of ethanol from Brazil reached record-high levels.

# THE SUPPOSED VIRTUES OF ETHANOL

Three factors are typically used to justify federal use mandates and subsidies for ethanol. First, it is claimed that adding ethanol to gasoline reduces air pollution and so yields environmental benefits. That may have been true fifteen or twenty years ago, but even the Environmental Protection Agency (EPA) acknowledges that ethanol offers no environmental advantages over other modern methods of making reformulated gasoline. Hence, neither the congressional mandate to add ethanol nor the 51-cent-per-gallon subsidy for its use as a fuel additive can be justified on environmental grounds.

A second argument advanced on behalf of ethanol is that it is "renewable," in that fields on which corn is grown to produce ethanol this year can be replanted with more corn next year. This is true enough, but we are in little danger of running out of "nonrenewable" crude oil any time in the next century. Indeed, proven reserves of oil are at record-high levels. Perhaps more to the point, the production of ethanol uses so much fossil fuel and other resources that under most circumstances, its production actually *wastes* resources overall compared to gasoline. In part, this is because ethanol is about 25 percent less efficient than gasoline as a source of energy. But it is also because the corn used to make ethanol in the United States has a high **opportunity cost.** If it were not being used to make fuel, it would be used to feed humans and livestock. Moreover, because ethanol production is most efficiently conducted on a relatively small scale, it must be transported by truck or rail, which is far more costly than the pipelines used for gasoline.

The third supposed advantage of ethanol is that its use reduces our dependence on imports of oil. In principle, this argument is correct, but its impact is tiny, and the likely consequences are not what you might expect. Total consumption of all **biofuels** in the United States amounts to less than 3 percent of gasoline usage. To replace the oil we import from the Persian Gulf with corn-based ethanol, at least *50 percent* of the nation's total farmland would have to be devoted to corn for fuel. Moreover, any cuts in oil imports will likely *not* come from Persian Gulf sources. Canada and Mexico are two of the three biggest suppliers of crude oil to the United States, and both countries send almost 100 percent of their exports to the U.S. market.

# THE POLITICAL ECONOMY OF ENVIRONMENTAL POLICY

All of this raises an interesting question. If ethanol doesn't protect the environment, conserve resources, or have any compelling foreign policy advantages, why do we mandate its use and subsidize its production? The answer lies at the heart of **political economy,** the use of economics to study the causes and consequences of political decision making. It is true that a critical component of what the government does (such as providing for national defense and law enforcement) provides an institutional structure necessary for the creation and retention of our total wealth. Nevertheless, the essence of much government policymaking, especially in the environmental arena these days, has nothing to do with making the size of the economic pie larger than it otherwise would be. Instead, many government policies are directed at dividing up the pie in new ways so that one group gets more resources at the expense of some other group. To do this successfully, politicians must be adept at concentrating the benefits of policies among a few favored recipients while dispersing the costs of those policies across a large number of disfavored individuals.

At first blush, such an approach sounds completely at odds with the essence of democracy. After all, under the principle of "one person, one vote," it seems that benefits should be widely spread (to gain votes from many grateful beneficiaries) and costs should be concentrated (so that only the votes of a few disfavored constituents are lost). The concept of **rational ignorance** explains what is really going on. It is costly for individuals to keep track of exactly how the decisions of their elected representatives affect them. When the consequences of political decisions are large enough to outweigh the **monitoring costs,** voters swiftly and surely express their pleasure or displeasure, both in the voting booth and in their campaign contributions. But when the consequences to each of them individually are small relative to the monitoring costs, people don't bother to keep track of them—they remain "rationally ignorant."

## ETHANOL WINNERS AND LOSERS

In the case of ethanol, about one-fifth of all ethanol for fuel is made by one company, Archer Daniels Midland (ADM). Clearly, even small changes in the price of ethanol are important to ADM. Because both federal use mandates and the federal ethanol subsidy increase the profitability of making ethanol, ADM has strong incentives to ensure that members of Congress are aware of the benefits (to ADM) of such policies. Similarly, corn farmers derive most of their income from sales of corn. Federal ethanol policies increase the demand for corn and thus increase its price. Because the resulting benefits are highly concentrated on corn farmers, each has a strong incentive to ensure that his or her members of Congress understand the benefits (to the farmer) of such policies.

Contrast this with the typical taxpayer or consumer of gasoline. It is true that the $3 billion or so spent on ethanol subsidies each year must come out of taxpayers' pockets. Nevertheless, this amount is spread thinly across tens of millions of federal taxpayers. Similarly, although the mandated use of ethanol in gasoline is estimated to raise the cost of gas by about 8 cents per gallon, this amounts to no more than $50 per year for the typical driver. Neither taxpayer nor motorist is likely to spend much time complaining to his or her senator.

Thus, it is that farmers and ethanol producers are willing to lobby hard for use mandates and subsidies at the same time that taxpayers and drivers put up little effective resistance to having their pockets picked. It may make for bad economics and lousy environmental policy, but it is classic politics.

## DISCUSSION QUESTIONS

1. Brazilian ethanol producers (who make ethanol from sugarcane) have lower production costs than U.S. producers. Indeed, even though it costs 16 cents per gallon to transport ethanol from Brazil to the United States, which also imposes an **import tariff** of nearly 60 cents per gallon on Brazilian ethanol, the United States still imports millions of gallons of ethanol per year from Brazil. If Congress really cares about protecting the environment and reducing our reliance on foreign crude oil, why do you suppose we have a large import tariff on ethanol?

2. If imports of Brazilian ethanol begin to rise sharply in the future, what do you predict will happen to the size of the import tariff levied on this good?

3. Why do you suppose the federal government gives special treatment to owners of fertile farmland rather than, say, automobile mechanics?

4. Use the theory of rational ignorance to explain why the ethanol subsidy is only 51 cents per gallon rather than, say, $5 per gallon.

5. The EPA has approved the use of up to 15 percent ethanol in fuel blends. Cars built before 2007 are at risk of considerable engine damage if they run on such "E15" fuel. Who will foot the bill for such damages, if they occur?

6. Why are foreign producers of products so often the subject of special taxes such as the tax on imported ethanol?

# PART FIVE

# Measuring the Macroeconomy

# CHAPTER 21

# Is GDP What We Want?

Economists disagree about a lot. One important point of disagreement has to do with how to measure things. For example, suppose you were interested in how the economy was doing, either over time or in comparison to other nations. Or perhaps you want to know how well different people across the country feel they are doing. Perhaps the most common way of addressing such issues would be with a measure linked to **gross domestic product (GDP)**. For example, almost all macroeconomic policy is driven by policymakers' perceptions of what is happening to a few key variables, and GDP is on just about everyone's list of key variables. Moreover, the human condition varies dramatically around the globe. Radical differences in prosperity and poverty from one nation to the next can be understood only if we begin with a clear awareness of what is being measured. And that measurement starts with GDP.

## What Does GDP Measure?

GDP is defined as the market value of new, domestically produced, final goods and services. There are four key elements of this definition:

1. *Market value*—GDP is calculated by multiplying the prices of goods and services by their quantities. Thus, it can move up or down just because of changes in the prices of goods and service. Most of our discussion will focus on **real GDP**, which adjusts GDP for changes in the **price level**. This way, we know that we are talking about the actual amounts of goods and services that are being produced.

2. *New*—The only goods and services that get into GDP are ones that are newly produced during the current accounting period, which normally is the current calendar year. Even though used cars, old houses, and even antiques are a source of satisfaction for many people, GDP focuses on those goods and services that are currently produced.

3. *Domestically produced*—If you were to look carefully at the components of a new car, you would find that much of that car was actually made in other nations, even if it is an "American" car. Similarly, much of the typical "Japanese" car sold in America is actually made in America. The GDP of a nation includes only those parts of cars (and other goods and services) that are made in that nation.

4. *Final goods and services*—Lots of intermediate steps go into producing goods and services, and typically many of these steps show up as separate transactions across the country. But because the value of each intermediate step is embedded in the value of the final product, we include only that final value in our measure of GDP. Otherwise, we would be double counting the final good and all of the components that go into it.

## IMPUTED AND MISSING INFORMATION

Real GDP, that is, GDP corrected for changes in the price level, is the official measure of the new, domestically produced, final goods and services in an economy. Although this number is widely used for many purposes, you should be aware of its limitations. First, some important parts of it are "imputed," or estimated, by the officials at the government agency that publishes the GDP numbers. For example, even though there is no "market" in owner-occupied housing, the Commerce Department has devised methods of estimating the implicit rental value of houses occupied by their owners, and it includes the aggregate value of these services in the published measure of real GDP. In a similar vein, farmers consume some of the food items they produce before those items ever get to the market. Again, the Commerce Department has devised ways to estimate the amount of such food. As with owner-occupied housing, these estimates are included in the official GDP numbers.

Despite the government's best efforts, there are some major omissions from published measures of real GDP. For example, do-it-yourself activities are not included in the official measures, even though they constitute the production of a service. If you take your car to a mechanic, the services performed on the car end up as part of measured real GDP.

But if you and a friend repair your car, these services are not included in the statistics. The biggest category of do-it-yourself services left out of the official GDP statistics consists of those performed in the house by homemakers. It is widely estimated, for example, that the *weekly* value of a homemaker's services is several hundred dollars, none of which is included in the official figures for real GDP.

Then there is the matter of the huge volume of transactions— hundreds of billions of dollars per year—in markets for illegal and underground activities. In some "true" measure of real GDP, we should probably add in these activities, which include prostitution and the illegal drug trade, because such goods and services presumably generate satisfaction to the individuals purchasing them. We should also include "underground" income that is the result of legal activities but is not reported. Some of this income goes unreported by individuals hoping to evade income taxes. But it also includes much of the income earned by illegal immigrants, who do not report their incomes simply because they do not wish to be deported.

## Are Subtractions Necessary, Too?

If we were able to adjust for the items mentioned in the previous section, we might agree that we have a solid measure of real GDP. Nevertheless, we might also feel that we should make some adjustments to real GDP to get a more accurate notion of the level of our material standard of living. For example, the government statisticians treat as equivalent the $5 you spend on gasoline to go on a date in the evening and the $5 you spend on gasoline for your trip to work in the morning. Clearly, however, most people would not think about these two expenditures in the same way.

The next category of items we might focus on is sometimes referred to as "regrettable necessities." This includes diplomacy, national security, police and fire protection, and prison facilities. These items typically don't yield consumer satisfaction in and of themselves. They are produced because they make it possible for us to enjoy the consumption of other goods. In this sense, we can think about regrettable necessities as intermediate goods that go into the production of other goods. As such, they probably should be subtracted from real GDP to get to a better measure of the final goods relevant to individuals, but the government statisticians won't hear of it.

It is also important to recognize that our urbanized, industrialized society has some drawbacks. Big cities make large-scale commercial activities (and thus more market goods) feasible. But they also bring with them a variety of urban disamenities, such as congestion, noise, and litter. If we are interested in some measure of welfare, we should make deductions from real GDP for such sources of dissatisfaction. (The same reasoning applies to pollution in general.) It is difficult to put a precise numerical value on them, however, and so none of the official statistics are adjusted.

## WHAT DOES GDP TELL US?

At this point you might well be wondering whether real GDP has any link at all to what we might think of as happiness or welfare. After all, if the time you spend tinkering on your classic car is *excluded* from real GDP, while the gas you burn stuck in traffic every morning is *included* in real GDP, it almost seems as though the government accountants have things upside down and backwards. Just as importantly, plenty of the items that are important on our GDP (fast food, for example) are a negligible part of GDP in other countries, while the items that are important to them (say, cassava root) are almost unknown to most of us. What, then, can we learn from comparisons of real GDP across nations? (The same query might be asked about comparisons of different time periods *within* a country. Whale oil was a big deal in 1840, just as laptop computers matter a lot today.)

For many years, economists thought that such comparisons, even though routinely made, might just as routinely mean nothing. Imagine, for example, that economies with lots more goods and services were also saddled with lots more crime and pollution and lots less leisure time. Under these circumstances, real GDP might bear no relationship whatsoever to the welfare, happiness, or satisfaction experienced by different people in different lands, or by people at different points in time in the same country. As it turns out, however, it now appears that real GDP might actually be quite useful in making these comparisons across people and countries, and over time.

## BRINGING IN HAPPINESS

Even as economists have been busy measuring real GDP, a variety of other researchers—such as sociologists, psychologists, and political scientists—have been asking people how happy or satisfied they are with their lives. Now, answers to questions such as these always need to be taken with a grain of salt and a dose of caution because "talk is cheap." That is, when you go to the store to buy something, you must make a real sacrifice to obtain the item. But when a person conducting a poll asks you whether you are happy or unhappy, it costs no more to check the box next to "happy" than it does to check the box next to "unhappy."

Keeping this caution in mind, economists Betsey Stevenson and Judson Wolfers thought it might be useful to see if there was any link between measures of real GDP and measures of happiness. Obviously, some adjustments were in order even before beginning. For example, some countries are large and some are small, so the researchers divided real GDP by population in each nation to obtain **real GDP per capita.** Similarly, the exact questions asked of people differed across nations and over time, so considerable work was needed to put all of the answers on a comparable footing. After all of this was done, however, the results were striking.

## REAL GDP AND HAPPINESS ARE STRONGLY LINKED

Stevenson and Wolfers found that there is a strong and consistent positive relationship between real GDP per capita and reported levels of happiness. Using data spanning many decades, and covering well over one hundred countries, the authors show that when per capita real GDP is higher, reported measures of satisfaction or happiness are higher also. Notably, there is no "satiation" point—that is, it appears that even the richest and happiest peoples have the opportunity to become even happier as their incomes rise further.

The authors examine the data in three different ways. First, they look at measures of income (real GDP per capita) and happiness (or reported well-being) across different people within the same country at one point in time. Then they examine income and well-being across different countries at the same point in time. And finally, they assess real per capita GDP and happiness over long periods of time within given countries. In each case, they observe the same strong positive relationship: People with higher real per capita incomes report being happier.

Obviously, real income is not the only factor that influences happiness. Gender, age, and many difficult-to-measure variables are important also. Moreover, it is entirely possible that some other factor is responsible for simultaneously creating high levels of income and happiness. Secure property rights and the rule of law are important in creating high levels of real GDP per capita. It may be the case that these same institutions also happen to make people happier, perhaps because they enhance personal liberty. Nevertheless, even though it may be true that "money can't buy happiness," the results of Stevenson and Wolfers make one point clear: Despite all of its imperfections, real GDP per capita is strongly linked to well-being, at least as perceived by the human beings being asked about such matters. And so, although GDP may not be a perfect measure of anything, we keep on using it because it seems to beat all of the alternatives.

## FOR CRITICAL ANALYSIS

1. How does one determine what is a final good or service and what is a regrettable necessity or an intermediate good? In other words, where does one draw the line?

2. Why is it important to carefully distinguish between GDP and real GDP?

3. Would you categorize each of the following expenditures as intermediate goods, regrettable necessities, or consumption goods: (a) a spare tire, (b) surgery to repair a badly broken arm, (c) a Botox injection to remove forehead wrinkles, (d) voice lessons, and (e) expenditures on your college education? Explain your reasoning in each case. Would your answers to (c) and (d) change if you knew that the purchaser was a professional singer who made many public appearances? Why or why not?

4. Over the past 40 years, growing numbers of women have entered the labor force, becoming employed outside the home. As a result, many women now hire people to do household tasks (such as child-care and house cleaning) that they used to do themselves. What impact does this "hiring out" of household tasks have on measures on GDP? Explain.

5. Over the past 40 years, the levels of water and air pollution in the United States have declined substantially in the United States. Would these environmental improvements likely be reflected in reported measures of well-being or happiness? Would they likely be reflected in GDP?

6. Are nations with large underground economies likely to be happier or unhappier than one would expect, given their *measured* levels of real per capita GDP? Explain.

# CHAPTER 22

# What's in a Word? Plenty, When It's the "R" Word

Incumbent presidents (and members of their political party) hate the "R" word. We speak here of **recession**, a word used to describe a downturn or stagnation in overall, nationwide economic activity. Politicians' attitudes toward recessions are driven by the simple fact that people tend to "vote their pocketbooks." That is, when the economy is doing well, voters are likely to return incumbent politicians to office, but when the economy is doing poorly, voters are likely to "throw the bums out." Interestingly, although *recession* is the word most commonly used to describe a period of poor performance by the economy, most people don't really know what the word means.

## THE NBER

Ever since its founding in 1920, a private organization called the National Bureau of Economic Research (NBER) has sought to accurately measure the state of overall economic conditions in the United States. (It also sponsors research on other economic issues.) Over time, the NBER developed a reputation for measuring the economy's performance in an evenhanded and useful way. As a result, most people now accept without argument what the NBER has to say about the state of the economy. And most notably, this means that it is the NBER that we rely on to tell us when we are in a recession.

If you are an avid reader of newspapers, you may have heard a recession defined as any period in which there are at least two quarters (three-month periods) of declining **real gross domestic product (real GDP)**. In fact, the NBER's recession-dating committee places little reliance on the performance of real (inflation-adjusted) GDP when deciding on the state of the economy. There are two reasons for this. First, the government measures GDP only on a quarterly basis, and the NBER prefers to focus on more timely data that are available at least monthly. Second, the official GDP numbers are subject to frequent and often substantial revisions, so what once looked like good economic performance might suddenly look bad, and vice versa.

Looking back at 2001 (a turbulent year), for example, the initial figures showed that real GDP declined in only one quarter during the year. But when the government finally finished all of its revisions to the data, it turned out that real GDP actually fell during *three* quarters of 2001. In 2007, the government issued a revision of its revised GDP figures for 2004–2006. Of the twelve quarters covered by this "revision of the revisions," the numbers for all twelve were changed: Two were revised upward and ten downward. One can easily see why an organization such as the NBER, which prides itself on reliability and accuracy, might be reluctant to place too much weight on measures of real GDP.

So what does the NBER use as its criteria in measuring a recession? Its official definition of a recession gives us some insight: "A recession is a significant decline in activity spread across the economy, lasting more than a few months, visible in industrial production, employment, real income, and wholesale–retail sales." Those are a lot of words to define just one term, but it's not too difficult to get a handle on it. The point to note at the outset is that the NBER focuses chiefly on four separate pieces of information:

- Industrial production
- Employment
- Real income (measured by inflation-adjusted personal income of consumers)
- Sales at both the wholesale and retail levels

All of these figures are reliably available on a monthly basis, and so every month, the NBER uses the latest figures on each to take the pulse of the economy. When all four are moving upward, that's generally good news. When all are moving downward, that's definitely bad news. And when some are moving in one direction and some in another direction, that's when expert judgment comes into play.

## THE THREE *D*'S

If the NBER recession-dating committee uses a strict formula to time the onset or end of a recession, the committee members don't reveal what it is. What they do reveal is that they are looking for three crucial elements, all starting with the letter *D*, when they officially announce the start or end of a recession:

1. *Depth.* If there is a downturn in one or more of the four key variables, the NBER focuses first on the magnitude of that downturn. For example, in an economy like ours with total employment of over 140 million, a drop in employment of 50,000 would not be crucial. But an employment drop of, say, one million surely would be considered significant.

2. *Duration.* Month-to-month fluctuations in economic activity are the norm in our economy. These fluctuations occur partly because our measures of economic activity are imperfect and partly because, in an economy as complex as ours, many things are happening all the time that have the capacity to affect the overall performance of the economy. Thus, if real personal income moves up or down for a month or even two months in a row, the recession-dating committee is likely to determine that such a change is well within the bounds of normal variation. But if a trend persists for, say, six months, the committee is likely to place a much heavier weight on that movement.

3. *Dispersion.* Because the NBER is trying to measure the overall state of the economy, it wants to make sure it is not being misled by economic developments that may be important to many people but are not reliable indicators of the overall state of the economy. For example, America is becoming less dependent on industrial production and more reliant on service industries. In addition, it is well known that industrial production is sensitive to sharp movements not shared by sectors elsewhere in the economy. So the NBER tempers the importance of industrial production by simultaneously relying on measures such as wholesale and retail sales to make sure it has a picture of what is happening throughout the economy.

## A Precise Answer

Having blended its four measures of the economy in a way that reflects its focus on the three *D*'s, the recession-dating committee makes its decision. A recession, in its view, begins "just after the economy reaches a peak of activity" and ends "as the economy reaches its trough" and starts expanding again. Between trough and peak, the economy is said to be in an **expansion.** Historically, the normal state of the economy is expansion. Most recessions are brief (usually ending within 12–18 months), and in recent decades, they have been rare. Our most recent recession began in December 2007 after six years of economic expansion, and ended in June 2009.

The four measures used by the NBER to date recessions generally move fairly closely together. Although individually they sometimes give conflicting signals for short periods of time, they soon enough start playing the same song. Nevertheless, some contention about the NBER's decisions remains. There are two sources of debate. One focuses on *potential* growth of economic activity, and the other highlights the importance of population growth.

The NBER defines a recession as an absolute decline in economic activity. But some economists note that at least for the past couple of centuries, growth in economic activity from year to year has been the norm in most developed nations, including the United States. Hence, they argue, a recession should be declared whenever growth falls significantly below its long-term potential. This dispute becomes more important when there is reason to believe that potential growth has shifted for some reason or when comparing the current performance of two nations that are growing at different rates. For example, suppose nation X has potential growth of 4 percent per year while nation Y has potential growth of only 2 percent per year. If both are actually growing at 2 percent, the unemployment rate in X will be rising, and some people would argue that this fact is sufficient to declare that X is in a state of recession. The biggest problem with this proposed measure of recession is that it is difficult to declare with confidence exactly what the potential growth rate of any country is.

The second point of contention starts with the observation that the population is growing in most countries. Hence, even if economic activity is growing, the well-being of the average citizen might not be. For example, suppose the population is growing three percent per year but real personal income is growing only two percent per year. Assuming that the other measures of activity were performing like personal income, the NBER would say the economy was in an expansion phase, even though **real per capita income** was declining. Some economists would argue that this state of affairs should be declared a recession, given that the term is supposed to indicate a less-than-healthy economy. This point has some validity. Nevertheless, there have not been many prolonged periods when the NBER has said the economy was expanding while real per capita income was falling.

Ultimately, of course, even if the recession-dating committee somehow tinkered with its methods to better acknowledge the importance of potential growth and population changes, some other issue would undoubtedly be raised to dispute the NBER's conclusions. For now, most economists are content to rely on the NBER to make the call. Most politicians are, too—except, of course, when it suits them otherwise. As for ordinary voters, well, even if they don't know how a recession is defined, they surely know what one feels like—and are likely to vote accordingly.

## For Critical Analysis

1. Why is it important, both for the political process and for our understanding of the economy, for the NBER to resist the temptation to change its definition of a recession to fit the latest political pressures or economic fads?

2. Do you think that voters care more about whether the NBER says the economy is in a state of recession or whether they and their friends and family members are currently employed in good jobs? Why do politicians make a big deal over whether the economy is "officially" in a recession or an expansion? (*Hint:* Is it hard for the average voter to tell what is going on in the economy outside his or her community, leaving the voter dependent on simple measures—or labels—of what is happening elsewhere in the economy?)

3. Examine the data from the last six recessions. (Good sources for data are www.nber.org/cycles/recessions.html, www.bea.gov, and www.globalindicators.org.) Rank them on the basis of both duration and severity. The first is easy; the second is more difficult: Is it possible that some people—either politicians or other citizens—might disagree about how to measure the severity of a particular recession? How would you measure it?

4. Return to the data you examined for question 3. Some people have called the recession of 2007–2009 the "Great Recession." Based on the data you think most relevant, is this latest recession worthy of being singled out as "Great"? Explain.

5. The stock market has been called a "leading indicator" of future economic activity, while the unemployment rate has been called a "lagging indicator" of past economic activity. Combine the data from questions 3 and 4, including data on the stock market and the unemployment rate to answer the following two questions:

   (a) How well do movements in a stock price index (such as the DJIA or the S&P 500) predict ahead of time the beginning or end of each recession?

   (b) How well do beginnings or endings of recessions predict future changes, up or down, in the unemployment rate?

6. Why do we bother to declare the beginning or end of something called a "recession"?

# CHAPTER 23

# The Great Recession

The period from 2004 to 2010 was arguably the most tumultuous in American history since the 1930s. We'll skip the details, but the year-by-year highlights shown in Table 23–1 should give you a flavor of the events that transpired over this recent period.

Home foreclosures hit record levels, millions of people lost their jobs, total output of goods and services fell by 6 percent, and the unemployment rate reached its highest level in nearly 30 years. Some people have even referred to the downturn of 2007–2009 as the "Great Recession." Was it really so bad, and if so, why? Just as importantly, what lessons can we learn for the future?

**Table 23–1** Key Economic Events of the Years 2004–2010

| Year | Events |
| --- | --- |
| 2004 | The Federal Reserve begins tightening monetary policy late in the year |
| 2005 | The buoyant housing market shows early signs of weakness |
| 2006 | Housing prices begin falling and foreclosures head upward |
| 2007 | Home foreclosures soar and the recession of 2007–2009 begins in December |
| 2008 | Widespread financial panic strikes in October and the recession deepens |
| 2009 | The recession ends in June after unemployment peaks at 10.1 percent |
| 2010 | Foreclosures continue but improving job market signals recovery is underway |

## The Years Before

The foundations for the recession of 2007–2009 were laid in policy choices by Congress over a long period leading up to the recession. In fact, we need to go back to 1995, when both Congress and the Clinton administration began pushing hard for banks and other mortgage-lending institutions to relax the standards applied to anyone seeking a home **mortgage.** The goal was to increase home ownership, particularly among lower-income U.S. residents.

Mortgage-lending institutions got the message. They began relaxing standards for down payments, credit histories, and other barometers of financial risk. Many of the new home loans they made were labeled subprime or Alt-A (so-called borderline mortgages). After the recession of 2001–2002, the two giant government-sponsored mortgage corporations, **Fannie Mae** and **Freddie Mac,** began pushing lenders to offer even more mortgage loans of dubious quality. Soon almost anyone could get a mortgage, and within a short period of time, a housing boom took flight. Low-income and even no-income individuals were realizing the American dream of home ownership—with lots of debt to pay back.

No lending institution, even the most risk-loving, would continue to make a larger and larger share of its loans to risky borrowers if it could not shift some or all of the risk elsewhere. Thus, financial firms invented and expanded a variety of securities to spread this risk. Included among these were:

- Mortgage-backed security (MBS )
- Asset-backed security (ABS )
- Collateralized debt obligation (CDO )

Although the details differed among them, all of these securities had the same organizing principle: A financial firm borrowed money using high-risk mortgages and other debts as collateral, and then lent the funds out to create more high-risk debts. The money kept flowing and the risks—which were considerable—were spread out over the many purchasers of these securities.

## Downturn And Panic

Late in 2004 the Federal Reserve began tightening credit, and by 2005, interest rates had started up. Under ordinary circumstances, the change in Fed policy likely would have produced, at worst, a mild recession, such as we observed in 2000–2001. But conditions were not ordinary. Many of the mortgage loans made in 2003–2005 entailed relatively low initial monthly payments that sharply escalated after two to three years. When these payments began rising on a wide scale in late 2005 and early 2006, many borrowers could not make those higher payments, and the housing **bubble** burst with a vengeance. Individuals who had purchased homes hoping to sell them for a quick **profit** found themselves "underwater," that is, the market values of their properties were suddenly less than what they owed. Many borrowers just *abandoned* their houses, refusing to make any more payments on their mortgages.

All of the entities (individuals, firms, even governments) that owned MBSs, ABSs, and CDOs were suddenly receiving billions of dollars less in monthly mortgage payments. Moreover, it was clear that the market value of these securities and obligations was going to turn out to be less than people had anticipated. Within a few months, hundreds of billions of dollars' worth of perceived wealth simply vanished—gone, just like the millions of homeowners who simply walked away from their mortgages and their homes. By late 2007 consumer and business spending was down and the recession had begun. And in 2008 when people began to realize just how worthless many of the fancy MBSs, ABSs, and CDOs were going to be, a financial panic developed and soon spread around much of the world.

## IN STEPS THE FED

Late in 2008, rapidly eroding confidence in America's financial system led to the near or total collapse of several major financial firms. Many commercial banks, investment banks, and even insurance companies were suddenly in dire condition, and potential borrowers across the country found themselves unable to obtain funds from anyone, at any rate of interest. The entire network of American financial markets was on the verge of a collapse that, if it had happened, might have produced conditions much like those experienced in the Great Depression of 1929–1933.

Mindful of the costs of inaction, the Fed moved swiftly to maintain and restore confidence in key components of the financial system. But its actions were considerably broader than ever before. Historically, for example, the Fed has lent funds to commercial banks and to the federal government itself. But in 2008, the Fed also lent hundreds of billions of dollars directly to nonbank corporations around the country. Moreover, the Fed began purchasing obligations of the government-sponsored mortgage market giants Fannie Mae and Freddie Mac, hoping to encourage more lending for home purchases. And finally, the Fed agreed to the following trade with commercial banks: It would exchange billions of dollars of risk-free federal **bonds** it held for billions of dollars of high-risk private bonds that they held. In effect, the Fed helped the banks remove high-risk assets of questionable value from their **balance sheets,** thus reducing the chances that skittish depositors might suddenly make large-scale withdrawals of funds from commercial banks.

The Fed's dramatic actions eventually brought the panic to a halt. Just as was envisioned when the Fed was created back in 1913, it served as a "lender of last resort" (see Chapter 32). The key difference compared to the past was that the Fed decided that practically *any* major company might qualify as worthy of lending by the Fed. While the long-run implications of this unprecedented change in Fed policy remain uncertain, one point is clear. The Fed's massive lending operations (which totaled over $1.5 *trillion* ) halted the panic and prevented the recession from getting much worse.

## How Bad Was It?

Even so, the recession of 2007–2009 was arguably worse than any other recession we've had since World War II. It also likely ranks among the half dozen or so worst we've had in our history. For example, during the latest recession, total employment fell 6 percent, compared to a mere 2 percent in the 2000–2001 recession, and 5 percent in 1948–1949, which had previously been the largest postwar drop. Similarly, total output in the economy fell 4.1 percent in 2007–2009. The largest prior decline in a postwar recession had been the 3.2 percent fall in 1973–1974. And although the unemployment rate (10.1 percent) did not get as high as it had in the 1981–1982 recession (10.8 percent), the jump in the unemployment rate was similar in both recessions—just over five percentage points.

By these measures, while the recession of 2007–2009 was large compared to other postwar recessions, it was minor compared to the Great Depression (1929–1933) and modest compared to the recessions of 1937–1938 and 1919–1920. But the latest recession will likely stick with the American people for a long time, for two well-deserved reasons. First, there is the matter of "what might have been" had the Federal Reserve not stepped in aggressively to end the financial panic of 2008. Many economists agree that if the Fed had not acted, the consequences could have rivaled those experienced in 1929–1933, when output fell 30 percent and the unemployment rate hit 25 percent.

Second, the housing market was utterly devastated in the recession of 2007–2009, to a degree not seen since the 1930s. Housing prices fell

40 percent, and millions of families lost their homes. The number of housing starts, which had previously peaked at two million per year, dropped to under 500,000. In many communities, housing constructions ground to a complete halt, often with houses simply left behind, partially finished.

## MORE ON THE FED

Amid the chaos surrounding the financial panic and the recession, not many commentators paid much attention to two changes in Fed policy that enlarged on a massive scale its role in allocating resources. First, the Fed asked for and received from Congress the legal authority to pay interest on the **reserves** held by the banking system. For many years before, economists had argued that the Fed should have the authority to pay interest on banks' **required reserves** —that is, those reserves that banks are legally mandated to hold. But with the blessing of Congress, the Fed has gone further than this, by paying interest on **excess reserves** also—that is, on the reserves banks hold over and above the legally required minimum. The problem with paying interest on excess reserves is that it discourages banks from making loans to individuals and businesses. Faced with a choice of making risky loans to the private sector or collecting guaranteed, risk-free interest from the Fed, many banks chose the risk-free option. The result is that excess reserves soared from their level of a few billion dollars to amounts well in excess of a *trillion* dollars— funds that were not available to private sector borrowers. Thus, for long after the panic of 2008 was over, recovery from the recession was impeded because banks have been earning interest on their excess reserves rather than making productive but risky loans to the private sector.

The sluggish credit market led the Fed to announce that—for the first time in its history—it needed to get involved in making loans to entities other than commercial banks or the federal government. Thus, since the fall of 2008, the Federal Reserve has been allocating credit all over the country, deciding who shall get loans (and thus survive) and who shall not (and thus face economic ruin). Although the U.S. Treasury has been widely criticized for bailing out investment banks and automobile companies, the Fed has quietly been reshaping credit markets on a grand scale, while attracting almost no attention from the press. On a scale unprecedented in American history, hundreds of billions of dollars' worth of resources are being allocated behind the closed doors of the Federal Reserve System's headquarters in Washington, DC—for reasons known only to the politically appointed government officials doing the allocating.

## WHAT HAVE WE LEARNED?

As we discuss more fully in Chapter 32, the latest recession confirms the pivotal role that the Federal Reserve can play when there is a financial panic. By acting as a lender of last resort, the Fed has the capacity to stave off economy-wide financial meltdowns. This was the role originally intended for the Fed back in 1913, and one that it failed to perform in 1929–1933. It is now clear that the Fed has the tools to do this should the need arise in the future.

A second key lesson of the recession of 2007–2009 is one that politicians don't seem to have absorbed. The attempts of Congress to artificially pump up home ownership in the United States chiefly encouraged financially ill-equipped individuals to purchase houses that they could not afford. When the housing market turned down, many of these people walked away from their obligations, with devastating consequences for the rest of the economy. Thus, Congressionally mandated housing policy set the stage for an unduly severe recession. There is no sign as yet, however, that the members of Congress recognize their role in this. The laws that encouraged high-risk lending to homeowners are still in place, and Fannie Mae and Freddie Mac are still doing their best to subsidize home purchases by individuals who are financially unprepared to meet their obligations. The risks of this policy are compounded by the Fed's decision to allocate credit on a grand scale throughout the economy. In America and elsewhere, government officials have a lousy historical track record when it comes to picking winners and losers in the marketplace. There is absolutely no reason that the officials at the Fed are likely to do any better—which means that many billions of dollars' worth of resources will likely end up being squandered by the Fed.

A third lesson is one that will only be learned in the future, likely sometime after you read these words. As we noted, the Fed engaged in roughly $1.5 trillion in new lending between late 2008 and 2010. In the long run, this is far more lending than the economy can possibly absorb without touching off a substantial inflation—perhaps one involving a *doubling* of the price level. No one thinks the Fed's intent is to permit such a massive increase in the price level, but no one is quite sure how the Fed will *avoid* it, without plunging the United States back into severe recession. Stay tuned, because by the end of the course in which you are using this book, economists will have a much better idea of how this next economic drama is going to work itself out.

## FOR CRITICAL ANALYSIS

1. What elements of the recession of 2007–2009 have led many observers to refer to it as the Great Recession? Do you think this title is warranted? Explain, using data to back up your conclusions.

2. What members of Congress have the most to gain by passing laws that subsidize the purchase of homes by high-risk, low-income individuals? What data would you need to test your hypothesis?

3. During the recession, Congress changed the law on unemployment benefits to enable people to collect such benefits for up to 99 weeks (the limit had previously been 26 weeks). What impact do you think this change in the law had on (i) employment, (ii) the duration of unemployment, and (iii) the unemployment rate? Explain.

4. How will financial institutions and other borrowers pay off the loans made to them by the Fed during the recession? What consequences do you think this will have for the economy?

5. Other possible measures of the severity of a recession are (i) decline in manufacturing output, (ii) decline in retail sales, and (iii) duration of unemployment. Based on these criteria, how did the recession of 2007–2009 stack up to other post–World War II recessions?

6. In general, should policy makers be more concerned with high inflation or high unemployment? The inflation rate in Zimbabwe recently got up to 230 *million* percent per year, at the same time that the unemployment rate hit 80 percent of the workforce. Is it possible that the policy choices that yield a high inflation rate also eventually produce a high unemployment rate?

# CHAPTER **24**

# The Case of the Disappearing Workers

Every month, the Bureau of Labor Statistics (BLS) goes out into the labor market to determine how many unemployed people there are in the United States. With the data it acquires, the BLS calculates the **unemployment rate.** This number is a key indication of how well the economy is doing. The unemployment rate is calculated in a seemingly straightforward way: It is the percentage of the total **labor force** that is (1) aged 16 and older but not institutionalized or in school, and (2) actively seeking employment but has not found it.

The reelection chances of incumbent presidents often hinge on the estimated rate of unemployment. Historically, when the unemployment rate is rising, the president's chances of reelection have been far worse than when the rate is stable or falling. As the old saying goes, "people vote their pocketbooks" (or in this case, their pay stubs).

For this and a variety of other reasons, understanding how the unemployment rate is measured is important for politicians and ordinary citizens alike. Remarkably, however, there is little consensus about the accuracy of unemployment statistics in the United States. First, consider the period when the United States had its highest measured rate of unemployment—the Great Depression, which started in 1929 and did not fully end until a decade later.

## TWENTY-FIVE PERCENT UNEMPLOYMENT—HARD TO IMAGINE

If you look at official government statistics on the unemployment rate during the Great Depression, you will find that in some statistical series, the rate hit 25 percent—meaning that one of every four Americans who were part of the labor force could not find a job during the depth of the depression. That high unemployment rate, of course, makes any **recession** since then seem insignificant in terms of the propostion of people adversely affected.

Some economists, though, are not so sure that one-fourth of the labor force was actually unemployed during the Great Depression. The reason is simple: At that time, the federal government had instituted numerous programs to "put people back to work." These included the Works Progress Administration (WPA), the Civilian Conservation Corps (CCC), and various lesser programs. Government statisticians decided that everyone working in these federally sponsored "make-work" programs would have been unemployed otherwise. Consequently, they decided to count these millions of Americans as unemployed. Michael Darby, an economist at UCLA, subsequently recalculated unemployment statistics for the depth of the Great Depression. After adjusting for people who were actually working but were counted as unemployed, he found a maximum unemployment rate of 17 percent. This number is still the highest we have had in modern times, but it is certainly not one-fourth of the labor force.

How much sense does Darby's adjustment make? The argument against the official government statistics is straightforward: The federal government taxed individuals and businesses to pay workers at the WPA and CCC. Had the federal government not levied the taxes to pay these new government employees, the private sector would have had more disposable income, more spending, and higher employment. Whether all of those people would have gotten private sector jobs is impossible to know, but it is clear that the official numbers greatly overstated the true unemployment rate during the Great Depression.

## DISCOURAGED WORKERS: A COVER FOR A HIGHER "TRUE" UNEMPLOYMENT RATE?

Certain individuals, after spending some time in the pool of the unemployed, may become discouraged about their future job prospects. They may leave the labor market to go back to school, to retire, to work full-time at home without pay, or just to take some time off. Whichever path they choose, when interviewers from the BLS ask these individuals whether they are "actively looking for a job," they say no. Individuals such as these are often referred to as **discouraged workers.** They might seek work if labor market conditions were better and potential wages were higher, but they have decided that such is not the case, so they have left the labor market. For years, some critics of the officially measured unemployment rate have argued that during recessions, the rising numbers of discouraged workers cause the government to grossly underestimate the actual rate of unemployment.

To get a feel for the labor market numbers, let's look at the 1990s, perhaps one of the greatest periods of rising employment in U.S. history. During that decade, the number of Americans who were unemployed fell by over five million. Moreover, far fewer workers settled for part-time jobs. Many who had been retired came back to work, and many of those about to retire continued to work. There were even large numbers of students who left school to take high-paying jobs in the technology sector.

The onset of the 2001 recession produced a turnaround in all of those statistics. The number of unemployed rose by about 2.5 million individuals. The number of part-time workers who indicated that they would like to work full-time rose by over a million. And the proportion of those out of work for more than half a year increased by over 50 percent.

According to some economists, another two million workers dropped out of the labor force—the so-called discouraged-worker problem. For example, University of Chicago economist Robert Topel claims, "The unemployment rate does not mean what it did 20 years ago." He argues that employment opportunities for the least skilled workers no longer exist in today's labor market, so such individuals simply left the labor force, discouraged and forgotten by the statisticians who compile the official numbers.

## ARE DISCOURAGED WORKERS A PROBLEM?

Other economists argue differently. They note that the labor market is no different from any other market, so we can examine it using **supply** and **demand** analysis, just as we do with any other good or service. The **labor supply curve** is upward-sloping. That means that as overall wages rise (corrected for inflation, of course), the quantity of labor supplied would be expected to increase. After all, when the inflation-corrected price of just about anything else goes up, we observe that the quantity supplied goes up, too. Therefore, argue these economists, the concept of discouraged workers is basically flawed. They say it makes no more sense to talk of discouraged workers than it would to talk of "discouraged apples" that are no longer offered for sale when the price of apples falls.

Because of the upward-sloping supply curve of labor, when **real wages** rise economy-wide, we expect that retirees and those about to retire will return to or remain in the labor market. We expect students to quit school early if the wages they can earn are relatively high. The opposite must occur when we go into a recession or the economy stagnates. That is, with reduced wage growth (or even declines in economy-wide real wages) and reduced employment opportunities, we expect more young people to stay in school longer, retirees to stay retired, and those about to retire to actually do so. In other words, we expect the same behavior in response to incentives that we observe in all other markets.

## Disability Insurance and Labor Force Participation

It is also worth noting that some, perhaps many, of the departures from the labor force by low-skill individuals may actually be prompted by certain government programs. We refer here to a portion of the Social Security program that has expanded dramatically over the past 20 years. It involves **disability payments.** Originally established in 1956 as a program to help individuals under age 65 who are truly disabled, Social Security Disability Insurance (SSDI) has become the federal government's second fastest growing program (after Medicare). The real value of benefits has steadily risen as the Social Security Administration (SSA) gradually made it easier for individuals to meet the legal criteria for "disabled" status. SSDI now accounts for over $100 billion in federal spending per year. Under SSDI, even individuals who are not truly disabled can receive payments from the government when they do not work.

In addition, because Social Security also offers Supplemental Security Income (SSI) payments for disabled people who have little or no track record in the labor force, some people are calling disability insurance the centerpiece of a new U.S. welfare state. Since 1990, the number of people receiving disability payments from the SSA has more than tripled to over eight million—perhaps not surprising when you consider that the real value of the monthly benefits a person can collect has risen almost 60 percent in the past thirty-five years. The federal government now spends more on disability payments than on food stamps or unemployment benefits.

What does this mean? Simply that people who might have worked through chronic pain or temporary injuries—particularly those without extensive training and education—have chosen to receive a government disability benefit instead. The average Social Security disability payment is about \$1,000 per month, tax-free. For many at the lower echelons of the job ladder, \$1,000 per month tax-free seems pretty good. Indeed, those receiving disability payments make up the largest group of the two million or so who left the labor force during the 2001–2002 recession. We suspect that when analysts go back and look at the recession of 2007–2009, they'll find the same story. And because people respond to incentives, we can be sure of one thing: Whatever happens to the economy in the future, if the real value of disability payments keeps rising, so will the number of people with disabilities.

## For Critical Analysis

1. To what extent do you believe that the existence of unemployment benefits increases the duration of unemployment and consequently the unemployment rate? (*Hint:* Use demand analysis and **opportunity cost.**)

2. Is it possible for the unemployment rate to be "too low"? In other words, can you conceive of a situation in which the economy would be worse off in the long run because there is not enough unemployment?

3. It is believed that much of the increase in the number of people collecting SSDI has resulted from decisions by workers at the Social Security Administration (SSA) to make it easier to qualify for benefits. How are the disability rules set by SSA workers likely to change depending on (a) whether the SSA budget is held constant or expands when the number of SSDI recipients rises, (b) the overall state of the economy, especially the unemployment rate, and (c) the likelihood that individuals with disabilities will be discriminated against in the workplace?

4. What would happen to the number of disabled people if Social Security disability payments were made subject to income taxes? Explain.

5. During the latest recession Congress increased the length of time people could receive unemployment benefits to 99 weeks (almost two years) from its previous level of 26 weeks (about six months). What impact do you think this change had on (i) the unemployment rate and (ii) the average duration of unemployment? Explain.

6. Imagine that at two different times—late 1933 (when the economy was struggling out of the depths of the Depression) and late 1939 (when the economy was expanding rapidly)—there were a million people on make-work government jobs who were officially classified as "unemployed." In which year (1933 or 1939) were these make-work employees more likely to have been displaced from private sector jobs and in which were they more likely to have been displaced from the ranks of the unemployed? Explain. How would this distinction factor into your thinking about whether such people should be officially classed as "employed" or "unemployed"? Explain.

# CHAPTER 25

# Poverty, Wealth, and Equality

In 1960, the poorest 20 percent of households in the United States received a bit over four percent of total income. Today, after half a century of government efforts to relieve poverty, the bottom 20 percent receives a bit less than four percent of total income. About 40 million Americans lived in poverty in 1960. About 40 million U.S. citizens *still* live in poverty, despite the expenditure of hundreds of billions of dollars in aid for the poor. In the richest country in the world, poverty seems remarkably resilient.

## FIRST, THE FACTS

If we are to understand why, we must begin by getting the facts straight. First, even though the *absolute* number of Americans living in poverty has not diminished over the past half-century, population growth has brought a sizable reduction in the *proportion* of Americans who are impoverished. As conventionally measured, more than 22 percent of Americans lived in poverty in 1960. Today, as we emerge from one of the worst recessions of our recent history, about 14 percent of the population is below the official poverty line.

Second, traditional methods of measuring poverty may be misleading because they focus solely on the *cash incomes* of individuals. In effect, government statisticians compute a "minimum adequate" budget for families of various sizes—the "poverty line"—and then determine how many people have cash incomes below this line. Yet major components of the federal government's antipoverty efforts come in the form of **in-kind transfers** (transfers of goods and services, rather than cash) such as Medicare, Medicaid, subsidized housing, food stamps, and school lunches. When the dollar value of these in-kind transfers is included in measures of *total* income, the **standard of living** of persons at lower income levels has improved substantially over the years.

There is disagreement over how much of these in-kind transfers should be included in measures of the total income of recipients.[1] Nevertheless, most observers agree that these transfers, plus the **Earned Income Tax Credit** (which gives special **tax rebates** to low-income individuals), are major sources of income for people at the bottom of the income distribution. Adjusting for these transfers and tax credits, it seems likely that over the past fifty years, the proportion of Americans living below the poverty line has been cut roughly in half. Just as important, the real standard of living for the poorest 20 percent of the population has doubled since the mid-1960s. In short, the incidence of poverty in this country has declined markedly over the past half-century, and individuals who remain officially classified as "poor" have a far higher real standard of living than the poor of the 1960s.

## The Impact of Income Mobility

Whatever measure of income we use, it is crucial to remember that most Americans exhibit a great deal of **income mobility,** tending to move around in the income distribution over time. The most important source of income mobility is the "life-cycle" pattern of earnings. New entrants to the workforce tend to have lower incomes at first, but most workers can enjoy rising incomes as they gain experience on the job. Typically, annual earnings reach a maximum at about age 55. Because peak earnings occur well beyond the **median age** of the population (now about age 37), a "snapshot" of the current distribution of earnings will find most individuals "on the way up" toward a higher position in the income distribution. People who have low earnings now are likely, on average, to have higher earnings in the future.

Another major source of income mobility stems from the operation of Lady Luck. At any point in time, the income of high-income people is likely to be abnormally high (relative to what they can expect on average) due to recent good luck—say, because they just won the lottery or just

---

1 There are two reasons for this disagreement. First, a given dollar amount of in-kind transfers is generally less valuable than the same dollar amount of cash income because cash offers the recipient a greater amount of choice in his or her consumption pattern. Second, medical care is an important in-kind transfer to the poor. Inclusion of all Medicaid expenditures for the poor would imply that the sicker the poor got, the richer they would be. Presumably, a correct measure would include only those medical expenses that the poor would have to incur if they were *not* poor and so had to pay for the medical care (or medical insurance) out of their own pockets.

received a generous bonus. Conversely, the income of people who currently have low incomes is likely to be abnormally low due to recent bad luck—for example, because they are laid up after an automobile accident or have become temporarily unemployed. Over time, the effects of Lady Luck tend to average out across the population. Accordingly, people with high income today will tend to have lower income in the future, while people with low income today will tend to have higher future income. Equivalently, many people living below the poverty line are there temporarily rather than permanently.

The importance of income mobility is strikingly revealed in studies examining the incomes of individuals over time. During the 1970s and 1980s, for example, among the people who were in the top 20 percent (quintile) of income earners at the beginning of the decade, fewer than half were in the top quintile by the end of the decade. Similarly, among the people who were in the bottom quintile at the beginning of the decade, almost half had moved out of that bracket by the end of the decade. Despite news stories that suggest otherwise, income mobility remains robust. From 1996 to 2005 (the decade most recently studied), *more than half* of the people who were in the bottom 20 percent income bracket in 1996 had moved out of that bracket by 2005.

## Appearances Versus Reality

Notwithstanding the data just cited, several forces have either increased income inequality in the United States or given the appearance of such an increase, so it is best to be clear about these. Consider first that a rising proportion of the population is *far* above the poverty line. In 1969, for example, about 4 percent of all people in America had earnings six times greater than the poverty-line level. Today, about 6 percent of Americans have earnings that high (above $150,000 for a family of four). Much of this jump in incomes at the top of the income distribution has come at the very top. Thirty years ago, for example, people in the top 10 percent of earners in America pulled in about 31 percent of total income. Today, they garner 37 percent. In even more rarified company, the top 1 percent of earners used to account for 9 percent of total income. Today, they take in 16 percent of income. So even though inflation-adjusted incomes are rising across the board, they appear to be rising the fastest at the very top. Economists are seeking to explain this pattern, which first became apparent during the 1990s. Much work remains to be done, but a few answers are emerging.

First, some key demographic changes are occurring in America. The nation is aging, and an older population tends to have more income inequality than a young population because older people have had more time to experience rising or falling fortunes. Americans are also becoming better educated, and this tends to increase income inequality. People with little education have incomes that tend to cluster together, while the incomes of well-educated people spread out: Some choose to convert their **human capital** into much higher incomes, while others convert it into added leisure time. Taken together, these two demographic changes, aging and education, can account for more than 75 percent of the *appearance* of greater income inequality.

Second, a substantial part of the rapid income growth at the top has really been a matter of accounting fiction rather than reality. Until the late 1980s, there were substantial tax advantages for the very wealthy to have a large portion of their incomes counted as corporate income rather than personal income. In effect, a big chunk of income for the wealthy used to be hidden not from the tax authorities but from the policymakers who worry about the distribution of income. Subsequent changes in the tax laws have since encouraged people to report this income as personal rather than corporate income. Their incomes haven't really changed; it just looks to policymakers like they have.

The third factor we need to account for is the difference in consumption bundles of those near the top of the income distribution and those near the bottom. High-income individuals tend to spend a larger proportion of their incomes on labor-intensive services (such as investment advice, personal care, and domestic help). Low-income individuals tend to spend a larger share of their incomes on nondurable goods, such as food, clothing, shoes, and toiletries. As it turns out, over the past twenty-five years, the items consumed by lower-income individuals have fallen markedly in cost relative to the items consumed by the wealthy. Rising **real wages** have pushed up the costs of service-intensive consumption, while growing international trade with China, India, and other developing nations has pushed down the relative costs of items important to low-income individuals. Overall, this difference in **inflation** rates between the people at the top and those at the bottom of the income distribution has effectively wiped out *all* of the seeming change in their relative incomes over this period.

## LIFE AT THE BOTTOM

Nevertheless, it is clear that many people at the bottom of the income distribution are struggling, so we need to take a look at what is going on here. One point is clear: Between 1990 and 2007, the United States experienced a huge influx of immigrants. Newcomers typically earn far less than long-term residents. When large numbers of them are added to the mix of people whose incomes are being measured, *average* income can fall, even when the incomes of all individuals are rising. Thus, immigration has created downward pressure on *measured* incomes at the bottom of the distribution. But new immigrants have also added to competitive pressures in labor markets for less skilled individuals. On balance, it appears that immigration has probably lowered the wages of high school dropouts in America by 4–8 percent. And although this seems small, remember that it is occurring among people whose incomes are already low. Both of these effects are likely to lessen and perhaps even reverse due to the recession of 2007–2009 because deteriorating economic conditions in America caused many recent immigrants to return to their homelands.

Public policy has also taken its toll on the incomes of people at the bottom. The war on drugs, for example, has saddled millions of individuals with criminal records, and the impact has been disproportionately greatest on African Americans, whose incomes were lower to begin with. For example, since 1990, more than two million African American males have served time in jail on serious (felony) drug charges. Once they return to the workforce, they find that their felony records exclude them from a great many jobs—and not just jobs at the top. Often convicted felons cannot find positions that pay more than $8 per hour. The result is that the incomes of such individuals are sharply diminished, which means more poverty.

There is one bright spot on the poverty policy front, however. It is the "welfare reform" program undertaken in 1996. Previously, low-income families had been eligible to receive—for an unlimited duration—federal payments called Aid to Families with Dependent Children (AFDC). The program was converted in 1996 into Temporary Assistance to Needy Families (TANF). Limits were placed on the length of time individuals could receive payments, and all recipients were given additional incentives and assistance to enhance their job skills and to enter or reenter the **labor force.** The full impact of this policy change is still being studied, but it now appears that it has modestly raised incomes among those at the bottom of the income distribution.

Although the resilience of poverty in America is discouraging to the poor and to those who study their plight, it is useful to consider these issues in an international context. In other industrialized nations, such as Japan and most countries in Europe, people at the bottom of the income distribution sometimes (but not always) fare better than the poor in America. Although the poor typically receive a somewhat larger *share* of national income than in America, the national income they share is lower. Hence, compared to America, the poorest 10 percent of the population has a higher average income in Japan and Germany but a lower average income in the United Kingdom and Italy.

In developing nations—which is to say, for the vast majority of people around the world—poverty has a completely different meaning than it does in America. In Africa and much of Asia, for example, it is commonplace for people at the bottom of the income distribution to be living on the equivalent of $400 per *year* or less—in contrast to the $10,000–$15,000 per year they would earn in America. This staggering difference in living standards is due to the vast differences in legal and economic **institutions** that are observed around the world. In America, as in many other industrialized nations, these institutions give people the incentives to put their talents to work and they also protect the fruits of their labors from expropriation by the government. Thus, the best anti-poverty program anyone has ever seen is the creation of an institutional environment in which human beings are able to make maximum use of the talents with which they are endowed.

## FOR CRITICAL ANALYSIS

1. Why do most modern societies try to reduce poverty? Why don't they do so by simply passing a law that requires that everybody have the same income?

2. How do the "rules of the game" help determine who will be poor and who will not? (*Hint:* How did the Civil Rights Act of 1964, which forbade discrimination on the basis of race, likely affect the incomes of African Americans compared to the incomes of white Americans?) Explain your answer.

3. Which of the following possible in-kind transfers do you think raises the "true" incomes of recipients the most: (a) free golf lessons, (b) free transportation on public buses, or (c) free food? Why?

4. Consider three alternative ways of helping poor people obtain better housing: (a) government-subsidized housing that costs $6,000 per year, (b) a housing **voucher** worth $6,000 per year toward rent on an apartment or a house, or (c) $6,000 per year in cash. Which would you prefer if you were poor? On what grounds might you make your decision?

5. How do government programs that provide benefits for the poor (such as food stamps and subsidized housing) change the incentives of people to be classified as "poor"? Explain.

6. One effect of the **minimum wage** is to reduce employment opportunities for minority teenagers. What effect do you think this has on the long-run poverty rate among minorities? Explain.

# CHAPTER 26

# Will It Be Inflation or Deflation?

During the summer of 2008, when gas prices were skyrocketing, the Department of Labor issued a frightening statistic: The **consumer price index (CPI)** had risen more than 5 percent over the prior 12 months, the biggest jump in nearly 20 years. A few months later, the average price of gasoline paid in the United States had dropped from over $4 per gallon to well under $2 per gallon. And as the price of gas was plummeting, **inflation** among primary commodities (such as lumber, metals, and grain) was collapsing as well. As a result, in the late summer and early fall, the overall inflation rate shrank to almost nothing. In fact, during several months in late 2008 and early 2009, overall consumer prices actually *fell*—there was **deflation.** This rapid turn of events quickly switched the Web site and news channel chatter about the problems of inflation into chatter about the prospects for sustained deflation. Before we try to sort out whether inflation or deflation is in your future, let's first make sure we know to what we are referring.

## A FORMAL DEFINITION OF INFLATION AND DEFLATION

Inflation is defined as a rise in the average of all prices, appropriately weighted for their importance in the typical consumer's budget. Inflation is not a change in one price. If the CPI rises by three percent over a 12-month period, what we know is that the appropriately weighted average of prices of goods and services in the United States went up by three percent relative to a year before. (Sometimes you will see references to **core inflation.** This is a measure of the overall change in prices *excluding* energy and food.)

If the rate of change in the **price level** is negative rather than positive, we have deflation—on average, prices are falling rather than rising. As our brief introduction suggests, people worry a lot about inflation, but they also worry about deflation. So we must ask: Are these concerns misplaced?

## THE DOWNSIDE OF DEFLATION

Deflation can be troublesome for the economy. One reason is that most of the debts in a modern society like ours are expressed in terms of dollars. When there is deflation, the **real purchasing power** of those dollars goes up. For creditors, this is good news because it means that people now owe them more, measured in terms of the goods and services those dollars will buy (so-called *real* terms). But for debtors, this is bad news, for exactly the same reason. Deflation raises the real burden of the debts they owe. Debtors have to pay back the sums owed with dollars that have a higher purchasing power than the dollars that were lent. In effect, during times of deflation, the inflation-corrected rate of interest (the **real interest rate**) goes up, imposing an added burden on debtors. Although it is possible that deflation's positive effects on creditors and negative effects on debtors could exactly cancel out, often it doesn't happen this way. The result can be significant economic dislocations.

There is also another problem with deflation. It never proceeds evenly and smoothly. During the Great Depression, when prices fell an *average* of about 8 percent per year for four straight years, this deflation did not proceed uniformly over time. Some months and years were worse than others. Moreover, the deflation did not proceed uniformly across all goods. House prices, for example, fell much more than clothing prices. Because of the erratic and unpredictable progression of deflation, individuals and businesses had to focus much of their attention on trying to predict the magnitude and timing of changes in the prices of goods and services. Had there been no deflation, they could have been producing new goods and services instead. The result was that the U.S. economy had fewer goods and services available for **consumption.**

## THE COSTS OF INFLATION

Inflation acts as a tax on people's holdings of money—that is, their holdings of **currency** and **checkable deposits.** All of us hold some currency and checkable deposits because of the convenience they provide. As a result, each of us loses **wealth** whenever there is inflation because the purchasing power of our money balances decreases at the rate of inflation.

Assume that you have $20 stashed in your wallet as an emergency cash reserve, that is, you have no immediate expectation of spending it. If at the end of one year there has been a 10 percent rise in the price level, the purchasing power of that $20 note will only be $18, measured in terms of taxi rides or sandwiches. You will have lost value equal to 10 percent times the amount of currency you kept in your wallet.

In essence, then, the purchasing power, or real value, of the money we hold depreciates when there is inflation. The only way we can avoid this type of **inflation tax** on the money we hold is to reduce our holdings of money. But doing this is not an easy matter. It is beneficial—productive—to have money on hand to pay for the things that we want when we want them rather than trying to purchase everything at the beginning of a pay period so as to minimize the dollars in our checkable accounts or in our wallets.

Thus, one cost to society of inflation is that it increases the cost of holding money. For society as a whole, we therefore use *too little* money during periods of inflation. This effect is greatest for currency because its real value falls one-for-one with each rise in the price level. The tax is much less for checkable deposits because many of these accounts pay some interest, and the **nominal interest rate** rises when the expected inflation rate rises.

We should also add that periods of inflation generate exactly the sort of prediction problems that arise when there is deflation. Inflation never proceeds evenly across time or across goods. As a result, during periods of inflation, consumers and businesses must spend some of their time trying to predict exactly how the inflation is likely to proceed. And this in turn means they are spending less time producing output that is available for consumption.

## INFLATION, DEFLATION, AND THE MONEY SUPPLY

Throughout the history of the world, there has been a consistent long-run relationship between the change in the price level over time and the change in the **money supply**—money in circulation. This relationship does not move in lockstep fashion in the short run. But it does hold, on average, over longer periods of time, and it is *sustained* inflation or deflation that is a cause for the greatest concern.

There are several ways to define a country's money supply. For our purposes, let's treat it as currency plus all of the funds in accounts that can be used for transactions, such as those accessible with debit cards. As already noted, a predictable long-term relationship has been observed between changes in the money supply and changes in the general price level: sustained, rapid monetary growth yields inflation, and sustained shrinkage in the money supply causes deflation. **Expansive monetary policy** on the part of the **Federal Reserve** caused the money supply to increase quite rapidly after the short **recession** in 2001–2002, for example. The expansion in the money supply continued through the decade. Not surprisingly, inflation crept upward, from 1.6 percent in 2001 to over 4 percent in 2007. And as inflation rose, so did concerns over how bad it would get.

## Deflation Discussions Front And Center

The talk of inflation came to a screeching halt at the end of the summer of 2008. Partly it was those plummeting gas and commodity prices that took the steam out of the inflation talk. But the financial panic of 2008 also changed sentiments about the likely course of the future price level.

Indeed, all of Washington, DC, and the financial world suddenly started worrying about deflation. According to Professor Frederic Mishkin of Columbia University, "If inflation expectations were to decline sharply, that would greatly increase the risk of deflation." Further, according to American Enterprise Institute researcher Desmond Lachman, "A deep and prolonged recession could raise the specter of deflation of the sort that plagued the Japanese economy." Lachman was referring to the 1990s, when Japan experienced a flat or declining price level (some economists refer to this as Japan's "lost decade").

Thus far, however, this talk of deflation has not turned out to be reality—and we doubt that it will. Among other things, the Fed reacted to the Panic of '08 with much easier credit policies, injecting more money into the economy. Initially, banks were not very amenable to lending out these new funds, so there were few signs of inflationary pressure in 2009 and 2010. But unless the Fed manages to move these funds out of the system as the economy recovers from the recession, inflationary trouble lies ahead.

So here is our prediction, notwithstanding the dire predictions of falling prices. Inflation is in your future. Eventually, all the increases in the money supply that were made possible by the Fed's credit expansion in 2008–2010 will be realized. As the economy accelerates, banks will be lending their plentiful **excess reserves.** The money supply will be growing, the demand for products will be rising, and the inflation rate will be rising. Thus, our bet is that by the time you read these words, talk of deflation will have stopped because inflation will be a regular part of life once again.

## FOR CRITICAL ANALYSIS

1. When the price of a barrel of petroleum increased greatly in 2008, every news article about rising oil prices had a negative slant. When the price of petroleum dropped by more than 50 percent later in the year, the press said little, and much of what the press said was negative. Those negative comments focused on fears that there would not be enough new exploration for oil in the future. Is it really possible for a rise in the price of a good to be "bad" and also for a drop in the price of that same good to be "bad"?

2. If the inflation rate is fully anticipated, what are the ways in which consumers and businesses can protect against the resulting loss of purchasing power?

3. Who are the people who are most affected by unanticipated inflation? Why?

4. Throughout much of 2010, the talk of deflation persisted, even though the price level was rising. It was as though people preferred to live in a world of rising, rather than falling (or even stable), prices. Can you suggest an explanation for people's preferences that there be inflation rather than deflation of stable prices?

5. Between 2008 and 2010 the Federal Reserve doubled the monetary base, which is enough, in the long run, to double the money supply. Given the observed long-run relationship between the money supply and the price level, how much can we expect the price level to rise, ceteris paribus?

6. During 2009 the Fed started paying interest to banks on the reserves they held. The Fed also seemed surprised that the banks then held on to their reserves rather than lending them out. Can you suggest a policy change that would induce the banks to lend out more of their reserves? What would you do if you wanted them to lend out even *fewer* funds to potential borrowers? Explain your answers.

# CHAPTER 27

# Is It Real, or Is It Nominal?

Every few years, some important commodity, such as gasoline, electricity, or food, experiences a spike in prices. Reporters examine such price spikes and plaster newspapers, magazines, and Web sites with the appropriate headlines—sometimes relentlessly, day after day. TV commentators interview frustrated and worried Americans who spout the expected negative reactions to the higher prices of essential items in their budgets. The world, it would seem, is coming to an end.

## WAS GAS REALLY EXPENSIVE?

Let's just take one often-in-the-press example, gasoline prices. The authors of the book you are reading are old enough to remember the TV interviews that ensued when the price of gas first hit the unprecedented level of $1 per gallon, back in 1980. The same types of interviews occurred when the price of a gallon of gas broke the $2 barrier, early in 2005, and lodged above $3 in 2007. Not surprisingly, virtually the same types of interviews occurred when the price of a gallon of gas rose above $4 in the summer of 2008. At each point in time, everyone interviewed had the same response, even though years had passed between the different price spikes: "I guess I'll just have to stop driving." "I'm going to get a bike." "I'm selling my big car and getting a small one." And of course, each time there was an accompanying story about how record numbers of people were (or soon would be) flocking to their neighborhood motor scooter dealerships.

If we wish to sensibly analyze the effects of higher prices on the quantity demanded and the quantity supplied of any good or service in this world, we can rely neither on what journalists report nor on what

Americans say when they are interviewed. After all, what is important is not what people say but what they do. As economists, we best understand consumers by their **revealed preferences.** Similarly, business people are best understood by their actions, not their words. What people do is reflected in how much they actually buy of any good or service after its price changes, not by their complaints to a TV reporter or what they post on their blog or on Facebook.

## RELATIVE PRICES, NOMINAL PRICES, AND INFLATION

For both microeconomic and macroeconomic analysis, the relevant price is the price *relative to* all other prices because people's decisions are based on **relative prices,** not **nominal prices.** The latter simply tell us the number of pieces of paper (dollar bills) you must hand over for a good. Nominal prices tell us nothing about the real sacrifice (measured in terms of other goods or of labor services) that one must make to obtain those goods. Relative prices reflect the real sacrifice involved in acquiring a good because they tell us the price of a good or service relative to the price of another good or service or to the average of all other prices. Relative prices tell us how much of other goods we must sacrifice.

Said another way, we have to separate out the rise in the general price level, called **inflation,** and the rise in the nominal price of a particular good or service. If *all* nominal prices went up exactly 3 percent, there would be no change in relative prices. This inflation of 3 percent would not change the real sacrifice entailed in acquiring any particular good. In the real world, even during periods of inflation, some prices go up faster than others and some prices even go down—witness the price of computing power, DVD players, and MP3 players. Nevertheless, if we want to predict people's behavior, we must know what has happened to the *relative* price of a good, and to determine this, we must adjust for inflation.

## GAS PRICES REVISITED

Now let's get back to our example of gasoline prices. Your grandparents might be able to talk about buying gas for 30 cents a gallon (its average nominal price most of the time between 1956 and 1964). Today, what you pay in dollars per gallon is many times that level. People still drive nonetheless—indeed, the use of gasoline for cars and trucks in the United States is roughly triple what it was when the nominal price of gas was only 30 cents. Something must have happened. The most important "something" is a general rise in *all* prices, including gasoline prices.

In the summer of 2008, the price of gasoline spiked over $4 per gallon. One presidential candidate argued that the government should intervene on gas prices to "give families some relief." Two-thirds of American voters at that time said they thought that the price of gas was "an extremely important political issue." (Of course, when gas prices started tumbling in the fall of 2008, there were not many front-page articles or TV interviews with happy consumers. And the politicians simply became silent on this subject.) Consider, though, that at its nominal price at the beginning of 2009, the *relative* price of gas was back down to about what it had been in 1960—after correcting for overall inflation. For many people, this is a shocking revelation. But correcting for inflation is absolutely essential if you want to sensibly analyze the price of anything over time. Often we talk about the **real price** of a good or service. This refers specifically to subtracting the rate of inflation from the change in a nominal price over time. Not surprisingly, we also do the same exercise when we want to go from **nominal income** to **real income** over time.

## THE IMPORTANCE OF HIGHER DISPOSABLE INCOME

Another fact is particularly relevant when thinking about the real burden of gasoline. People are becoming more productive over time because they are getting better educated and because ongoing technological change enables us to produce more with a given input of our time. As a result of this higher **productivity**, U.S. consumers' **disposable incomes** generally rise from one year to the next—and certainly rise on average over longer periods of time. As Americans become richer on average, they are financially able to handle even higher relative prices of those items they wish to purchase, gasoline included.

To help us understand this point better, researchers Indur Goklany and Jerry Taylor came up with an "affordability index." They compared family income to the price of gas from 1949 to 2008. They arbitrarily set 1960 at an affordability index of 1. Relative to this, a higher affordability index number means that something is more affordable. Even when gas was $4.15 per gallon, the affordability gas index was 1.35. In other words, the ratio of the average person's disposable income to the price of gasoline was higher by about 35 percent in 2008 than it was in 1960—gasoline was *more* affordable than it had been back in 1960, when your grandparents were filling up their tanks at 30 cents a gallon. That's hard to believe for some of us but true nonetheless. And once gas prices turned down at the end of 2008, the gas affordability index rose even more, passing 2, meaning that gasoline was more than twice as affordable at the beginning of 2009 as it had been in 1960. A subsequent rise in gas prices meant that by 2011 gas was "only" about 50 percent more affordable than it had been in 1960.

## PRODUCT QUALITY CHANGES

The quality of gasoline typically does not change much over time. But the quality of many other products often changes significantly over time, usually for the better. Often we forget about this crucial aspect when we start comparing prices of a good or service over time. If you ask senior citizens today how much they paid for their first car, you might get prices in the range of $2,000–$5,000. The average new car today costs around $30,000 (in nominal dollars). By now, of course, you know that if you want to compare these numbers, you have to first account for the inflation that has occurred over whatever time period you are examining. In this case, adjusting for inflation still means that the relative price of a car appears to be about 50 percent higher than it was, say, fifty years ago.

Does that necessarily mean that a car is really 50 percent more expensive than it was in 1960? Probably not. We must take into account improved quality features of cars today compared to those of the past. Today (unlike fifty years ago), the average car has the following:

- Antilock computer-controlled power brakes
- Power steering
- Digital radio with CD or MP3 player
- Air conditioning
- Steel-belted radial tires
- Cruise control
- Power windows and locks
- Air bags
- Fifty percent better fuel economy

The list of improved and new features is actually much longer. Today, the average car is safer, breaks down less often, needs fewer tune-ups, has a host of amenities that were not even dreamed of fifty years ago, and almost certainly lasts for at least twice as many miles. If you correct not only for inflation but also for these quality increases, the relative price of cars today has almost certainly *fallen* appreciably in the past fifty years, in spite of the "sticker shock" that you may experience when you go shopping for a new car. That is, appearances to the contrary, the inflation-corrected **constant-quality price** of automobiles is actually lower today than it was five decades ago.

# DECLINING NOMINAL PRICES

The necessity of adjusting for inflation and quality changes continues to apply even when we are examining goods whose nominal prices have declined over time. A good example is computing power. The nominal price of the average personal computer has gone down in spite of general inflation over the past several decades. These days, a Windows-based desktop computer has an average price of about $500. For a laptop, the average price is a bit over $600. A decade ago, the average machines in each category would have had nominal prices of twice as much. You might be tempted to conclude, then, that the price of personal computing has fallen by 50 percent. You'd be wrong: The price has actually fallen by *more* than 50 percent.

Why? There are two reasons. First, over the past 10 years, the average dollar prices of all goods increased by 30 percent. That is how much overall inflation there has been. That means that the *relative* price of the average computer has fallen by two-thirds, which, of course, is greater than 50 percent. But even here we are missing something extremely important: The quality of what you are buying—computing power—has skyrocketed. The processor speed of the average computer today is at least ten times greater than it was 10 years ago and is increasing exponentially. Moreover, hard drives are bigger, monitors are flat-screen LCDs instead of bulky old cathode ray tubes, laptops are lighter, RAM is larger—the list of improvements goes on and on. And despite people's frustrations with both the hardware and software of the personal computer today, long-time users can tell you that both are vastly more reliable than they were a decade ago. Thus, if you only look at the inflation-corrected decrease in computer prices, you will be underestimating the *true* decrease in the relative price of computers.

The moral of our story is simple. At some point in your education, you learned that "what goes up must come down." Now you know that when it comes to prices, it is often the case that "what goes up has actually gone down." It is a lesson worth keeping in mind if you really want to understand the behavior of consumers and businesses alike.

## FOR CRITICAL ANALYSIS

1. Create a list of goods (or services) whose quality has improved over time in such a way that the current prices of these commodities do not accurately reflect their real prices, even after adjusting for inflation. Now see if you can come up with a list of items whose quality has systematically *decreased* over time. Can you suggest why it is easier to find examples of the former than the latter?

2. The demand for small-engine motor scooters jumped when the price of gasoline started moving up in the summer of 2008. Make a prediction about the demand for this form of transportation in, say, two years from today. Explain your answer.

3. Explain why you will make more accurate predictions if you focus on the changing incentives people face rather than listening to what they say they are going to do.

4. When the price of gasoline rose to $4 from $2 per gallon, media commentators spoke as though people were headed to the poor house as a result. But here are some other facts: The average car is driven about 12,000 miles per year and gets about 24 miles per gallon. Even if people did not drive less when the price of rose, by how much did the average driver's "real" income fall due to the $2 per gallon rise in the price of gas? Given that per capita income is almost $50,000 per year, what is this income change in percentage terms? Show all calculations.

5. One implication of the **law of demand** is that the pain to a consumer of a price increase is always *less* than suggested by multiplying the price increase by the amount of the product consumed before the price increase. Explain why.

6. The law of demand also implies that the pleasure that comes from a fall in the price of a good is always *more* than implied by simply multiplying the price cut by the amount of the good consumed before the change. Explain why.

PART SIX

# Fiscal Policy

# CHAPTER 28

# Are You
# Stimulated Yet?

George Bush supported one. Barack Obama proposed one too. And Republicans and Democrats in both houses of Congress ended up passing two of them. With all of this backing, surely economic stimulus packages must be good for the economy, right? Well, maybe not. Let's see why.

## STIMULUS PACKAGES

As implemented by the U.S. (or foreign) governments, so-called economic stimulus packages generally contain some combination of two elements: higher government spending and lower government taxes. One consequence of such packages is that the size of the government **deficit** grows, implying that the **national debt** must get larger. Higher debt is merely a side effect of a stimulus package, however. The *objective* of such packages is to increase total spending in the economy, raise employment, and reduce the unemployment rate.

Proposals for stimulus packages generally come during economic recessions, when gross domestic product (GDP) is depressed and the unemployment rate is elevated. At first blush, it seems like a government stimulus is exactly what we need at such times. After all, government spending is part of GDP, so more government spending seemingly must, as a matter of definition, generate more GDP. And because the things that the government buys (such as cement for new highways) are produced using labor, it seems pretty clear that more people will be hired, thereby cutting the unemployment rate. Alternatively, to the extent that part of the stimulus comes in the form of a tax cut, this puts more **disposable income** in the hands of consumers, some or all of which will presumably be spent by them. Again, production of goods and services rises and the unemployment rate falls. Either way, it seems, a government stimulus package is the sure-fire way out of a recession. Before we jump to this conclusion, however, it will be wise to take a closer look.

## TAX CUTS

Let's look first at the tax cuts that are often components of stimulus packages. To do so, imagine for the moment that we keep government spending at current levels and simply cut the taxes we are collecting from people during the current period. Such an action is what people have in mind when they refer to a "tax cut." To fully appreciate the effects of a tax cut, however, we must carefully specify how it is conducted. For example, in the "Economic Stimulus Act of 2008" the tax cut consisted of **lump sum tax rebates.** Each eligible person received $300, regardless of income, with another $300 for each dependent child.[1] In contrast, tax cuts pushed by Presidents Kennedy in the 1960s, Reagan in the 1980s, or Bush in the early 2000s reduced the **marginal tax rate** for many taxpayers. That is, the taxes taken out of additional dollars of earned income were reduced. This not only lowered the individual's **tax liability** (total taxes owed) it also increased the incentive to work more, produce more, and thus earn more, because taxpayers could keep more of what they earned.

However the tax cut is implemented, it is clear that if the government is going to pay for its spending, at least initially it must borrow, that is, run a budget deficit. Now, unless potential lenders are convinced they will be repaid, they will not lend. And the only way for the government to repay its loans is to collect *more* taxes in the future, indeed taxes that are higher by enough to repay both the principle and the interest on the loan.

Now we see the problem with trying to stimulate the economy by cutting taxes: A reduction in *current* taxes must be met by an even larger increase in *future* taxes. For a given level of government spending, taxes *cannot* actually be reduced, they can at best only be moved around in time. Thus, although a "tax cut" puts more current disposable spending in the hands of consumers, it also loads them up with an even bigger added debt burden. In the case of tax cuts of the rebate variety, this is the end of the story. The added debt burden will weigh on the spending decisions of consumers, so there is no necessary reason to think

---

1 For individuals earning over $75,000 or couples earning over $150,000 the rebate was gradually phased out to zero, and thus technically not lump sum. This actually tended to discourage some work effort among these individuals, which would tend to *reduce* real GDP. This effect was likely quite small, however, because the dollar amounts were small.

that consumers will spend more today. They may (and typically do) just save most of the increase in disposable income so they'll be ready in the future when their bigger tax bills come due. Of course, consumers may not *think* this way about their taxes at all. But the key point is how they *behave*. And the fact is that many consumers act *as though* they are quite conscious of the added burden of future taxes they bear when current taxes are cut. Hence, tax rebates such as contained in the Economic Stimulus Act of 2008 typically cannot do much to stimulate the economy in any important way.

Reductions in marginal tax rates offer hope of something more. Again, we cannot expect people to go on a spending spree just because taxes have been moved around in time. But there is an added feature with lower marginal tax rates. People have an incentive to work more, produce more, and thus earn more, because they get to keep a larger share of what they earn. This feature of this type of tax cut does indeed stimulate the economy, although it does so from the supply side (labor supply rises), rather than the demand side.

## SPENDING INCREASES

Now, what about the other half of stimulus packages—higher spending by the government? To sort this out, we will first have to distinguish between two broad types of government spending: that which is a substitute for private spending and that which is not. For example, although the government spends plenty on education (primary, secondary, and college), so do private citizens. The government spending is a substitute for private spending, and when the government spends more on education, private spending on education falls. This offsetting change in private spending clearly reduces the potential stimulus effect of the government. Indeed, in some cases, education included, it appears that *all* of the higher government spending is offset by lower private spending. The stimulus effect in this case is obviously zero.

Of course, plenty of government programs don't compete directly with private spending. For example, most defense spending (such as expenditures on the war in Afghanistan) does not compete with private spending. Also, some so-called infrastructure spending, such as on highways and bridges, competes little with private spending. Thus, when government defense or infrastructure spending goes up, there is no direct dollar-for-dollar cut in private spending, as there can be with items like education. Nevertheless, there are generally substantial *indirect* impacts on private spending—impacts that can markedly reduce the stimulating effects of the government spending. Let's see why.

## Indirect Offsets in Private Spending

As we suggested above, the real burden of the government is its spending. Taxes are simply the means of deciding who shall bear that burden. Thus, for a given level of other expenditures, when defense or infrastructure spending rises, taxes *must* rise, at some point now or in the future. And because consumers know this, they will typically make some provision for it, by reducing their own spending. This clearly dampens the overall stimulus effect of the higher government spending.

There is another potential offset when government spending rises. If the government "finances" this spending by borrowing rather than raising current taxes, the result can be upward pressure on interest rates. Higher interest rates in turn reduce the attractiveness of consumer durable goods (such as houses and cars) and also reduce the profitability of business investment spending. Thus, when larger government deficits push up interest rates, private consumption and investment spending will decline, once more dampening any hoped-for stimulus.

## Delays in Spending

As amazing as this may seem, there is yet one more obstacle in the path of stimulus spending—time. Despite all the headlines about so-called "shovel ready" projects and "immediate action," there are usually long delays in implementing the spending portion of stimulus packages. Let's consider one simple example. As part of the 2009 stimulus pushed by President Obama and passed by Congress early in that year, more than a dozen states were supposed to get federal funds for building or expanding light rail commuter systems. Ultimately, two of the states (Wisconsin and Ohio) decided that the benefits of this spending to them would not outweigh the costs. Hence, these states declined to accept the money for light rail systems, hoping the federal government would let them keep the money and use it to repair and expand their roads and bridges. In fact, late in 2010 (nearly two years after the stimulus package was passed) President Obama ordered that the rejected funds be redirected to the dozen states that had accepted the rail funding. Well into 2011 most of these funds were still unspent, as were many billions of dollars of other funds included in the "2009" stimulus package.

Not all spending is delayed this much, of course (although some can be delayed even more). But the key point is simple. Despite all of the claims politicians make about taking "immediate action," it just doesn't work out this way. In fact, over the span of the last fifty years or so, much of the government spending supposedly designed to help pull us out of recessions was not actually spent until well after these recessions were over.

## The Stimulus that Mostly Wasn't

The 2009 American Recovery and Reinvestment Act (ARRA), President Obama's first major piece of legislation, received lots of media attention, in no small part because of its size—$862 billion. But its impact on aggregate demand appears to have been minimal. One reason stems from the fact that a large portion of the legislation called for grants to state and local governments. The law's backers argued that these funds would immediately be spent by the recipients on all sorts of new programs, thereby stimulating the economy. In fact, the state and local governments used almost *all* of these transfers to reduce their borrowing. Thus, the mechanics went like this: the federal government borrowed funds (about $120 billion per year during each of the first two years), lent those funds to the states, which then borrowed $120 billion less. Net effect: federal debt up, state and local debt down, and aggregate spending unchanged.

The ARRA was also touted as being big on infrastructure—roads, bridges, and so forth. In fact, the legislation itself never called for more than about 10 percent of its funds to be used in this way, and by two years after its passage, only a small fraction of this had been spent. Indeed, the ARRA appears to have yielded almost no increase in government spending on goods and services, at least through 2010. Twenty-one months into the act's existence, government purchases of goods and services had risen only $24 billion, and infrastructure had gone up only $3 billion. In a $14 trillion economy, these sums are trivial.

## Is Stimulus Possible?

As you may have gathered, our overall conclusion is that, unless marginal tax rates are reduced, we should typically not expect government stimulus packages to actually stimulate the economy very much. Lump sum tax cuts are not really tax cuts at all, and higher government spending levels are routinely offset in whole or in part by cuts in private spending. But notice our use of the word "typically." There is indeed a set of circumstances in which stimulus packages have the potential to live up to their billing. Fortunately, these circumstances don't come around very often. Indeed, the only time they may have been observed is during and immediately after the Great Depression (1929–1933).

A series of declines in aggregate demand over the period 1929–1933 ended up pushing economy-wide output down by 30 percent and raising the unemployment rate to an unprecedented 25 percent of the labor force. By the depths of 1933, many people had been unemployed for years and they and their families were living hand to mouth. They were

**cash-constrained.** Every time their income changed by a dollar, so too did their spending. Thus, when so-called "relief" spending by the federal government began, most people worried not a bit about the future tax liabilities that might be involved. Moreover, much of the spending was on items (such as the Hoover Dam, and Post Office and other public buildings) that did not compete directly with private spending.

This set of circumstances meant that the government stimulus spending during the 1930s did help increase total spending and also helped get people back to work. Indeed, it was during this period of time that stimulus spending first gained credibility among both economists and politicians. But the circumstances of the 1930s were extreme. No recession since then has come remotely close to being as severe, not even the recessions of 1981–1982 and 2007–2009. Moreover, since the 1930s credit markets have become much more developed. People have credit cards and lines of credit and thus the ability to continue spending even when their incomes decline. To be sure, a prolonged period of unemployment can eventually exhaust these reserves. Fortunately, the number of people who find themselves in such circumstances is generally small, even in recessions. As a result, the stimulating effects observed for stimulus packages during the 1930s cannot be expected to be repeated, unless of course the 1930s somehow repeat themselves.

So our moral is that if you are not yet feeling stimulated by federal spending increases or tax cuts, don't feel left out. You have plenty of company.

## FOR CRITICAL ANALYSIS

1. Why is it in the interest of politicians to promote the notion that unemployment can be lowered if federal spending is increased?

2. If the unemployment rate can be reduced by cutting taxes, why don't we cut taxes to zero, at least during recessions?

3. During World War II, federal spending rose to roughly 50 percent of total spending in the economy, from its prewar level of just under 10 percent. How was this possible—that is, what spending had to decline to make it feasible for the federal share of spending to rise by a factor of five?

4. Some people argue that unemployment benefits (i.e., cash payments by the government to people who are unemployed) help stimulate the economy. The reasoning is that without the benefits the incomes of unemployed people would be lower, and thus their spending on goods and services would be lower. Keeping in mind that unemployment

benefits are generally no more than 40–50 percent as large as the typical earnings of people when working, answer these questions:

(a) How do unemployment benefits change the incentive to be *employed*? Explain.

(b) Is it possible that a system of unemployment benefits could actually cause total spending in the economy to *fall*? Explain.

5. If current taxes are reduced by way of a lump sum rebate, does the consumer response likely depend on how long it will be before taxes are actually raised to pay off the debt incurred by the government? In answering, be sure to account for the fact that the longer the delay in raising taxes, the greater will be the interest debt that accrues.

6. Who is more likely to think of a cut in current taxes as being a true reduction in taxes: a young worker with several young children or an older retiree with no children? Explain.

# CHAPTER 29

# Health Care Reform

The trite but true saying "Nothing is more important than your health" should be replaced these days with another: "Nothing is more important than who pays for health insurance and health care." The most massive change in the history of our nation's health care insurance and delivery systems occurred in 2010 with the passage of health care "reform." The stakes are big. Americans spend 17 percent of total national annual income on health care—we are, indeed, the world's health-care spending champions.

## How About the Uninsured?

So what about all those people who are said to be shut off from this health care system because they lack health insurance? The typical claim in the debate over health care reform was that 15 percent of Americans lacked coverage—but like many numbers you hear in political debates, this one needs to be taken with a grain (or perhaps a shaker) of salt. Of the forty-five million people said to lack health coverage in America, about eighteen million were aged 18–34, a group for which health expenditures are far lower than average. About twelve million were fully eligible for publicly provided (and paid-for) health insurance, but chose not to take it. And among all of the uninsured, fully half were uninsured only part of each year. The bottom line is that only about 3 percent of Americans (fewer than one in thirty) were likely to have a significant demand for health insurance and yet be unable to get insurance on a persistent basis. For these individuals, the lack of insurance was an onerous, often terrifying, fact of life. But it is important to keep in mind that the number of people in this group is a far cry from the numbers that are normally bandied about.

## Rising Health Care Costs in America

Fifty years ago, spending on health care in this country was not even 6 percent of national income. Today it is 17 percent, about equally divided between public spending and private spending. And there is no doubt that even as we speak, health care costs have been rising in America. There are at least four reasons why health care costs have gone up so much:

1. *An aging population:* The top 5 percent of health care users incur more than 50 percent of all health care costs. Senior citizens (all of them covered by Medicare) make up most of the top users. It is not surprising, therefore, that as our population ages, we will be spending more on health care. Currently, about 13 percent of U.S. residents are over 65. By 2035, this number will have risen to 22 percent. Given that the elderly consume in excess of four times as much per capita health care services as the rest of the population, the demand for such services is certain to go up with our aging population.

   Of course, populations in Western Europe, Canada, Japan, and other industrialized nations are rising as well. But there the elderly have not played as big a role in pushing up health care costs as in America. The reason is simple. In those other nations, which have national health insurance systems, the elderly are sharply limited on the amount of health care they are allowed to utilize. This is much different from the U.S. Medicare system, which effectively lets senior citizens choose to have whatever health care services they wish.

2. *More expensive technologies:* Each advance in medical technology brings with it more expensive equipment and prescription drugs. A magnetic resonance imaging (MRI) scanner costs at least $2 million. A positron emission tomography (PET) scanner costs over $4 million. Each time these machines are used, the fees range to as high as $2,000 per procedure. New drugs for cancer can easily cost $250,000 for one course of treatment. Innovation in medicine has played a key role in improving the quality of health care in America, and neither innovation nor spending on it is about to stop. Therefore, we can expect increasing expenditures in medicine just because of advances in equipment and drugs.

3. *When someone else pays:* Between the government (through **Medicare** and **Medicaid**) and insurance companies, more than 80 percent of health care spending is paid for by someone else—a **third party.** Less than 20 percent is paid directly by individuals. This was not always the situation. In 1930, third parties paid only about 4 percent of health care expenditures.

When someone else pays for medical services, we encounter the problem of **moral hazard:** Payment by third parties creates a larger quantity demanded. You may think that people do not react to the price of medical services, but they do. When Medicare went into effect in 1965, the volume of federal government–reimbursed medical services increased by more than 65 percent above what was anticipated when the program was made into law. And when senior citizens received new coverage for prescription medicines in 2003, their spending on prescriptions ended up being *double* the forecast.

Consider an example: If you have a health insurance policy that pays everything, then you have little incentive to reduce your medical care purchases. Why not see a doctor about every sniffle "just in case"? If, in contrast, you have to pay the first $1,000 out of your pocket before an insurance company (or the government) will start paying for your medical care expenses, you will react differently. You will engage, at a minimum, in more wellness activities and you will be less inclined to seek medical care for minor problems. Physicians in hospitals face a type of moral hazard problem, too. If they are reimbursed for every procedure by an insurance company or by the government, they will tend to ask for more tests and procedures "just in case." That means we pay more for medical care.

4. *Obesity:* The Centers for Disease Control and Prevention (CDC) have estimated that almost one-third of Americans are obese. In contrast, fifty years ago obesity was a rarity. The CDC estimates that today about 10 percent of total U.S. medical expenditures are attributable to obesity. About half of these expenditures are being paid for by Medicare and Medicaid. Many expenditures for obese people relate to obesity-caused type 2 diabetes—a disease that is rising at a record rate in the United States. As obesity rises, spending on medical care will follow.

## HEALTH CARE REFORM TO THE RESCUE?

A bitterly fought battle over the health care system occurred in the U.S. Congress until new health care legislation was signed into law by President Obama in 2010. After briefly reviewing the key aspects of the two-thousand-plus pages of the new law on this matter, you will see that not all of the promised results can actually come to fruition, especially the promise that "spiraling health care costs will come down."

Here is a brief point-by-point summary of the federal government's new national health care program:

1. *Health care regulations*—Health insurance companies must cover everyone who applies, including those with preexisting medical problems. (As explained below, this new rule will weigh heavily (and expensively) on young people.)

2. *Individual mandate*—Just about everyone living in the United States must either purchase health care coverage or pay a fine up to $750 per year for an individual or $2,250 per year per family (twenty-one states have challenged this mandate in federal court).

3. *Employer mandate*—Firms with more than 50 employees must offer health insurance coverage or pay an annual fine of up to $750 per employee who obtains federal subsidies for such coverage.

4. *Health care insurance subsidies*—A variety of subsidies and tax credits will be provided to lower-income people and smaller firms.

5. *Higher taxes*—A special tax rate of 3.8 percent will apply to nearly all income earnings above $200,000 for individuals and $250,000 for a married couple.

## THE MORAL HAZARD PROBLEM WILL WORSEN

You have already been introduced to the moral hazard problem that arises when third parties pay for medical care. Health care reform will worsen moral hazard. Once the national health care program fully goes into effect, tens of millions of U.S. residents are going to be paying a smaller percentage of their health care expenses themselves than they did previously. Consequently, the direct price paid by them for health care services will fall and thus the quantity of health care services demanded will rise. Also, because health insurers will be required to cover this expanded consumption of medical services, total expenditures on health care will increase even faster.

Finally, the moral hazard problem will become worse because more U.S. residents will face reduced incentives to make decisions that promote better health. As people have more health problems as a consequence of this increase in moral hazard, the demand for health care will increase. And as you know, when demand rises, so too will prices and expenditures.

## WHY YOUNG PEOPLE WILL PAY MORE

The new law means that soon everyone must buy health insurance. The law also states that insurance companies must give full coverage to those with preexisting illnesses, but without charging them a higher rate. What does that mean? Simply that healthy young people—who will be required to buy insurance policies—will not pay a low price that reflects the low risk of them getting sick. One analysis conducted for the *Associated Press* estimates that beginning in 2014 young adults seeking coverage in the individual health insurance market will pay almost 20 percent more for the same coverage that they could buy today. To see why this is likely to be an understated impact of the new rules, consider this fact: Typically, insurance companies have charged six or seven times as much to older customers as to younger ones in those states that had no restrictions. The new federal law limits this ratio to three to one. That means that a 60-year-old can be charged only three times as much as a 25-year-old. So, who gets stuck? Young adults will, in the form of higher premiums.

## WON'T EXTRA PREVENTIVE CARE
## CUT HEALTH CARE SPENDING?

Supporters of health care reform argue that it will encourage a lot more preventive care, thereby reducing overall health care spending. But Stanford University Medical Professor Abraham Verghese argues that spending more on preventive care will actually drive costs *up*, not down. First of all, everyone knows what illness prevention strategies we can do as individuals—lose weight, eat better, exercise more, smoke less, and wear a seat belt while driving a car. These are cheap, save lives, and cut health care costs.

All other preventive strategies end up costing the economy more. Increased medical screening leads to discovering more potential medical problems and therefore more expenses in the form of additional screening tests and medications. Professor Verghese uses the following example. A test that discovers high cholesterol in a person who is feeling fine is really the discovery of a risk factor and not a disease. Elevated cholesterol levels mean that you have a greater chance of having a heart attack. You could reduce your cholesterol levels through weight loss, better diet, and lots of exercise. Or, you can take a pill every day in the form of a drug called a statin. That pill will reduce your cholesterol levels. Using a statin in the general population costs about $150,000 for every *year* of life it saves in men and costs even more in women. Sorry, no savings to be found here.

## There are Indeed no Free Lunches

From the onset, the health care debate was couched in absurd contradictions, at least for those who understand limited resources versus unlimited wants, **budget constraints,** and supply and demand. No legislation that promises to subsidize tens of millions of U.S. residents who currently have no health care insurance can possibly lead to lower overall medical care expenditures. That does not mean that such legislation is wrong—that's a value judgment and not a conclusion arising from economic analysis. Nevertheless, it is past time that everyone who takes place in the discussion of health care acknowledges one simple fact. Throughout all recorded history, when any good or service becomes cheaper to the person who uses that good or service, quantity demanded will rise, no matter what the political arguments are to the contrary.

## The Macroeconomic Effects of Health Care Reform

Let there be no doubt about it—the most recent health care reform legislation is going to impact the rest of the U.S. economy in significant ways. It will have effects on labor markets, markets for goods and services, and the budgets of federal and state governments. Let's consider these effects in order:

1. *Labor market effects*—The new legislation requires many firms to provide health care insurance when they are currently not providing it. The result will be an increase in the effective wage rates that these firms must pay for each unit of labor. The increased effective wage rate will induce firms to reduce the quantity of labor demanded. The result: Other things being equal, U.S. employment will be lower than it otherwise would have been had there been no mandate requiring firms to pay for employee health care coverage.

2. *Markets for goods and services*—The increase in labor costs that firms will incur in hiring each unit of labor will clearly increase average and marginal costs of production. This will induce firms to decrease their output in all prices. The result: Other things being equal, equilibrium prices will rise in a number of markets and consumers will pay higher prices for many goods and services.

3. *The impact on government budgets*—The new taxes for higher-income people mentioned on page XX went into effect in 2011, so tax revenues began flowing into the new federal health care program immediately. Because federal government expenditures on this new

program are being phased in gradually, the program initially will be financed by the revenues collected in advance. According to most experts, though, the new tax revenues will be insufficient to cover the increases in government health care spending that is going to occur in future years. Ultimately, the federal government will have to search for additional ways to reduce its health care expenditures—such as **price controls** on hospitals and physicians—or increases in tax rates and new taxes. Note that the federal program does not include revenues for states to cover the higher expenses of additional people admitted to the Medicaid program, which state governments administer. Consequently, state governments will also face pressures to increase tax rates or to reduce health care service costs.

## FOR CRITICAL ANALYSIS

1. Is it correct to apply standard economic analysis to something as important as medical care? Why or why not?

2. What are some of the ways in which government could force individuals to undertake their own illness-preventing activities?

3. If the government attempts to reduce health care expenditures by lowering the fees that physicians can charge for certain procedures, what might be the result in the short run? In the long run?

4. Why don't most current health care insurance plans cover preexisting illnesses? Who benefits from this current general rule? When health care reform legislation abolishes this rule, who will be hurt?

5. Currently, most U.S. residents cannot buy health care insurance coverage from a company based in another state. The new legislation leaves this restriction in place. Who benefits from this situation? Who loses?

6. What is special about health care that justifies so much government intervention? In other words, what problems would arise if the health care sector were completely unregulated and unsubsidized?

# CHAPTER **30**

# The Fannie Mae, Freddie Mac Flimflam

Between 1995 and 2010, the U.S. housing market went on the wildest ride in its history. Over the years 1995–2005, median real (inflation-adjusted) house prices soared 60 percent nationwide and then promptly crashed, falling 40 percent from 2006 to 2010. Over the same period, the proportion of Americans who owned homes, normally a variable that changes quite slowly, leapt from 64 percent to 69 percent and then quickly dropped back to 67 percent. Meanwhile, the number of new houses built each year soared from 1.4 million to 2 million and then plunged to 500,000 per year.

But what really got people's attention—and created huge pressures on financial markets here and abroad—was the fact that just as quickly as people had snapped up houses during the boom years of 1995–2005, they simply *abandoned* their houses beginning in 2006, refusing to make any more payments on their mortgages. In a typical year, about 0.3 percent of homeowners (fewer than one out of three hundred) stop making mortgage payments and thus have their houses go into foreclosure, a process in which the borrower must give up any **equity** (ownership) in a home because of a failure to meet payment obligations. The foreclosure rate doubled to 0.6 percent in 2006, doubled again in 2007, and rose yet again in 2008, 2009, and 2010. In some hard-hit states, such as Nevada, foreclosures exploded to more than *ten times* the normal nationwide rate, with one home out of thirty going into foreclosure each year.

Across the country, people were literally walking away from their homes, leaving them in the hands of banks and other lenders. These lenders then took huge financial losses when forced to sell the abandoned properties in a market in which house prices were already falling. The result was further downward pressure on prices, which gave more owners the incentive to walk away from their homes, which raised foreclosures, and so forth. Within just a few years, the housing market was more depressed than it had been at any time since the Great Depression of the 1930s. In fact, to see what happened, we need to go back and start our story during that very period.

## SOME HOUSING HISTORY

Prior to World War II, most home mortgages were of short duration, such as one or two years (rather than fifteen to thirty years, which is common now). During the Great Depression, many risk-weary lenders refused to renew mortgages when they came due. The state of the economy was such that most borrowers were unable to repay immediately, and so their homes were foreclosed. In response, the U.S. government in 1934 created the Federal Housing Administration (FHA), to guarantee some home mortgages from default, and in 1938 created the Federal National Mortgage Association (FNMA, known as Fannie Mae), to purchase mortgages from the FHA, enabling the latter to guarantee still more mortgages. In 1968, Congress authorized Fannie Mae to buy mortgages from virtually all lenders, and it also created Ginnie Mae (the Government National Mortgage Association), authorized to bundle up, guarantee, and sell home mortgages issued by the FHA. Two years later, in 1970, Congress created Freddie Mac (the Federal Home Mortgage Loan Corporation) to offer competition to Fannie Mae. Both Fannie Mae and Freddie Mac are referred to as **government-sponsored enterprises (GSEs).** They are technically independent of the federal government, but both are subject to congressional oversight and, it turns out, to political pressure to do what Congress wants them to do. Ginnie Mae is part of the U.S. Department of Housing and Urban Development and thus under the direct budgetary control of Congress.

It has been clear from the inception of each of these agencies that the intent of Congress has been to promote home ownership in the United States, especially among lower-income individuals. Ultimately, the only way to do this is to reduce costs for borrowers. The agencies have done this in a variety of ways, including allowing people to make down payments of as little as 3.5 percent of the value of the house, as opposed to the 10–20 percent required by private lenders.

Going back as far as 1993, Fannie and Freddie have taken special measures to subsidize the highest-risk borrowers, along the way racking up huge potential risks. But beginning soon after the recession of 2001, Congress made it clear to Fannie, Freddie, Ginnie, and the FHA that even more should be done. In fact, powerful Democratic Representative Barney

Frank explicitly told the agencies that they needed to "roll the dice" in the housing market, that is, take on more risk by insuring, guaranteeing, or making home mortgage loans to people who were much worse credit risks than normal. The organizations responded with enthusiasm, helping to spark the housing boom that finally ended up crashing. Two things made the outcome of this behavior singularly costly. First, at the behest of Congress, the agencies focused most of their efforts on subsidizing purchases by the least creditworthy customers. Second, when it became apparent just how extensive the foreclosure losses were going to be, Congress not only bailed out the agencies by giving them more taxpayer cash but also told them to continue doing more of the same. The result will be huge tax bills for you.

## Rolling the Dice

The two riskiest types of mortgages are called subprime and Alt-A, respectively. Subprime mortgages are those made to borrowers who are considered to have a much higher than normal risk of defaulting. These people have relatively poor credit scores and the size of the mortgage they are getting is high relative to their ability to repay. Alt-A mortgages are generally those that either are missing some key documentation (such as proof of the borrower's income) or have especially low down payments. Either way, Alt-A mortgages are riskier than the typical mortgage.

By 2008, Fannie Mae and Freddie Mac either owned or were guaranteeing nearly ten million subprime and Alt-A mortgages. The outstanding balance on these loans was $1.6 *trillion*, a potential liability of $8,000 for each U.S. taxpayer. What made this worse, however, is that since the early 1990s Fannie and Freddie had routinely misrepresented just how risky their portfolios were becoming, reporting that their subprime and Alt-A mortgages were "prime" mortgages (the highest quality, least risky category).

## Bailouts

As we saw, both Fannie and Freddie were established as GSEs, that is, privately owned, but publicly sponsored, or endorsed. Although the federal government did not formally guarantee either organization, many people regarded such a guarantee as being implicit. And indeed, when it became apparent in September 2008 that both organizations were **insolvent** (their liabilities exceeded their assets), that implicit guarantee became reality. The federal government initially offered up $200 billion in explicit guarantees. Since then, the size of the guarantee—many people refer to it as a bailout—has been increased twice. Most recently, the Obama administration announced that there was *no limit* on how much the federal government was willing to invest in Fannie and Freddie. Although the Congressional Budget office claims that the cost to taxpayers is likely to be "only" $389 billion, potentially the taxpayer liability is many trillions of dollars.

At this point, you might think that Fannie and Freddie would change their behavior, perhaps by turning to lower-risk loans, or even trying to clean up their balance sheets by getting rid of the worst loans. In fact, both agencies have done just the reverse, getting involved in even riskier loans, and helping borrowers avoid their debts at little or no cost to the borrowers. The result is that the likely cost to taxpayers continues to rise.

## CASH UNLIMITED

As a practical matter, Fannie Mae and Freddie Mac have gotten themselves involved in almost every nook and cranny of the U.S. housing market. Consider just two examples. First, plenty of people in the housing market are either "underwater" (the value of their home is less than what is owed on it) or simply unable or unwilling to continue making payments on the mortgage. Fannie and Freddie have been actively engaged in a loan forgiveness program for many of these people, although this is not what the program is called. Essentially, the two agencies have been purchasing existing mortgages that are in default and then "modifying" them by reducing the amount the borrower owes. Rather than reporting this as a debt forgiveness (something that likely would not set well with homeowners who are still paying their bills), Fannie and Freddie just report the forgiveness as a "credit-related expense."

Of course, some people just cannot or will not continue making payments, even when offered a substantial reduction in the amount of the mortgage. In these cases, Fannie and Freddie have been taking over ownership of the homes—at a rate of one every ninety seconds. By 2010 the two agencies owned 170,000 homes, more houses than are located in Seattle. After putting still more cash into the properties (about $10,000 per house) to ready them for sale, the agencies then hand them over to real estate agents to sell for whatever price they can get—which of course is always far below what was owed on them. And the borrowers? Well, they are off the hook, replaced by the taxpayers.

## IT MAY GET WORSE

The meltdown in housing markets slowed the issuance of new mortgages by banks, and thus slowed the growth of Fannie and Freddie. While this may help reduce future losses by these two organizations, it won't stem the overall flood of losses. Why not? It's simple. The FHA has dramatically *increased* the amount of lending it is undertaking, and as a practical matter virtually all FHA loans are made to borrowers who are riskier than average. Moreover, the risks of FHA loans are enhanced by the fact that it requires a down payment of only 3.5 percent of the value of the home. Some experts now believe that up to one in ten of all FHA loans will end up in default—which means that taxpayers will be footing the bill.

Just how costly the federal involvement in mortgage markets will become is anyone's guess. In the meantime, the federal government seems determined to keep the cash flowing, which means that your tax bill will keep on growing. How high it will go, no one knows.

## For Critical Analysis

1. Who benefits from the actions of Fannie and Freddie?

2. There are approximately 220 million taxpayers in the United States, at least as measured by the number of tax returns filed with the IRS. But only about half of these "taxpayers" end up paying income taxes. (Some of the others pay only Social Security or Medicare taxes, while some actually *receive* payments, under the Earned Income Tax Credit program.) Considering that Fannie and Freddie are now owners or guarantors of almost $5.5 trillion in mortgages, what is the maximum potential liability for each of the taxpayers who actually pay income taxes?

3. How does the FHA requirement of a low down payment affect the incentive of the borrower to default on his or her mortgage, that is, stop making the payments? What impact does this have on taxpayer liability for these loans? Explain.

4. What characteristics of the people in a congressional district would help explain whether the member of Congress representing that district favored or opposed the actions of Fannie Mae and Freddie Mac? Explain.

5. Why do low-income and high-risk borrowers receive subsidies from Fannie, Freddie, Ginnie, and FHA? Make sure you address the question of why doesn't the government simply hand them cash every year, rather than subsidizing their purchases of houses.

6. Given the huge losses incurred by Fannie and Freddie as a result of "rolling the dice," why do you suppose Congressman Barney Frank hasn't been voted out of office?

# CHAPTER 31

# Big Bucks
# for Bailouts

Alstom, American International Group (AIG), Anglo Irish Bank, Bear Stearns, Citigroup, General Motors (GM), Chrysler, Freddie Mac, and Fannie Mae. What do these companies—which are based in a variety of nations and offer different products—all have in common? They have been "saved" by government (read: taxpayer) subsidies. They were, according to proponents of these subsidies, just "too big to fail." Now that concept—too big to fail—could be looked at in the alternative. Perhaps those companies were too big to save—at least from the points of view of taxpayers and the long-run efficiency of each country's economy. We shall first look at what "too big to fail" means, and then examine this concept in the context of what has been called **industrial policy**.

## THE LOGIC (OR ILLOGIC) BEHIND
## TOO-BIG-TO-FAIL POLICIES

The people who support preventing very large corporations from failure, whether those companies are manufacturers of high-speed trains, insurance providers, investment banks, commercial banks, automobile producers, or large guarantors of mortgages, sincerely believe that a failure of a very large corporation can create **systemic risk**, that is, threaten a widespread reduction in economic activity throughout an economy.

Consider two contrasting examples. Your local CD retailer is having a tough time competing against online downloads. Eventually, the company goes out of business, laying off its three employees and abandoning the rented retail space in the local mall. There are no systemic risks with such an event. A few people have to look for jobs and the landlord of the rented space has to find another tenant, but that is the extent of the impact of the firm's closure.

Now consider GM. For years prior to its partial takeover by the government, it was losing hundreds of millions, even billions, of dollars per year. Over the past half century or so, during good economic times GM routinely agreed to generous labor contracts. During bad economic times, it was stuck with high labor costs, including high pension benefits. By the time the recession of 2007–2009 rolled around, GM was simply uncompetitive due to its high costs. Just as the company was about to go under, it was saved by the U.S. government (with subsequent help from the Canadian government). Those who argued for government intervention claimed that GM's bankruptcy would put several hundreds of thousands of people out of work and lead to a vicious cycle of increasing unemployment throughout the United States and elsewhere. In other words, GM was too big to fail and had to be saved. The systemic risks were supposedly too great to let it go under.

## THE MORAL HAZARD PROBLEM WITH "SAVING" LARGE CORPORATIONS

When large corporations are "saved" by the government, the taxpayers who actually pay the bill also face the possibility of a **moral hazard** problem. Why? Consider how labor leadership and management in corporations can reason if they believe they are candidates to be "saved." Believing that they will not be allowed to fail, they can engage in activities that are not necessarily in the long-term interests of the company. (And, we should add, not in the interests of the taxpayers (that's you and us) who will be subsidizing them.)

When times are tough, the head of a labor union whose workers produce GM's cars knows that the union does not have to "give back" very much to the company in terms of lowered fringe benefits and lower wages. Why should it? The company is too big to fail, after all. The managers of GM act the same way: They know that during tough times they don't have to institute dramatic cost-saving actions because—you guessed it—GM is too big to fail.

This moral hazard problem influenced the behavior of all of the large corporations that were saved by taxpayers in the United States— Chrysler, Citicorp, Goldman Sachs, and AIG, among others. Those companies' workers and managers were no longer subjected to an unfettered competitive marketplace, and they acted accordingly. The result was (and continues to be) the **inefficient** use of resources. Costs were not trimmed where and when they should have been, excessive risks were assumed, and so forth. As a result, resources were not employed in their most productive uses. So, not only are taxpayers footing the bill, but also the economy will in general grow less rapidly than it would have without the subsidies to the too-big-to-fail corporations.

## Industrial Policy is Back in Fashion

The latest worldwide recession officially lasted from 2007 to 2009, but its reverberations may still be going on as you read this. The recession brought back in vogue something called **industrial policy**. The too-big-to-fail policies examined above are just an example of this policy. The way President Barack Obama put it in 2009 was this: The government must make "strategic decisions about strategic industries." The $800 billion stimulus legislation in that year earmarked billions of taxpayer dollars for investment in "strategic" sectors, such as renewable energy, advanced vehicles, and high-speed rail systems. But the United States was not alone. At about the same time, Japan announced that it would create a strategy to make sure that its key industries would not be "left behind." France declared that it would invest in "strategic" industries, too, although the government there used the phrase "national champions." The bottom line is that an essential part of the new industrial policy in Europe and Asia, as in America, has been to lavish taxpayer subsidies on banks, carmakers, and other favored industries.

If we define industrial policy as attempts by governments to promote the growth of particular industrial sectors and companies, history does not shed a favorable light on these policies. Simply claiming, as Obama did when he visited Detroit in 2010, that taxpayer subsidies "saved jobs" does not really tell us anything. After all, the correct analysis of any industrial policy must compare costs with benefits. How much did those "saved" jobs cost the economy?

Consider the example of the semiconductor industry. Japan spent somewhere between $20 and $50 billion (estimates differ) during the early 1980s to make the Japanese firms in this industry competitive. All that money was spent for naught. None of the Japanese firms appreciably improved their market shares, and the two world leaders in the industry today are American (Intel) and South Korean (Samsung). Singapore spent about $15 billion in 1995 as part of a similar drive, as did China in 1999. Both policies were failures—no companies from either nation have managed to crack the top ten.

Britain tried similar maneuvers, just as it tried to prop up some of its ailing car companies. Both efforts failed. France spent billions trying to construct an information technology industry, a move that ultimately failed also. The simple fact is that the more globally competitive an industry is, the harder it is for government industrial policy to effectively promote companies in that industry. And because virtually all major industries are globally competitive, this means that industrial policy is destined to fail.

## PICKING WINNERS—NOT AS EASY AS IT SEEMS

Most industrial policy is based on the belief of government officials that they are able to pick winners. Whether the selection process is undertaken in a poor country or in a rich country does not seem to matter, for reasons that are easy to understand. Consider the incentives facing government employees in charge of industrial policy compared to the incentives of decision makers in the private sector. First, the government policymaker is using other people's money—taxpayer dollars, yen, or euros. It is difficult for us to imagine that a government employee using other people's money is going to make better predictions about which industries or companies are going to be winners in the future than someone who has "skin in the game." After all, if the government employee is wrong, the financial consequences are minimal. Her or his life savings are not at stake.

There is also a certain amount of arrogance involved in a government official deciding where best to move resources in the economy. Under what circumstances would such an official have better information about future demands for certain products or services than people in the private sector? There are almost none of which we can think.[1] After all, those who pick winners in the private sector are rewarded handsomely and can become millionaires or even billionaires. In contrast, a government official who is successful in this endeavor might move up a grade level in civil service rating or perhaps be mentioned as an exemplary employee. Small peanuts, we would say.

## CREATIVE DESTRUCTION AND BANKRUPTCY

Do you know what a Polaroid camera is? Probably not, because that good has virtually disappeared due to competition from a better instant photography medium—digital cameras. Do you know what an eight-track cassette tape is? Probably not. It was replaced by the compact disc, which is now becoming obsolete because of competition from online music downloading. Have you ever heard of FedMart? Probably not.

---

1 The (possible) exceptions involve industries (such as aerospace) where correct decision making is heavily dependent on "top secret," government-held information.

It was eventually put out of business by innovative competitors, such as WalMart.

A Harvard economist named Joseph Schumpeter (1883–1950) had a term for the death of certain companies over time—**creative destruction**. He used this term to describe the process by which the economy is transformed by innovation. In his view (now generally shared by economists), innovative entry by entrepreneurs is the economic force behind sustained long-term **economic growth**. In the process of innovation, the value of established companies (and many of their specialized workers) is destroyed. Of course, at the same time, even *more* value is created elsewhere by the innovation. Indeed, the process of creative destruction is at the heart of sustained economic growth.

We see most dramatically the process of innovative destruction at work when we see companies going **bankrupt**. Many companies simply disappear when they go bankrupt, forcing employees to seek work elsewhere. Other companies emerge from bankruptcy leaner and better able to compete. When a bankrupt company emerges from bankruptcy, most of its creditors and shareholders have lost considerable sums. Many of its workers have been laid off or have had to accept reduced salaries and benefits, even if they previously had a union contract. That is what would have happened, without taxpayer subsidies, for GM, Chrysler, Citicorp, Goldman Sachs, and AIG.

## BUT WHAT ABOUT SAVING JOBS?

Whether bankruptcy is involved or not, creative destruction necessarily means that people will have to move from one job to another—old jobs are eliminated, new ones created. Supporters of the too-big-to-fail theory (and of industrial policy in general) always argue that they are only trying to "save jobs." It is true that such taxpayer subsidies may protect the jobs of those in the subsidized companies or industries. But that is hardly job-saving **fiscal policy**. Every subsidy to save a job in a company or industry has to be paid for. Either there is less government spending (and presumably fewer jobs) elsewhere or taxes must be raised, which means less taxpayer spending (and presumably fewer jobs) elsewhere. Therefore, a job "saved" in one company or industry ultimately leads to job *losses* in unsubsidized companies and industries. (In fact, there is every reason to believe that the jobs lost will *exceed* the jobs saved—see Chapter 7.) Economists are fond of saying that there is no such thing as a free lunch, and this principle applies to any fiscal policy justified as being purportedly "job saving."

## Negative Industrial Policy

Despite all the talk by politicians about "saving" jobs, governments at all levels in the United States regularly have acted in ways that *reduce* employment. Indeed, the tax and regulatory policies of the federal government and many state governments have fostered a climate of **deindustrialization**. We have the second highest corporate tax rate in the world. Perhaps equally important, federal government regulations add dramatically to the cost of production in this country. Estimates of the annual costs go as high as $1.7 trillion for federal regulations, or about 12 percent of annual national income.

Businesses in the United States today are also facing regulatory uncertainty. They do not know whether there is going to be a tax on carbon output. They certainly do not know how to estimate the costs of the 2,400-page health care law, or the 2,300-page financial services law, both passed in 2010. The latter requires that 243 new rules be written and no one knows what they will be. The former involves over a hundred new agencies, all of which will write new rules. All of this uncertainty puts U.S. companies at a disadvantage to their competitors in other countries, particularly in Asia.

The bottom line is simple. Despite their willingness to spend your money on bailouts, politicians don't actually seem too interested in promoting the policies that would encourage long-run recruiting and retention of workers. Once again, good politics makes bad economic policy.

## For Critical Analysis

1. Who benefits and who loses from our "too-big-to-fail" policies?

2. Why do you think politicians are more active creating industrial policies during recessions than during boom times?

3. Estimated U.S. taxpayer subsidies in green energy technology through 2013 are about $125 billion. Under what circumstances does the federal government need to undertake these subsidies as opposed to letting private companies themselves pay for such investments?

4. Outline the scenario of what would have happened to GM had the federal government allowed it to go bankrupt on its own several years ago?

5. What is the incentive that private companies have to "pick winners"?

6. Is there any way to stop creative destruction?

# PART SEVEN
# Monetary Policy

# CHAPTER 32

# The Fed and Financial Panics

The Panic of 1907 began after a failed attempt by Otto Heinze to "corner the market" on **shares of stock** in the United Copper Company. Heinze had expected the demand for United's shares to increase in the near term and thought that if he bought up enough shares quickly at low prices, he could turn around and sell them at a handsome **profit.** His judgment proved wrong, and Heinze had to sell out at devastatingly low prices. Not only did his stock brokerage firm go out of business as a result. More disastrously, the public's confidence in the financial condition of banks that had large holdings of United Copper shares evaporated. Confidence also plummeted regarding the financial health of several banks with whom Otto's brother Augustus was associated.

All of these banks suffered **bank runs,** in which large numbers of customers simultaneously withdrew their deposits, and some ultimately failed as a result. The banking panic soon spread more widely, threatening the security of the entire financial system. It was eventually halted only when the famed financier J.P. Morgan induced a large number of banks to join a consortium and mutually stand behind each other's financial obligations.

## BIRTH OF THE FED

The Panic of 1907 achieved notoriety at the time by causing the recession of 1907–1908, but the panic's longer-term importance lies elsewhere. Hoping to avoid a repeat of 1907's financial meltdown, Congress in 1913 established the **Federal Reserve System,** commonly referred to as the **Fed.** The Fed is now the nation's monetary authority and, among other things, our first line of defense against financial panics.

As had been true in prior financial panics, the crux of many banks' woes in 1907 was their inability to convert their assets into the cash that panicked depositors desperately wanted. So the Fed was created to serve as "lender of last resort" to the nation's **commercial banks.** Congress empowered the Fed to lend funds to banks to meet whatever demands that depositors put on the banks, regardless of how great those demands might be. The intention was that there would never be another financial panic in the United States, an objective that, if achieved, would significantly reduce the number and severity of the nation's economic **recessions.**

## OPPORTUNITY AND FAILURE

The Fed's first real chance to perform as lender of last resort—the function for which it was created—came in 1930 when several prominent New York banks got into financial difficulties. Customers of those and other banks started withdrawing funds, fearing that their banks might be weak. This spreading lack of confidence was exactly the scenario the Fed was created to defend against—yet it did nothing. The result was a banking panic and a worsening of the economic downturn already under way.

The next year, the Fed had two more opportunities to act as lender of last resort when confidence in banks sagged, yet in both cases it again failed to act. The results were recurring bank panics in 1931 and an intensification of what was by then an extremely severe recession. Early in 1933, eroding public confidence in the banking system gave the Fed yet another opportunity to step in as lender of last resort, and *again* it failed to do so. The resulting banking panic was disastrous and ushered in the deepest stages of what has come to be known as the Great Depression. It is little wonder that Herbert Hoover, who was president of the United States at the time, referred to the Fed as "a weak reed for a nation to lean on in time of trouble."

## LESSONS LEARNED

Thirty years after the end of the Great Depression, Nobel laureate Milton Friedman and Anna Schwartz published *A Monetary History of the United States.* Among other things, this book laid out in detail the story of the Fed's failings during the 1930s. The book's lessons were absorbed by at least two people who have since served as the head of the Fed—Alan Greenspan, who was chair of the Fed from 1987 to 2006, and Ben Bernanke, who succeeded Greenspan.

Greenspan's opportunity to have the Fed serve as the banking system's lender of last resort came in September 2001, in the wake of the terrorist attacks on the World Trade Center towers. Banks found themselves in need of a quick infusion of funds as panicked depositors made large-scale withdrawals of cash. The Fed quickly stepped in to provide funds to banks, enabling them to meet the demands of depositors without having to sell off assets quickly at depressed prices. A terrorist attack had surely never been contemplated by the legislators who created the Fed. Nevertheless, the Fed acted vigorously as a lender of last resort and thus certainly achieved the objectives of its creators—prevention of financial panic.

## THE PANIC OF '08

Only 2 years after he replaced Greenspan as chair of the Fed, Ben Bernanke had an even bigger opportunity to put the Fed to work. Late in 2008, rapidly eroding confidence in America's financial system led to the near or total collapse of several major financial firms. Many commercial banks, investment banks, and even insurance companies were suddenly in dire condition. Potential borrowers across the country found themselves unable to obtain funds from anyone, at any rate of interest. Although circumstances differed from 1907 in that commercial banks were not at the center of the panic, there was no doubt about one point: The Panic of '08 was just as threatening to the U.S. economy as its century-old predecessor had been.

Mindful of the costs of inaction, the Fed moved swiftly to maintain and restore confidence in key components of the financial system. But its actions were considerably broader than ever before. Historically, for example, the Fed has lent funds to commercial banks and to the federal government itself. But in 2008, the Fed also lent hundreds of billions of dollars directly to nonbank corporations around the country, including tens of billions to insurance giant AIG. The Fed also began purchasing obligations of government-sponsored **mortgage** market giants Fannie Mae and Freddie Mac, hoping to encourage more lending for home purchases. And finally, the Fed agreed to the following trade with commercial banks: It would exchange billions of dollars of risk-free federal **bonds** it held for billions of dollars of high-risk private bonds that they held. In effect, the Fed helped the banks remove high-risk assets of questionable value from their **balance sheets,** thus reducing the chances that skittish depositors might suddenly make large-scale withdrawals of funds from commercial banks.

## THE SURGE IN EXCESS RESERVES

On many of their deposits, commercial banks are required to keep a minimum amount of **reserves** on hand, either in their vaults or on deposit with the Fed. These are referred to as **required reserves.** Any reserves above these minimum required levels are called **excess reserves.** Over the past 70 years, bank holdings of excess reserves have generally been quite small, amounting to no more than a few billion dollars for the entire banking system. And this is not surprising. In normal times, banks generally keep only enough excess reserves to handle day-to-day transactions with depositors because they can earn interest on any funds they lend out.

By 2009, excess reserves soared to more than $800 billion, and eventually topped $1.2 *trillion.* Total reserves (required plus excess) were up sharply because the Fed was giving banks reserves in return for other assets. Among the purchases were commercial paper (debts issued by private companies), securities backed by credit card debt and home mortgages, and even home mortgages themselves. But almost all of the Fed-provided reserves simply sat there—either in bank vaults or on deposit with the Fed—because banks lent almost none of them out.

Banks across the country held on to the excess reserves for three reasons. First, the sagging economy meant that borrowers were riskier and hence less profitable at any given interest rate. Second, depositors were greatly concerned about the financial condition of commercial banks. The banks therefore wanted plenty of funds on hand—in the form of excess reserves—in case they had to meet increased withdrawal demands by depositors. Oddly enough, the third reason for the failure of banks to lend out reserves was a new policy implemented by the Fed itself.

## PAYING INTEREST ON RESERVES

In 2008, the Fed began paying interest on the reserves held by commercial banks, something it had never done before. And it was paying interest not just on required reserves but on *excess* reserves as well. This policy encouraged banks to hold excess reserves rather than to lend the funds to customers. Thus, the payment of interest on commercial bank reserves made it *more difficult* for companies and individuals to get loans. (See Chapter 33 for more on this.)

On balance, it remains to be seen whether the Fed actions during the last recession lived up to the expectations that the Fed's founders had more than a century ago. By providing funds to banks and other financial institutions, the Fed helped reduce the impact of the financial panic and helped prevent widespread runs on commercial banks. Nevertheless, the Fed decision to pay interest on reserves markedly discouraged banks from lending those reserves to companies and households across the land. This surely *slowed* recovery from the recession. Only time and further study will tell whether, on balance, the Fed's actions during the recession made us better off—or worse off.

## For Critical Analysis

1. How did the Fed's long-standing policy of not paying interest on bank reserves act much like a tax on bank reserves?

2. If the Fed continued to pay interest on required reserves but stopped paying interest on excess reserves, how would bank lending incentives be changed?

3. If the Fed had not injected reserves into the banking system in 2008, what would have been the consequences for the banks and for **aggregate demand**?

4. By late 2010 concerns over bank solvency had faded. How did this change likely alter the incentives of banks to lend out excess reserves? What are the implications for aggregate demand? Explain.

5. In the long run, if the Fed fails to remove the excess reserves from the banking system, what will the banks do with them? What are the implications for inflation? Explain.

6. The Fed was given great power in 1913 to undertake potentially beneficial actions. Did this also give it great power to engage in potentially *harmful* actions? Explain why or why not.

# CHAPTER 33

# The Fed Feeding Frenzy

"QE1 didn't seem to work. But QE2 looks hopeful. When will QE3 have to be undertaken?"

If you have no idea what the above quote means, you are not alone. Here is the origin of the abbreviation "QE." Financial reporters decided a few years ago to accept a new term for an old concept. That term is **quantitative easing (QE).** Consequently, "QE1" is a reference to the Fed's expansionary monetary policy during the latest serious recession, in 2008 and 2009. QE2 refers to the Fed's expansionary monetary policy that started in November 2010. QE3—who knows?

## MONETARY POLICY—THE WAY IT USED TO BE

Historically, the Fed's main tool for monetary policy has been the purchase and sale of U.S. government securities, usually **Treasury bills.** When the Fed has wanted to engage in expansionary monetary policy, it bought U.S. Treasuries in the **open market,** thereby increasing **reserves** in the banking system. **Excess reserves** (those over and above legally **required reserves**) were used by banks to expand loans. In the process, the **money supply** grew, which increased aggregate demand. Contractionary monetary policy was just the opposite—the Fed sold U.S. government securities, thereby reducing reserves. The end result was a decrease in the money supply in circulation and a decrease in aggregate demand.

That was then, but Fed monetary policy changed quite abruptly in response to the financial panic in late 2008.

## THE FED STARTED TO LIKE OTHER ASSETS

During the first 95 years of its existence, the Federal Reserve dealt with U.S. government securities only. All that changed in 2008 when the Fed decided that it had to target specific sectors in our economy. So, instead of engaging in traditional expansionary monetary policy, the Fed started buying assets other than U.S. government securities. This was something that had never been done before.

The assets purchased by the Fed included (and still include) short-term corporate debt, short-term loans to banks, **mortgage-backed securities,** mostly issued by the government-sponsored corporations Fannie Mae and Freddie Mac, other debt issued by Fannie Mae and Freddie Mac, and preferred shares in the former investment bank Bear Stearns and in the insurance company American International Group (AIG). Oh, and let's not forget that for well over a year the Fed engaged in **foreign currency swaps** with other countries—perhaps that was considered the icing on the larger cake.

All of those purchases of all of those assets clearly increased the size and composition of the Fed's **balance sheet.** For much of its more recent existence, the Fed "owned" anywhere from several billion to several hundred billion dollars of U.S. Treasury securities. But by 2011, the Fed's assets totaled close to $2.5 trillion (including many hundreds of billions in "new" securities it had bought as part of its quantitative easing policy).

So, in a sentence, the Fed's traditional monetary policy abruptly changed in 2008. Rather than seeking to stimulate the entire economy in general, the Fed decided to provide credit to parts of financial markets (and even specific corporations) that it believed were being abandoned by private lenders. Never before in its history had the chair of the Fed and its board of directors used such discretionary policy to benefit specific sectors of the economy.

## WHY WASN'T THERE AN OUTBREAK OF INFLATION?

With traditional monetary policy analysis, when the Fed aggressively adds to the money supply in circulation by buying U.S. government securities, the banking system suddenly has excess reserves. Not wanting to lose out on potential income from those excess reserves, depository institutions increase their loans, the money supply rises, and aggregate demand increases. At least that's the way economists used to tell the story.

While QE1, QE2, and so forth, got the headlines, however, there was a revolution in central banking in the United States. Starting on October 1, 2008, the Fed began paying interest on reserves—*all* reserves, including excess reserves. While some monetary economists for years have argued that interest should be paid on required reserves, none ever demanded that interest be paid on excess reserves, too. This policy change by the Fed converted excess reserves into an income-earning asset for banks, and thus fundamentally altered the nature of the conduct of monetary policy.

If you are the manager of a bank and know that the Fed will pay interest on excess reserves, you are not so keen to loan out those reserves to businesses and individuals. After all, if you make loans to businesses and individuals, you run a risk. During the recession of 2007–2009, that risk appeared to be much greater than normal. Why not just sit back, collect interest checks from the U.S. government on all of your reserves, and wait to see what happens?

Well, that is exactly how most banks have proceeded over the past few years. The numbers tell the story. When they didn't earn interest, excess reserves were a drag on bank profits, and so banks kept them to a minimum. Typically, excess reserves for the entire banking system averaged $2–$3 billion. During 2011 they peaked at over $1.2 *trillion*, and since then have routinely been from $800 billion and up, depending on the day. Thus, most of the reserves injected into the banking system from 2008 to 2011 ended up not in new loans, new money, and new spending. Instead, they ended up sitting in the form of new excess reserves. That means that the "expansionary" quantitative easing of the Fed was almost completely offset by its decision to pay interest on excess reserves. The result was little increase in aggregate demand and little upward pressure on inflation—at least in the short run.

## ON WANTING MORE INFLATION

For several years, the Fed has told reporters and experts alike that it was worried about **deflation**. Deflation has been associated with bad times—the Great Depression in the United States, for example, and the "lost decade" of the 1990s in the Japanese economy. In justification of its quantitative easing (QE2) in November 2010, the Fed pointed to the "need" for a little bit of inflation, to avoid a deflationary downward spiral.

Actually, as measured by the personal consumption expenditure price index, there had been inflation running at about 1.2 percent annually, a number that was bumping up around 2 percent toward the end of 2010 and into 2011. In other words, based on the Fed's historically preferred price index, there has been no sign of deflation, so it is strange that the Fed has argued in favor of quantitative easing to avoid deflation. The source of the Fed's deflation worries is easily identified, though. Without much publicity, in 2010 the Fed switched from the personal consumption expenditure price index to the consumer price index (CPI) as its preferred measure of inflation. The CPI gives almost double the weight to housing prices than does the personal consumption expenditure price index. Given that housing prices fell quite dramatically during the years 2006–2010, it is not surprising that the CPI has showed some deflation, especially in 2008.

## GETTING BACK TO QUANTITATIVE EASING

Even if the Fed's argument about deflation is based on no more than a switch in price indexes, its desire to prime the pump for the faltering U.S. economy is genuine. The recession that started in December 2007 pushed the unemployment rate above 10 percent, and the rate was slow to drop back below 9 percent. So the Fed argued that QE2 would lower long-term interest rates and thereby give the economy a boost.

When the Fed buys up government and other debt obligations, it will push investors into stocks and corporate bonds—raising the latter's values and lowering interest rates. Lower borrowing costs should help some homeowners refinance their mortgages. Some businesses will be helped, too, because they will have access to cheaper credit. Such analysis is quite traditional and at times has worked—*in the short run*. In the long run, in contrast, large-scale purchases of debt, whether labeled quantitative easing or not, will simply lead to a higher rate of inflation and a return of interest rates to their previous and even higher levels.

So, the Fed might well be thought of as being on a tightrope of its own making. The huge infusion of reserves into the banking system helped moderate the recession of 2007–2009, but the payment of interest on reserves slowed the recovery from that recession. The presence of large excess reserves presents a huge potential threat of inflation down the road, but if the reserves are pulled out of the banking system too fast, the economy will surely sink back into recession. It is the classic case of the two-handed economic policy problem. On the one hand, the economy is threatened by severe inflation. On the other hand, it is threatened by a relapse into recession. Stay tuned, for this is one drama that will work itself out in front of your very eyes.

## FOR CRITICAL ANALYSIS

1. Why do increases in the money supply in circulation ultimately lead to inflation?

2. Was the Fed justified in targeting specific sectors of the economy during the financial panic of 2008? Why or why not?

3. When the Fed buys U.S. government securities, how does it pay for them?

4. Is there any risk to the Fed in holding mortgage-backed securities and debt issued by Fannie Mae and Freddie Mac? If so, what is it?

5. Why did excess reserves increase so much in recent years?

6. Why have banks been so reluctant to loan funds to businesses in recent years?

# CHAPTER 34

# Deposit Insurance and Financial Markets

During the Panic of '08, the federal government announced a key new policy: It was insuring against loss all bank deposits up to $250,000 per account. So if your depository institution happened to be holding some toxic (possibly even worthless) **mortgage-backed securities**, you were home free. The bank could suffer terrible losses, even go out of business, and yet your accounts, up to $250,000 each, would be guaranteed by the full faith and of the U.S. government—which is to say, the U.S. taxpayer.

If you happened to notice the announcement of this policy, you may have wondered to yourself, why would the government do this? For example, although the federal government bought **shares of stock** in numerous banks at the same time, it most assuredly does not guarantee the value of those shares. Why treat deposits differently? A more subtle question is this: How do banks and other **depository institutions** behave differently because of this special deposit insurance? And you might even have wondered whether *your* behavior is likely to be any different because of this insurance. To get a handle on these and other questions, we must look back to the 1930s, before the notion of deposit insurance had even been conceived.

## RUNS ON BANKS

**Bank runs** are defined as the simultaneous rush of depositors to convert their deposits into **currency.** Until the federal government set up deposit insurance in 1933, runs on banks were an infrequent but seemingly unavoidable occurrence, sometimes becoming widespread during economic **recessions.** The largest number of bank runs in modern history occurred during the Great Depression. As a result, more than *nine thousand* banks failed during the 1930s.

Just put yourself in the shoes of the depositor in a typical bank in 1930 and remember that you are a **creditor** of the bank. That is to say, your deposits in the bank are its **liabilities.** Suppose a rumor develops that the **assets** of the bank are not sufficient to cover its liabilities. In other words, the bank is, or will soon be, **insolvent.** Presumably, you are worried that you won't get your deposits back in the form of currency. Knowing this, you are likely to rush to the bank. All other depositors who hear about the bank's supposedly weak financial condition are likely to do the same thing.

This is the essence of a bank run: Regardless of the true state of the bank's financial condition, rumors or fears that a bank is in trouble can cause depositors to suddenly attempt to withdraw all of their funds. But many assets of a bank are in the form of loans that cannot immediately be converted into cash. Even if solvent, the bank is said to be **illiquid** because it doesn't have enough cash on hand to meet the demands of fearful depositors. And when it attempts to get that cash by selling some assets, any resulting decline in the market value of those assets can quickly turn a **solvent** bank into an insolvent one.

Bank runs can be disastrous for the economy because when they occur, the nation's **money supply** shrinks as people pull cash out of banks and stuff it under their mattresses (or wherever they think it might be safe). This in turn causes **aggregate demand** to fall, leading to higher unemployment, business failures, and yet more concerns for the solvency of banks. Quickly enough, the result can be an economic recession and widespread hardship.

## DEPOSIT INSURANCE

When bank failures hit four thousand in 1933, the federal government decided to act to prevent further bank runs. That year, Congress passed, and the president signed into law, legislation creating the Federal Deposit Insurance Corporation (FDIC) and the next year created the Federal Savings and Loan Insurance Corporation (FSLIC). Many years later, in 1971, the National Credit Union Share Insurance Fund (NCUSIF) was created to insure credit union deposits, and in 1989, the FSLIC was replaced by the Savings Association Insurance Fund (SAIF). To make our discussion simple, we will focus only on the FDIC, but the general principles apply to all of these agencies.

When the FDIC was formed, it insured each account in a commercial bank against a loss of up to $2,500. That figure has been increased on seven different occasions, reaching $250,000 in 2008. The result of federal deposit insurance is that there has not been a widespread bank run in the United States since the Great Depression, despite numerous bank failures in the interim. Even during the Panic of 2008, when confidence in many financial institutions collapsed, federally insured depository institutions continued to operate. Indeed, total deposits in them actually rose. The good news about federal deposit insurance is that it has prevented bank runs. But this has come at a significant cost, arising largely due to the unintended consequences of deposit insurance.

## ADVERSE SELECTION

Suppose someone offers you what is claimed to be a great **investment** opportunity. That person tells you that if you invest $250,000, you will make a very high rate of return, say, 20 percent per year, much higher than the 3 percent your funds are currently earning elsewhere. No matter how much you trusted the person offering you this deal, you would probably do some serious investigation of the proposed investment before you handed over fifty thousand hard-earned dollars. You, like other people, would carefully evaluate the risk factors involved in this potential opportunity.

For example, if you use part of your **savings** to buy a house, you will undoubtedly have the structural aspects of the house checked out by an inspector before you sign on the dotted line. Similarly, if you planned to purchase an expensive piece of art, you surely would have an independent expert verify that the artwork is authentic. Typically, the same is true every time you place your accumulated savings into any potential investment: You look before you leap. In circumstances such as these, there is initially **asymmetric information**—in this case, the seller knows much more than the potential buyer. But with diligence, the buyer can eliminate much of this gap in knowledge and make a wise decision.

Now ask yourself, when is the last time you examined the financial condition or lending activities of the depository institution at which you have your checking or savings account? We predict that the answer is never. Indeed, why should you investigate? Because of federal deposit insurance, you know that even if the depository institution that has your funds is taking big risks, you are personally risking nothing. If that depository institution fails, the federal government will—with 100 percent certainty—make sure that you get 100 percent of your deposits back, up to the insurance limit.

So here we have it, the first unintended consequence of depository insurance. Depositors like you no longer have any substantial incentive to investigate the track record of the owners or managers of banks. You care little about whether they have a history of risky or imprudent behavior because at worst you may suffer some minor inconvenience if your bank fails. So unlike in the days before deposit insurance, the marketplace today does little to monitor or punish past performance of owners or managers of depository institutions. As a result, we tend to get **adverse selection**—instead of banks owned and operated by individuals who are prudent at making careful decisions on behalf of depositors, many of them end up run by people who have a high tolerance for taking big risks with other people's money.

## Moral Hazard

Now let's look at bank managers' incentives to act cautiously when making loans. You must first note that the riskier the loan, the higher the interest rate that a bank can charge. For example, if a developing country with a blemished track record in paying its debts wishes to borrow from a U.S. depository institution, that country will have to pay a much higher interest rate than a less risky debtor. The same is true when a risky company comes looking for a loan: If it gets one at all, it will be at a higher-than-average interest rate.

When trying to decide which loan applicants should receive funds, bank managers must weigh the trade-off between risk and return. Poor credit risks offer high **profits** if they actually pay off their debts, but good credit risks are more likely to pay off their debts. The right choice means higher profits for the bank and likely higher salaries and promotions for the managers. The wrong choice means losses and perhaps insolvency for the bank and new, less desirable careers for the managers.

To understand how bank mangers' incentives are changed by deposit insurance—even for managers who otherwise would be prudent and conservative—consider two separate scenarios. In the first scenario, the bank manager is told to take $250,000 of depositors' funds to Las Vegas. The rules of the game are that the manager can bet however he or she wants, and the bank will *share* the winnings *and losses* equally with the deposit holders whose funds the manager has in trust. In the second scenario, the same bank manager with the same funds is given a different set of rules. In this case, the bank doesn't have to share in any of the losses, but it will share in any of the gains when betting in Las Vegas.

Under which set of rules do you think the bank manager will take the higher risks while betting in Las Vegas? Clearly, the manager will take higher risks in the second scenario because the bank will not suffer at all if the manager loses the entire $250,000. Yet if the manager hits it big, say, by placing a successful bet on double zero in roulette, the bank will share the profits, and the manager is likely to get a raise and a promotion.

Well, the second scenario is exactly the one facing the managers of federally insured depository institutions. If they make risky loans, thereby earning, at least in the short run, higher profits, they share in the "winnings." The result for them is higher salaries. If, by contrast, some of these risky loans are not repaid, what is the likely outcome? The bank's losses are limited because the federal government (which is to say you, the taxpayer) will cover any shortfall between the bank's assets and its liabilities. Thus, federal deposit insurance means that banks get to enjoy all of the profits of risk without bearing all of the consequences of that risk.

So the second unintended consequence of deposit insurance is to encourage **moral hazard.** Specifically, bank managers of all types (risk lovers or not) have an incentive to take higher risks in their lending policies than they otherwise would. Indeed, when the economy turned down in the early 1980s, we got to see the consequences of exactly this change in incentives. From 1985 to the beginning of 1993, a total of 1,065 depository institutions failed, at an average rate of more than ten times that for the preceding 40 years. The losses from these failures totaled billions of dollars—paid for in large part by you, the taxpayer.

What, then, might be expected from the 2008 insurance hike to $250,000? Well, in the short run, confidence in banks was renewed and depositors were encouraged to keep more funds in banks. This was good news, for it helped the economy adjust to the financial shocks of 2008–2009. But the bad news will be forthcoming in the long run: The higher deposit insurance limits will encourage both adverse selection (more risk-loving bank managers) and moral hazard (more risk taking by bank managers of all stripes). Eventually, the lending standards of banks will deteriorate to the point that losses mount once again—paid for in part by you, the taxpayer.

## Paying for Deposit Insurance

For the first 60 years or so of federal deposit insurance, all depository institutions were charged modest fees for their insurance coverage. Unfortunately, the fee that these depository institutions paid was completely unrelated to the riskiness of the loans they made. A bank that made loans to Microsoft was charged the same rate for deposit insurance as a bank that made loans to a start-up company with no track record whatsoever. Hence, not even the fees paid by banks for their insurance gave them any incentive to be prudent. This is completely unlike the case in private insurance markets, in which high-risk customers are charged higher premiums, giving them at least some incentive to become lower-risk customers.

In the early 1990s, the federal government made a feeble attempt to adjust fees for depository insurance to reflect the riskiness of their lending activities. But the political strength of the depository institutions prevented any fundamental change in the system. In 2008, the insurance fees paid by depository institutions were doubled, but even this was not enough to keep up with the added risks of the higher insurance limits. In 2009 the insurance rules were changed again. There are now four risk categories for banks, with different insurance premiums charged in each category. Although this is an improvement on the past, most experts believe that the system still not adequately charge banks for the risks they impose on the insurance system. That is, the premiums are not nearly enough to cover the likely losses of the riskiest banks or enough to get them to change their risky behavior.

So while your banker is headed to Vegas, you'd better plan on staying at home to work. Sooner or later, as a U.S. taxpayer, your bill for deposit insurance will come due.

## FOR CRITICAL ANALYSIS

1. If federal deposit insurance costs nothing, who pays when an insured depository institution fails and its depositors are nonetheless reimbursed for the full amount of their deposits?

2. In a world without deposit insurance, what are some of the mechanisms that would arise to "punish" bank managers who acted irresponsibly? (*Hint:* There are similar types of mechanisms for consumer goods and in the stock market.)

3. Explain how "experience rating" of insurance—charging higher premiums to higher-risk customers—affects the incidence of both adverse selection and moral hazard.

4. Why doesn't the federal government fully price bank failure risks?

5. How would the chance of a major economic depression change if federal deposit insurance were eliminated?

6. Why doesn't the federal government offer automobile accident insurance?

# CHAPTER 35

# Credit Card Crunch

By the time you read this, you may already have had a credit card application denied or an existing card canceled. No, we are not talking about the credit card cutbacks that resulted from the recession of 2007–2009. We are referring to the effects of new **Federal Reserve** regulations (expanded by Congress) that are said to benefit you but have in many cases had exactly the opposite effect.

We speak of federal restrictions on the interest rates and fees that credit card firms may charge their customers. Since 2010, such firms are sharply limited in their ability to raise interest rates on existing credit balances, even if interest rates soar elsewhere in the economy. Moreover, the companies are limited in the fees they may charge customers who have little or no credit background or customers who have a troubled credit history. The result is a reduction in the credit available and credit that is more, not less, expensive to obtain.

## CREDIT CARD COMPLAINTS

If you have had a credit card for several years or know people who have, you have likely heard one or more "horror stories" about outrageous late fees or sky-high interest rates or other charges imposed by credit card companies. Some of these incidents are no doubt the result of unscrupulous practices by companies that prey on naïve consumers. Some companies have actually been able to commit fraud under the guise of being a credit card issuer.

But the vast majority of all credit cards are issued by companies that are in the business for the long haul. The interest rates and fees they charge are competitively determined and dependent on the (often substantial) risks of dealing with their cardholders. The practices of companies such as these are generally beyond reproach. Nevertheless, in 2008, the Fed and the other federal agencies that regulate credit card firms decided that the fly-by-night operators needed to be reined in. Congress got involved in 2009, passing legislation that buttressed the Fed's rules. Hence, a sweeping new series of regulations have been instituted, taking full effect in 2010. A positive result of the regulations is that some customers will be protected from fraudulent activities. Those elements of the new rules have proved beneficial to a limited set of consumers. But the new rules also severely hamper the way the *reputable* companies do business. The result of this has been less credit and more expensive credit—a lesson you may already have learned the hard way.

## PRICE CONTROLS ON CREDIT CARDS

Among the myriad details of the new credit card regulations, the key provisions are those that limit the interest rates and fees that companies may lawfully charge. For example, firms are limited in the circumstances under which they can raise the interest rates they charge. Moreover, higher rates can only be applied to new charges, not to past balances—even if market interest rates in general have increased or the borrower has become a worse credit risk since the card was issued. Credit card firms are also limited in the fees they may charge when customers exceed their preset credit limits and the fees that they may charge for the subprime credit cards they issue to people with bad credit ratings.

As a practical matter, these provisions effectively act as **price controls**—legal limits on the prices that may be charged for goods or services. Here the controls are upper limits on prices, which means that interest rates and fees on credit cards are kept below their competitive levels. This causes firms' revenues to fall relative to their costs, which in turn reduces **profits** and discourages the firms from supplying the good in question, in this case consumer credit. On the other side of the market, because the legal maximum price is below the equilibrium price, people respond according to the law of **demand.** They try to obtain more of the good. In this case, consumers try to borrow more via credit cards. Because the quantity demanded rises and the quantity supplied falls, an excess quantity demanded is the result: People want to acquire far more than firms are willing to provide. In this case, desired borrowing goes up while desired lending goes down. Ultimately, the excess quantity demanded must be rationed somehow. The result is a series of readily predicted—and generally wasteful—consequences in the market. Let's see what those are.

## Less Credit

The first and foremost effect of the price controls is to reduce the amount of credit available to consumers. Firms have reduced the number of credit card offers they make, for example, because the expected profit from those cards is reduced by the limits on interest rates and fees. Many thousands of customers have had existing cards canceled because the new regulations made those cards unprofitable for the issuing companies. Credit card companies are also denying more consumer applications for credit cards because the firms are no longer able to cover the expected costs of issuing and servicing the cards of high-risk customers. And finally, when the companies do issue credit cards, they are generally imposing lower credit limits (maximum balances that consumers may have). This is because, for a customer with any given credit rating, the higher the credit balances, the higher the expected costs for the supplier of credit. Quite simply, as credit balances rise relative to a person's ability to pay, the chances rise that there will be late payments or no payments at all. Under the new rules, firms are less able to recoup those higher losses, so they have cut credit limits.

## More Expensive Credit

Paradoxically, the net effect of limits on interest rates and fees has been to *raise* effective costs for many, perhaps most, customers. This is because the limits on interest rates and fees have reduced the amount of credit supplied and thus produced an excess quantity demanded, which, as we have noted, must be rationed somehow. To achieve this rationing, the cost to consumers of that credit must rise. There is simply no way to avoid this in a world of **scarcity.**

Some of these higher costs have come in the form of more onerous application procedures, which now require more documentation and verification. But there is another and even more important way that the cost of credit is driven up by the price controls on credit cards. Many people have been forced to turn to consumer finance companies, which typically charge interest rates of 30–40 percent per year, rather than the 15–30 percent routinely charged on credit card balances. In other instances, the new regulations have made life even worse than this for people with bad credit histories. Many of these individuals are now forced to obtain so-called payday loans.[1] These loans, usually made for

---

[1] One variant of these loans is sometimes called a "check into cash" transaction. Here is a simple example: The borrower receives $100 in cash today in return for writing the lender a personal check for $120, which the lender agrees not to cash until 2 weeks have passed. This deal translates into an implicit interest rate of about 10 percent *per week.*

one week to one month at a time, often carry interest rates as high as 500 percent per year! Thus, some of the people supposedly helped by the new regulations actually end up paying far more for their credit than they did before—as much as twenty times more.

## THE POOR GET POORER

Of course, the developments of which we have spoken so far—reduced credit opportunities and higher credit costs—are not borne equally by all potential customers. In particular, affluent customers with top credit ratings have been essentially untouched. The fees and interest charges most affected by the new regulations are those that apply to people with poor credit ratings—generally, low-income individuals. As a result, it is these people, the ones supposedly helped, who are actually hurt the most. It is their applications that are being denied, and they are the ones turning to consumer finance companies and payday loan operations. For the well-to-do, it is business as usual. For the disadvantaged, it is one more example of a government regulation for which the principal consequences are "unintended," which is to say, directly contrary to the avowed purpose of the regulations.

## WASTED RESOURCES

Not surprisingly, the new limits on interest rates and fees must be enforced, so the regulations have spurred growth in the bureaucracies of the Fed, the Office of Thrift Supervision, and the Federal Deposit Insurance Corporation. The credit card firms also face higher costs due to these regulations because they must demonstrate compliance with them and keep additional records. And because caps on rates and fees have forced the firms to conduct more credit checks and require more documentation, additional resources are being expended here. These are all resources that could have been put to good use elsewhere but are instead being used to implement and enforce the new price controls.

## SAVERS LOSE TOO

Clearly, the new rules on interest rates and fees reduce the amount of credit extended to consumers. This means that the people who ultimately provide the funds for that credit lose too, because there is less demand for their savings. You might think that it is the credit card companies that are the ultimate source of those funds, but you would be wrong. In fact, it is ordinary savers who provide the funds that are lent to consumers by means of credit cards. The credit card companies merely act as intermediaries, moving the funds from savers to borrowers. Thus, people who have savings accounts or money market funds or small certificates of deposit are all now earning lower interest rates on their deposits because the interest rates paid by borrowers are controlled by the government.

## THE BOTTOM LINE

The new price controls for credit cards have made the market less effective in allocating funds from savers to borrowers. As a result, our **wealth** as a society has been reduced. But at least the new rules enable us to see some key public policy principles in action:

*There is no free lunch.* It is nice to think that with the stroke of the regulatory pen, we might "make it so." But in a world of scarcity, that simply doesn't happen. Price controls distort incentives, raise costs, and reduce opportunities. Moreover, they are costly to implement and enforce, and they generally do not accomplish their avowed purpose, which is to help the disadvantaged.

*People respond to incentives.* When there is a reduction in the profits of making loans via credit cards, fewer of those loans are made. And when that happens, people have an incentive to turn elsewhere for funds. Even though those alternative sources are far more costly, they are not as costly for the borrowers as the option of doing without. And so people do what they must because they can no longer do what they wish.

*Things aren't always what they seem.* A superficial look at the credit market seems to suggest that people are better off because many of the people who do still have credit cards are paying lower interest and lower fees. But such a look misses the higher costs people are paying elsewhere and the losses that result because some people are unable to obtain any credit at all due to the new controls.

*Policies always have unintended consequences, and so their net benefits are almost always lower than anticipated.* Surely Congress and policymakers at the Fed didn't go into the regulatory process intending to reduce credit opportunities for low-income individuals. Nor did they hope to increase the credit costs that such individuals must actually bear to obtain credit under the new rules. But this is exactly what has happened, meaning that the rules produced fewer net benefits than the authors of the new rules intended.

So if you are one of the people who was turned down for a credit card, had one canceled, or was forced to turn to a higher-cost source of credit, there should be one consolation in all this: At least you have received an education in how the public policy process works in practice.

## FOR CRITICAL ANALYSIS

1. Why do you suppose the government regulates interest rates on consumer credit (as with credit cards) but generally does not do so with commercial credit (as with loans to businesses)?

2. What do controls on interest rates do to the incentive of consumers to lie on their credit applications in an effort to qualify for a credit card?

3. More than 65,000 individuals and businesses submitted comments on the Fed's regulations when they were first proposed. How might a look at these comments (which are a matter of public record) help you identify individuals and businesses who are likely to gain or lose as a result of the regulations?

4. Why would a limit on interest rates on *old* credit card balances reduce the incentive of firms to issue *new* cards?

5. If government-imposed limits on interest rates are such a good idea, why not just make it illegal to charge *any* interest on *all* loans? What would be the consequences of such a policy?

6. The new limits on credit cards were imposed at a time that interest rates throughout the economy were at record-low levels. What will happen to the magnitude of the adverse effects of these limits as interest rates rise generally? Be explicit. Consider all of the adverse effects mentioned in this chapter. Who will be blamed for these consequences?

# Glossary

**abject poverty:** surviving on the equivalent of $1 or less of income per person per day

**adjustable-rate mortgage (ARM):** debt used to finance house purchases, the interest rate on which changes depending on current market conditions

**adverse selection:** a process in which "undesirable" (high-cost or high-risk) participants tend to dominate one side of a market, causing adverse effects for the other side; often results from *asymmetric information*

**aggregate demand:** the total value of all planned spending on goods and services by all economic entities in the economy

**appropriations bills:** legislation that determines the size of government discretionary spending

**asset:** any valuable good capable of yielding flows of income or services over time

**asset-backed security (ABS):** a bond that has other assets (such as home mortgages) as collateral

**asymmetric information:** a circumstance in which participants on one side of a market have more information than participants on the other side of the market; often results in adverse selection

**average tax rate:** total taxes divided by income

**balance sheet:** a written record of assets and liabilities

**bank run:** an attempt by many of a bank's depositors to convert checkable and savings deposits into currency because of a perceived fear for the bank's solvency

**bankruptcy:** a state of being legally declared unable to pay one's debts so that some or all of the indebtedness is legally wiped out by the courts

**Bankruptcy Code:** the set of federal laws and regulations governing the process of declaring bankruptcy

**bond:** a debt conferring the right to receive a specific series of money payments in the future

**bondholders:** the owners of government or corporate bonds

**book value:** asset valuations that are based on the original purchase price of the assets rather than current market values

**bubble:** an episode in which asset prices exceed their values based on economic fundamentals, as determined by real future profits or service flows

**budget constraint:** all of the possible combinations of goods that can be purchased at given prices and given income

**budget deficit:** the excess of government spending over government revenues during a given time period

**business cycles:** the ups and downs in overall business activity, evidenced by changes in GDP, employment, and the price level

**capital account surplus:** a net inflow of capital funds (loans and investments) into a nation

**capital ratio:** the value of assets divided by the value of debt

**capital stock:** the collection of productive assets that can be combined with other inputs, such as labor, to produce goods and services

**cash flow:** cash receipts minus cash payments

**central bank:** a banker's bank, usually a government institution that also serves as the country's treasury's bank; central banks normally regulate commercial banks

**checkable deposits:** accounts at depository institutions that are payable on demand, either by means of a check or by direct withdrawal, as through an automated teller machine (ATM)

**civil law system:** a legal system in which statutes passed by legislatures and executive decrees, rather than judicial decisions based on precedent, form the basis for most legal rules

**collateral:** assets that are forfeited in the event of default on an obligation

**collateralized debt obligation (CDO):** an obligation to pay that is guaranteed by the pledge of another asset

**commercial bank:** a financial institution that accepts demand deposits, makes loans, and provides other financial services to the public

**common law system:** a legal system in which judicial decisions based on precedent, rather than executive decrees or statutes passed by legislatures, form the basis for most legal rules

**comparative advantage:** the ability to produce a good or service at a lower opportunity cost compared to other producers

**constant-quality price:** price adjusted for any change in the quality of the good or service

**consumer price index (CPI):** a measure of the dollar cost of purchasing a bundle of goods and services assumed to be representative of the consumption pattern of a typical consumer; one measure of the price level

**consumption:** spending by consumers on new goods and services

**core inflation:** a measure of the overall rate of change in prices of goods, excluding energy and food

**cost of living:** the dollar cost (relative to a base year) of achieving a given level of satisfaction

**creative destruction:** the ultimate outcome of a competitive process in which innovation continually creates new products and firms and replaces existing firms and products

**credit-default swap:** a financial contract in which the buyer of the swap makes a series of payments to the seller, who agrees to makes a pay-off to the buyer if an underlying financial instrument (such as a bond) goes into default

**creditor:** an institution or individual that is owed money by another institution or individual

**currency:** paper money and coins issued by the government to serve as a medium of exchange

**default:** failure to meet obligations, for example, the failure to make debt payments

**default risk:** an estimation combining the probability that a contract will not be adhered to and the magnitude of the loss that will occur if it is not

**deficit:** excess of government spending over tax receipts during a given fiscal year

**deflation:** a decline in the average level of the prices of goods and ser-vices

**deindustrialization:** a process of social and economic change caused by the removal or reduction of industrial capacity or activity in a country or region

**demand:** the willingness and ability to purchase goods

**depository institutions:** financial institutions that accept deposits from savers and lend those deposits out to borrowers

**depression:** a severe recession

**direct foreign investment:** resources provided to individuals and firms in a nation by individuals or firms located in other countries, often taking the form of foreign subsidiary or branch operations of a parent company

**disability payments:** cash payments made to persons whose physical or mental disabilities prevent them from working

**discouraged workers:** persons who have dropped out of the labor force because they are unable to find suitable work

**discretionary spending:** government spending that is decided on anew each year, rather than being determined by a formula or set of rules

**disposable income:** income remaining after all taxes, retirement contributions, and the like are deducted

**dividends:** payments made by a corporation to owners of shares of its stock, generally based on the corporation's profits

**drift:** the average annual rate at which stock prices change over a long period of time

**dumping:** the sale of goods in a foreign country at a price below the market price charged for the same goods in the domestic market or at a price below the cost of production

**dynamic economic analysis:** a mode of analysis that recognizes that people respond to changes in incentives and that takes these responses into account when evaluating the effects of policies

**Earned Income Tax Credit:** a federal tax program that permits negative taxes, that is, that provides for payments to people (instead of collecting taxes from them) if their incomes go below a predetermined level

**economic growth:** sustained increases in real per capita income

**elasticity:** a measure of the responsiveness of one variable to a change in another variable

**entitlement programs:** government programs for which spending is determined chiefly by formulas or rules that specify who is eligible for funds and how much they may receive

**equity:** assets minus liabilities; net asset value

**European Central Bank (ECB):** the central bank for the group of nations that use the euro as their monetary unit

**European Union (EU):** a supranational entity resulting from an agreement among European nations to closely integrate the economic, political, and legal systems of the twenty-seven individual member nations

**excess reserves:** funds kept on hand by commercial banks to meet the transactions demands of customers and to serve as precautionary sources of funds in the event of a bank run; may be held as vault cash or as deposits at the Fed

**exchange rate:** the price of a currency expressed in terms of another currency

**expansion:** a period in which economic activity, measured by industrial production, employment, real income, and wholesale and retail sales, is growing on a sustained basis

**expansive monetary policy:** actions that tend to increase the level or rate of growth of the money supply

**expected rate of inflation:** the rate at which the average level of prices of goods and services is expected to rise

**face value:** the denomination in terms of a unit of account expressed on a coin or unit of currency

**fair-value accounting:** an accounting method in which the reported values of assets are adjusted to reflect (estimates of) the current market values of those assets rather than their purchase prices or their stated maturity value

**Fannie Mae:** U.S. government–sponsored enterprise established in 1938 to facilitate the market in home mortgages

**federal budget deficit:** the excess of the national government's spending over its receipts

**federal funds rate:** the nominal interest rate at which banks can borrow reserves from one another

**Federal Reserve System (the Fed):** the central bank of the United States

**fiscal policy:** discretionary changes in government spending or taxes that alter the overall state of the economy, including employment, investment, and output

**fiscal year:** the accounting year used by a government or business; for the federal government, the fiscal year runs from October 1 to September 30

**flexible exchange rates:** exchange rates that are free to move in response to market forces

**foreclosure:** the legal process by which a borrower in default under a mortgage is deprived of his or her interest in the mortgaged property

**Freddie Mac:** U.S. government–sponsored enterprise established in 1970 to facilitate the market in home mortgages

**fully funded pension liability:** an obligation to make postretirement contractual payment made to an individual that is guaranteed by a sufficient amount of assets as to make the payment virtually certain

**gains from trade:** the extent to which individuals, firms, or nations benefit from engaging in voluntary exchange

**globalization:** the integration of national economies into an international economy

**government-sponsored enterprise (GSE):** a federally chartered corporation that is privately owned, designed to provide a source of credit nationwide, and limited to servicing one economic sector

**gross domestic product (GDP):** the dollar value of all new, domestically produced final goods and services in an economy

**gross public debt:** all public debt, including that owned by agencies of the government issuing it

**hedge funds:** investment companies that require large initial deposits by investors and pursue high-risk investments in the hope of achieving high returns

**human capital:** the productive capacity of human beings

**illiquid:** when used in reference to a company or person—having insufficient cash on hand to meet current liabilities; when used in reference to an asset—that which cannot be easily and cheaply converted into cash

**in-kind transfer:** the provision of goods and services rather than cash, as in the case of Medicare, Medicaid, or subsidized housing

**incentives:** positive or negatives consequences of actions

**income mobility:** the tendency of people to move around in the income distribution over time

**industrial policy:** a set of government actions that attempt to influence which firms succeed and which fail

**Industrial Revolution:** the widespread radical socioeconomic changes that took place in England and many other nations beginning in the late eighteenth century, brought about when extensive mechanization of production systems resulted in a shift from home-based hand manufacturing to large-scale factory production

**inefficient:** an outcome that fails to maximize the value of a resource

**inflation:** a rise in the average level of the prices of goods and services

**inflation tax:** the decline in the real value or purchasing power of money balances due to inflation

**inflationary premium:** the additional premium, in percent per year, that people are willing to pay to have dollars sooner rather than later simply because inflation is expected in the future

**inside information:** valuable information about future economic performance that is not generally available to the public

**insolvent:** describing a financial condition in which the value of one's assets is less than the value of one's liabilities

**insourcing:** the use of domestic workers to perform a service traditionally done by foreign workers

**institutions:** the basic rules, customs, and practices of society

**interagency borrowings:** loans from one part of the federal government to another

**interest group:** a collection of individuals with common aims

**intermediate goods:** goods that contribute to present or future consumer welfare but are not direct sources of utility themselves; typically, they are used up in the production of final goods and services

**investment:** the creation of new machines, factories, and other assets that enable the production of more goods and services in the future

**investment bank:** a financial institution that helps companies or municipalities obtain financing by selling stocks or bonds on their behalf

**investment security:** a debt obligation for which the default risk is low

**labor force:** individuals aged 16 and over who either have jobs or are looking and available for work

**labor supply curve:** a schedule showing the quantity of labor supplied at each wage rate

**liabilities:** amounts owed; the legal claims against an individual or against an institution by those who are not owners of that institution

**loophole:** a provision of the tax code that enables a narrow group of beneficiaries to achieve a lower effective tax rate

**lump sum tax rebates:** fixed cash payments made by a government to taxpayers that are independent of taxpayer income

**mandates:** in the context of governments, regulations or laws that require other governments, private individuals, or firms to spend money to achieve goals specified by the government

**margin:** increment or decrement

**marginal tax rate:** the percentage of the last dollar earned that is paid in taxes

**mark to market:** an accounting practice in which the reported values of assets are adjusted to reflect (estimates of) the current market values of those assets rather than their purchase prices or their stated maturity value

**median age:** the age that separates the older half of the population from the younger half

**median income:** the income that separates the higher-income half of the population from the lower-income half

**Medicaid:** joint federal–state health insurance program for low-income individuals

**Medicare:** federal health insurance program for individuals aged 65 and above

**medium of exchange:** any asset that sellers will generally accept as payment **mercantilists**—believers in the doctrine of mercantilism, which asserted (among other things) that exports were the principal objective of international trade because they permitted the accumulation of gold

**microeconomics:** the study of decision making by consumers and by firms and of the market equilibria that result

**monetary policy:** the use of changes in the amount of money in circulation to affect interest rates, credit markets, inflation (or deflation), and unemployment

**money supply:** the sum of checkable deposits and currency in the hands of the public

**moral hazard:** the tendency of an entity insulated from risk to behave differently than it would behave if it were fully exposed to the risk

**mortgage-backed security (MBS):** a debt obligation that pledges home mortgages as collateral

**mortgages:** debts that are incurred to buy a house and provide that if the debt is not paid, the house can be sold by the creditor and the proceeds used to pay that debt

**mutual funds:** a pools of money that are invested in assets, often shares of stock in corporations

**national debt:** cumulative excess of federal spending over federal tax collections over time; total explicit indebtedness of the federal government

**natural resource endowments:** the collection of naturally occurring minerals (such as oil and iron ore) and living things (such as forests and fish stocks) that can be used to produce goods and services

**negative tax:** a payment from the government to an individual that is based on the individual's income

**net public debt:** the portion of the public debt that is owned outside of the government issuing it

**net worth:** the excess of assets over liabilities

**nominal income:** income expressed in terms of a monetary unit, such as the dollar

**nominal interest rate:** the premium, in percent per year, that people are willing to pay to have dollars sooner rather than later

**nominal prices:** the exchange value of goods, expressed in terms of a unit of account, such as the dollar or the euro

**normal good:** a good for which the demand increases as people's income or wealth grows

**official, reported economy:** commercial transactions on which taxes are paid, regulations are obeyed, required paperwork procedures being adhered to

**open market:** the market for U.S. Treasury securities

**opportunity cost:** the highest-valued, next-best alternative that must be sacrificed to obtain something

**outsourcing:** the use of labor in another country to perform service work traditionally done by domestic workers

**pay-as-you-go system:** a scheme in which current cash outflows are funded (paid for) with current cash inflows

**payroll taxes:** taxes that are levied on income specifically generated by workforce participation and that are generally earmarked for spending on specific programs, such as Social Security

**per capita income:** GDP divided by population

**per capita real net public debt:** net public debt, deflated by the price level and divided by the population

**perfectly inelastic:** having an elasticity (or responsiveness) of zero

**permanent income:** the sustained or average level of income that one expects will be observed over a long period of time

**physical capital:** the productive capacity of physical assets, such as buildings

**price controls:** government rules that limit the prices firms may charge for the goods or services they sell

**price level:** the average current-year cost, measured relative to the average base-year cost, of a typical basket of goods and services

**productivity:** output per unit of input

**profits:** the difference between revenue and cost

**progressive tax system:** a set of rules that result in the collection of a larger share of income as taxes when income rises

**property and contract rights:** legal rules governing the use and exchange of property and the enforceable agreements between people or businesses

**proportional tax system:** a set of rules that result in the collection of an unchanging share of income as income changes

**protectionism:** economic policy of promoting favored domestic industries through the use of high tariffs and quotas and other trade restrictions to reduce imports

**protectionist:** any attitude or policy that seeks to prevent foreigners from competing with domestic firms or individuals

**public debt:** the amount of money owed by a government to its creditors

**purchasing power:** a measure of the amount of goods and services that can be purchased with a given amount of money

**purchasing power parity (PPP):** the principle that the relative values of different currencies must reflect their purchasing power in their home countries

**quantitative easing (QE):** Federal Reserve policy that entails the purchase of various financial assets, conducted in an effort to increase aggregate demand

**quota:** a limit on the amount of a good that may be imported; generally used to reduce imports so as to protect the economic interests of domestic industries that compete with the imports

**real gross domestic product (real GDP):** the inflation-adjusted level of new, domestically produced final goods and services

**real income:** income adjusted for inflation; equivalently, income expressed in terms of goods and services

**real interest rate:** the premium, in percent per year, that people are willing to pay to have goods sooner rather than later

**real per capita income (real GDP per capita):** GDP corrected for inflation and divided by the population—a measure of the amount of new domestic production of final goods and services per person

**real price:** price of a good or service adjusted for inflation; equivalently, the price of a good or service expressed in terms of other goods and services; see *relative prices*

**real purchasing power:** the amount of goods and services that can be acquired with an asset whose value is expressed in terms of the monetary unit of account (such as the dollar)

**real tax rate:** share of GDP controlled by the government

**real wages:** wages adjusted for changes in the price level

**recession:** a decline in the level of overall business activity

**regressive tax system:** a set of rules that result in the collection of a smaller share of income as taxes when income rises

**relative prices:** prices of goods and services compared to the prices of other goods and services; costs of goods and services measured in terms of other commodities

**required reserves:** funds that a commercial bank must lawfully maintain; they may be held in the form of vault cash or deposits at the Fed

**reserves:** assets held by depository institutions, typically in the form of currency held at the institution or as non-interest-bearing deposits held at the central bank, to meet customers' transaction needs and Fed legal requirements

**resources:** any items capable of satisfying individuals' desires or preferences or suitable for transformation into such goods

**revealed preferences:** consumers' tastes as demonstrated by the choices they make

**rule of law:** the principle that relations between individuals, businesses, and the government are governed by explicit rules that apply to everyone in society

**saving:** an addition to wealth, conventionally measured as disposable personal income minus consumption

**savings:** one's stock of wealth at a given moment in time

**scarcity:** a state of the world in which there are limited resources but unlimited demands, implying that we must make choices among alternatives

**securitized:** describing cash flow–producing assets pooled and repackaged into securities that are then sold to investors

**share of stock:** claim to a specified portion of future net cash flows (or profits) of a corporation

**shareholders:** owners of shares of stock in a corporation

**Social Security:** the federal system that transfers income from current workers to current retirees

**solvent:** describing a financial condition in which the value of one's assets is greater than the value of one's liabilities

**standard of living:** a summary measure of the level of per capita material welfare, often measured by per capita real GDP

**static economic analysis:** a mode of analysis that assumes for simplicity that people do not change their behavior when incentives change

**stock:** as applied to measurement, an amount measured at a particular moment in time

**stockbroker:** a middleman who sells shares of stock to individuals

**subprime mortgages:** *mortgages* that entail the higher risk of loss for the lender

**subsidies:** government payments for the production of specific goods, generally intended to raise the profits of the firms producing those goods

**supply:** the willingness and ability to sell goods

**systemic risk:** hazard that is felt or experienced throughout an entire economy

**tariff:** a tax levied only on imports; generally used to reduce imports so as to protect the economic interests of domestic industries that compete with the imports

**tax bracket:** a range of income over which a specific marginal tax rate applies

**tax credit:** a direct reduction in tax liability, occasioned by a specific set of circumstances and not dependent on the taxpayer's tax bracket

**tax evasion:** the deliberate failure to pay taxes, usually by making a false report

**tax liability:** total tax obligation owed by a firm or individual

**tax rate:** the percentage of a dollar of income that must be paid in taxes

**tax rebate:** a return of some previously paid taxes

**third party:** in the context of health insurance, it is an entity other than the insured or the service provider that has a financial obligation in the transaction; typically an insurance company or government

**trade barrier:** a legal rule imposed by a nation that raises the costs of foreign firms seeking to sell goods in that nation; they include tariffs and quotas

**trade deficit:** an excess of the value of imports of goods and services over the value of the exports of goods and services

**trade surplus:** an excess of the value of exports of goods and services over the value of the imports of goods and services

**Treasury bills:** short-term notes of indebtedness of the U.S. government

**underground economy:** commercial transactions on which taxes and regulations are being avoided

**unemployment benefits:** regular cash payments made to individuals, contingent on their status as being unemployed

**unemployment rate:** the number of persons looking and available for work, divided by the labor force

**unfunded pension liabilities:** obligations to make postretirement contractual payment to individuals that are not guaranteed by a sufficient amount of assets as to make the payment virtually certain

**unfunded taxpayer liabilities:** obligations of taxpayers for which no specific debt instruments have been issued

**voucher:** a written authorization, exchangeable for cash or services

**wealth:** the present value of all current and future income

**wealth tax:** a tax based on a person's net worth

**World Trade Organization (WTO):** an association of more than 150 nations that helps reduce trade barriers among its members and handles international trade disputes among them

**write off:** declare to be worthless